The Birth of British Television

D0303586

WITHDRAWN

LIVERPOOL JMU LIBRARY

3 1111 01422 1137

The Birth of British Television

Mark Aldridge

© 2012 Mark Aldridge

All rights reserved. No reproduction, copy or transmission of this publication may be made without written permission.

No portion of this publication may be reproduced, copied or transmitted save with written permission or in accordance with the provisions of the Copyright, Designs and Patents Act 1988, or under the terms of any licence permitting limited copying issued by the Copyright Licensing Agency, Saffron House, 6–10 Kirby Street, London EC1N 8TS.

Any person who does any unauthorized act in relation to this publication may be liable to criminal prosecution and civil claims for damages.

The author has asserted his right to be identified as the author of this work in accordance with the Copyright, Designs and Patents Act 1988.

First published 2012 by
PALGRAVE MACMILLAN

Palgrave Macmillan in the UK is an imprint of Macmillan Publishers Limited, registered in England, company number 785998, of Houndmills, Basingstoke, Hampshire RG21 6XS.

Palgrave Macmillan in the US is a division of St Martin's Press LLC, 175 Fifth Avenue, New York, NY 10010.

Palgrave Macmillan is the global academic imprint of the above companies and has companies and representatives throughout the world.

Palgrave® and Macmillan® are registered trademarks in the United States, the United Kingdom, Europe and other countries

ISBN 978–0–230–27769–4 paperback
ISBN 978–0–230–27768–7 hardback

This book is printed on paper suitable for recycling and made from fully managed and sustained forest sources. Logging, pulping and manufacturing processes are expected to conform to the environmental regulations of the country of origin.

Library of Congress Cataloging-in-Publication Data

Aldridge, Mark.
    The birth of British television : a history / Mark Aldridge.
        p. cm.
    Includes index.
    Summary: "This is the story of how television in Britain developed
    from whimsical techno-fad to everyday household object. With
    coverage of pioneering early domestic models and influential
    international developments, the text tracks the energetic
    inventors, cynics, developers and beneficiaries who ensured the
    creation of this beloved medium"-Provided by publisher.
    ISBN 978–0–230–27769–4 (pbk.)
    1. Television broadcasting-Great Britain-History. 2. Television-
    Great Britain-History. I. Title.
    HE8700.9.G7A43 2011
    384.550941-dc23   2011034398

10   9   8   7   6   5   4   3   2   1
21 20 19 18 17 16 15 14 13 12

Printed and bound in Great Britain by
CPI Antony Rowe, Chippenham and Eastbourne

Contents

List of Illustrations

Acknowledgements

Principally, my thanks must go to Lucy Mazdon and Michael Williams who provided me with a great deal of advice and constructive criticism when this research was first undertaken as a PhD project. Their feedback was always delivered in a friendly, prompt and helpful manner. I would also like to thank the other members of staff in the Film Studies department of the University of Southampton, especially Tim Bergfelder and Michael Hammond, who have all been encouraging and helpful at various stages of my research. Similarly, I have greatly appreciated the support of my colleagues at Southampton Solent University, including Jacqueline Furby, Claire Hines, Darren Kerr, Donna Peberdy and Karen Randell.

My research was assisted by the excellent staff at both the Post Office archive and the BBC's Written Archive Centre. I would particularly like to thank Erin O'Neill and Fallon Lee for their guidance through the maze of BBC files. Additionally, I would like to thank Simon Vaughan of the Alexandra Palace Television Society and Clare Colvin of the Royal Television Society for their help in providing research material and many of the photographs reproduced in this book. Special thanks must go to John Trenouth and Donald F. McLean, both of whom read my manuscript and offered invaluable advice, corrections and comments.

I am also grateful for the help and support offered by Sebastian Buckle, Shauno Butcher, Peter Carlton, Nick Gates, James Howells, Andy Murray, Kelly Robinson, Cliff Shelton, Ingrid Stigsdotter, Paul Vanezis and Nicky Williams. At Palgrave Macmillan, I have been ably assisted by Rebecca Barden and Paul Sng, who have guided this process smoothly and efficiently. Finally, I would like to thank my parents, Gary and Sarah, and my sister Jo, without whom I would never have been in a position to be able to write this book.

Introduction

When the BBC launched the world's first regular, high-definition television service on 2 November 1936 it was the culmination of decades of technological innovations. More than this, however, the service meant that the principle of television had finally found its place. Television was to be situated alongside radio, as a public service funded by a licence fee and operating as a monopoly for several years. This placement is now little commented on, with the BBC's role in television broadcasting generally assumed to be a foregone conclusion given their control of radio. This book dispenses with this somewhat retrospective perspective, instead exploring the extent to which the early development of television in Britain demonstrated a range of aims and expectations for the medium.

In order to rationalise this emphasis it is useful to think back to 1935. At this point there had been serious development of television for over a decade, and this had been increasingly formalized in the UK. Television had initially been the work of backroom inventors since the earliest experiments in the late 19th century, with many working on a small range of theoretical concepts for moving images at a distance. By the mid-1930s the developments had finally reached the point where the technology was deemed workable, and in the UK it was placed into the care of the British Broadcasting Corporation. The BBC's template of public service broadcasting had been successfully and exclusively applied to all public radio transmissions in the United Kingdom since 1927, but the emergence of television raised a new problem. Should it operate alongside radio broadcasts, or be treated as a separate entity? The eventual placement of television within a framework of public service broadcasts was not a decision that was taken lightly. A parliamentary committee, overseen by Lord Selsdon,[1] endeavoured to fully assess the possible avenues for television broadcasting. Whilst the committee was looking for a single way forward, this book does not overlook the other potential uses for television that would ultimately be abandoned, partly as a result of their decision. It presents the changing expectations of, and rationale for, television and encourages the reader to consider exactly what led to the system of television with which we are now so familiar. Starting with the work of private inventor John Logie Baird, and his presentation of 'television' (really a reproduction of shadow images) in 1925, and continuing until the earliest official, high definition, regular broadcasts in 1936, this book explores how attitudes and expectations developed so that the heavy involvement of the BBC came to be seen as the best option for the future of the medium. It asks what was expected of television, and to what extent its early broadcasts conform to those aims and presumptions.

The aim is not only to tell the story of the birth of television in Britain, but to encourage those studying the period to consider the options available to those who played leading roles in the medium's establishment, and examine why the basic tenets of television broadcasting came to be. The book is designed to cater both for those researching the period in depth and for those looking for a detailed overview of the crucial developments of the period. For those using the book as a study aid, there is contextual material throughout. This includes the box-outs that situate the British history within international and contemporary developments. Similarly, each section concludes with 'Points to Consider', designed for student discussion. This allows those who wish to use this book for research to concentrate on the main bulk of the book, while those exploring the period for the first time can draw on this additional material as they find necessary.

Situating this History

Clearly, this is not the first book to explore the early development of British television. Of particular note are the relevant sections in Asa Briggs' five volume *History of Broadcasting in the United Kingdom* covering the medium's emergence. The comprehensiveness of Briggs' history is both impressive and valuable, as he examines the development of broadcasting from the perspective of the institutions that played a role in the changes in radio and television. In doing this he also signposts the wider thinking behind many of the decisions made. Although this book draws on some of the same primary material as Briggs, its approach has been somewhat different. Briggs necessarily internalises every development within the large organisations, drawing our attention to the relevance of decisions and developments in relation to the BBC and government in particular. However, the overall structure of this book allows consideration of the developments outside public organisations in more depth. Conversely, Briggs' history is fixed in its viewpoint. It looks out from the vantage point of these institutions, with their importance and roles emphasised.

Briggs' work is not the only study to have looked at early television, of course. There have already been explorations of drama productions in this early period (Jason Jacobs' *The Intimate Screen*[2]) and nostalgic collections of reminiscences from the perspective of both the actors and the personnel who were making these early television productions (Kate Dunn's *Do Not Adjust Your Set*[3]) and the audience themselves (David Lazell's *What's On The Box?*[4]).

Similarly, there have been examinations of the developments in the field of television prior to the official launch, such as R.W. Burns' *British Television: The Formative Years*[5], which often focuses on the technical developments, as does Albert Abramson's *The History of Television, 1880–1941*[6]. There is also Paddy Scannell's examination and attempted definition of the concept of public service broadcasting, which provides a useful examination of this key term as a springboard into discussion of television's role.[7] Additionally, there have been several biographies of Baird, who also wrote his own memoirs, many of which are useful sources for helping our understanding of the man and his motivations.

This study will be examining a limited time frame with a wide breadth of approach, aiming to dissect the developments that affected the roles of each in the early years of television. In this respect there are some similarities to Bruce Norman's *Here's Looking at You*,[8] which covers the period of television to 1939. Norman's history quotes heavily from interviews, with an emphasis on telling the story through the eyes of those who were involved in some capacity. As Norman says, 'The official records tell one story of the birth of television, the people involved tell another.'[9] Along the same lines, the material collated by Donald F. McLean for his CD-ROM project *The Dawn of Television Remembered* creates a substantial and important resource.[10] Not only is this an audio documentary but it includes unedited interviews with some of those involved. While these are rarely referenced directly in this study their existence was of considerable assistance in gaining a sense of the individuals' attitudes and feelings at this crucial time. Similarly, McLean's book *Restoring Baird's Image* has been a valuable reassessment of the role of Baird in the early development of television.

Despite the value of these various studies of this period in television history, it is unfortunate that there have not been more in-depth examinations. As John Corner has put it, 'the study of television, like the study of media more generally, has suffered from a lack of historical studies,'[11] and it is certainly true that there are relatively few close examinations of this crucial period of television history, although there is a superfluity of basic, brief overviews. This book helps to redress the balance by highlighting the extent to which there is still so much more to be said about this earliest period in particular. Wider historical analyses that incorporate early television often fail to give the period the same level of analysis and historical narrative afforded later periods, possibly for reasons that will soon become clear; a problem that is compounded by the lack of studies that concentrate on the pre-war period in its own right. Even excellent broader histories, such as Andrew Crisell's *An Introductory History of British Broadcasting*,[12] give little attention to this period of television's development. In this case, Crisell dedicates less than two pages, of three hundred, to television broadcasts prior to 1946, indicating the extent to which early television is generally left unexplored.

This study assigns rather more importance to this period of television history. The aim is not to present a cosy and nostalgic exploration of a period that undoubtedly features many interesting characters, nor to assess these early years as part of a particular element's wider history. The latter approach tends to either emphasise the aspects of television's early development that were ultimately adopted or simply footnote the entire period as a prelude to the issue of programming. Even Briggs inevitably places the early development of television within wider concerns of the ongoing development of the fledgling BBC. The placement of early television's development within a wider history of any kind (whether it be a biography of John Logie Baird or a history of the BBC) implies the importance of that aspect of television. While this presents a risk for this study, as each section concentrates on what I argue is a key part of our understanding of television's development, I have chosen aspects of television's development in this period that are deliberately broad and can give us the widest possible understanding of individual and overall attitudes towards the system. Often these differ and there was certainly no consensus of opinion towards television. This is the fact which makes this study of such interest and value; the best way to understand television's emergence as a popular medium is by understanding the reasons behind the particulars of its official launch.

Exploring Multiple Perspectives

The period covered by this book ranges from Baird's 1925 demonstrations until the official launch of the medium on 2 November 1936, assessing points that were of importance at the time in the run-up to the launch alongside developments that are of more retrospective interest. At times it is necessary to show that later developments had their roots in the very earliest years of television, even if these other periods of television are generally beyond the scope of this study. One section explores pre-war programming on the official BBC service, for example, so as to show the culmination of the previous developments. However, more importantly, a forward-looking perspective allows us to examine possibilities for television that were not to be, or that were short-ived. This type of analysis is aided by the other key part of my approach, the decision to examine key areas of development thematically, rather than take a strictly chronological approach.

One of the prominent figures in the field of private experimentation was John Logie Baird, examined in the first section of the book. He is the person most commonly associated with television's early years and was often described (many claim spuriously) as the 'inventor' of television. Whatever the truth may be, Baird played an integral role in the early years of television's development, and his career helps to demonstrate how television was not the result of a single concerted effort to create a workable system. Instead, it was preceded by years of experimentation in different areas, both amateur and professional, from small scale projects like that of Baird and his associates to that of the BBC and latterly Marconi-EMI. There is a degree of controversy concerning the role of Baird and other private television enthusiasts in the development of television, and this section addresses the concerns levelled at their work.

It was not private enterprise that launched a fully-fledged television service in the UK from 1936, however. Accordingly the second section looks at the role of the institutions in the development of television, particularly the impact of granting the BBC an exclusive licence (initially at least) and dictating a public service remit. Using a wealth of original documentation, this section considers what these public institutions planned to achieve with the system, and what role they played in the shaping of television.

The third section examines the wider views of television from those who did not have a vested interest in the product. This takes the form of examining the reports in the press relating to two key periods in the medium's early development. The first follows Baird's 1926 private demonstration in front of invited members of the press and The Royal Institution. The second is the year of the official launch of the medium itself in 1936, with the run-up to the event itself gaining some interest in the national press. These reports help to demonstrate the wider perceptions of the medium and can indicate the attitudes of the public at large to some degree. From this we can see an intriguing vista of attitudes when comparing the 1926–7 with 1936; we will see that some stances and opinions would change between the two periods while others would not.

This examination of changing attitudes leads to Section Four, which reconstructs and examines the content of television as it was when launched in 1936. Utilising aspects of Jason Jacobs' methodology, this compares productions of differing complexity, looking beyond the dramatic productions that Jacobs analysed so well. By using the existing fragments of information available, this section shows how the key factors examined to that point culminated in a medium that was certainly unique and remarkably similar to television as we now know it. While styles of programming may change, the basic aims and overall content of television was essentially a similar mix to modern channels. This section is a rare opportunity to explore this often overlooked, but nevertheless exciting, period of television. Television programming encompassed a broad range of subjects, but this was compounded by the service's limited resources. Through the combination of many different sources this analysis results allows a good understanding of the early television schedules which allows the significance, or otherwise, of many aspects of early television history to be properly assessed.

The rationale for separating the important movements behind television's development is that it makes it clearer that the BBC's involvement with television was not a foregone conclusion. Other approaches tend to use the corporation's involvement as the backbone of the analysis, but this emphasises the successful policies and the paths eventually taken, which goes against this book's approach. Of much more interest, as far as this study is concerned, is the very fact that there was never a clear and unobstructed route for television to take in order to become a mass medium. Indeed, television's very placement in the mainstream was still unclear even by the time of its launch. Therefore, in order for us to see why those who were working on television independently saw a future for the medium in the private sphere as well as those working for the public bodies of the BBC and the Post Office we must analyse the developments in their proper context.

For example, there is the consideration that Baird applied for his first licence to transmit television on 4 January 1926,[13] 12 months before the BBC made the transition from a private company to a public corporation. While the presumption may be that television followed where radio had gone, in this earliest period the use of radio as a system of public service broadcasting was only starting to come to fruition. As a result, it is understandable that a new system of broadcasting may seem to have been not only possible, but potentially desirable so as to usurp the stranglehold that the BBC then had over broadcasting. Previous histories of early television have often declined to take these other possibilities seriously, treating them as a diversion to the 'true' history of television under the control of the BBC. This book tackles the subject differently by electing to consider the reasoning behind these alternatives, once more using them to aid our examination of attitudes towards the development of television.

A Necessary Methodological Approach

To an extent, this book's methodological approach is dictated by external circumstances, which also offer an explanation for early television's relative lack of analysis. The most important element is perhaps also the most obvious to those who know television's history. While there is a complete record of programming shown on the main terrestrial channels in the last two decades, prior to that point there are significant gaps in the archives. The proportion of programmes now lost generally increases the earlier the period. If we move as far back as pre-war television, the amount of existing programming is almost negligible. There are some examples of items shown on television before the Second World War still in existence, but none of them are complete and original live shows. As a result, they are far from representative of the majority of output. They variously take the form of newsreels, specially shot films to showcase the service, a handful of mute extracts recorded off-screen and some extracts of broadcasts that predated the official 1936 launch. As John Caughie has pointed out, the technology for recording early broadcasts did not exist in this early period, and recording of this seemingly ephemeral medium was not considered a priority even when it did become possible, meaning that 'While cinema historians have a continuous, though incomplete, history of films from the 1890s, television has a pre-history in which programmes themselves do not exist in recorded form.'[14] Certainly this lack of existing recordings of early programming creates more problems than those faced by the early film historian. Famous 'lost' movies include the Lon Chaney horror film *London After Midnight* (d. Tod Browning, US: MGM, 1927) and Laurel and Hardy's *Hats Off* (d. Hal Roach, US: Hal Roach Studios, 1927) alongside numerous others from cinema's first forty years in particular that no longer appear to exist. Nevertheless, a substantial range of important films remain, along with a wealth of less renowned features. There is a traceable history for film, with the holes in its history largely failing to detract from an overall understanding of its ongoing development.

For television, the lack of recordings from this early period clearly creates more of a problem. While some academics, such as Charles Barr,[15] have called for more attention to be paid to early television, how can the content of television broadcasts be examined in any depth when there are no recordings of the shows themselves and the time passed is so great that most (if not all) television historians will not have seen any broadcasts at the time in question? While it is certainly difficult to gain an understanding of what was shown on television in this time, it is not impossible. It calls for what Caughie has called 'an archaeological, rather than strictly historical procedure'.[16] Jason Jacobs has most clearly demonstrated a workable way of analysing early television in his aforementioned book *The Intimate Screen*. Here, Jacobs successfully 'reconstructs' programming using original documentation, but television was not completely ephemeral. While recordings were not made, there is a great deal of peripheral material that affords an insight into transmissions. On the most basic level, the *Radio Times* published a special 'Television Edition' within London from November 1936, which allows us to at least see which programmes were broadcast at which times with relative ease, along with the BBC's own Programme as Broadcast documents which list the proper timings alongside some useful extraneous detail for many schedules. However, the intricacies of productions cannot be demonstrated by a two sentence synopsis at best. As a result, further research is needed, and thankfully the BBC's own Written Archive Centre can supply further material that can help us to gain a more specific impression of the programmes as they would have been seen. The most useful material is within the production file of each programme. Not every programme has a file that still exists, but of those that do, several include items such as floorplans which help to indicate what would have been seen on screen. There is no logic behind which productions had files which survive; some were simply better documented and filed than others at the time (there being no directive to keep items related to productions for historical reasons), while many have subsequently been destroyed, especially during the Second World War. When they exist, these floorplans show where the cameras and sets would be placed, and camera scripts can often demonstrate more specific actions. These can be used to help us in our understanding of early television, as demonstrated in Section Four.

However, for most of the period in question this book is assessing the historical developments behind the scenes, and more specifically the personal ideologies that would influence the operation of the medium. Some of the previous histories, most especially Briggs', outline the developments in some detail but this examination returns to the source material for the most part. To a large extent this is because this study will be using the source in a different way, with less interest in telling the overall story of television's development, in favour of an examination of hopes and predictions for the technology. In part, this original documentation is once more drawn from the BBC's own Written Archive Centre, where there is a wealth of material both personal and official. In some respects, it is difficult to argue with Raphael Samuel's claim that 'The BBC is, or ought to be, a researcher's dream'[17] when one considers the wealth of material of all kinds kept by the corporation. As he goes on to say, the BBC has always been 'obsessed with monitoring its own performance, minuting every stage in its decision-making processes, punctilious in timetabling its programmes'; that the result of this is that the researcher is presented with 'vast amounts of paperwork' to sift through is equally undeniable.[18] But the BBC has never kept 'a record of everything' as Samuel also claims.

This is one of the great frustrations faced by the BBC researcher, namely that there can so often be exasperating holes in any set of records relating to a given programme, person or period. The contents of the treasury-tagged manila folders in the Written Archive Centre range from the impressively comprehensive to the disappointingly incomplete. Some programme files contain everything from the first contracts to carefully trimmed cuttings of reviews in the press, whereas other programmes often do not have a file at all, especially in this earliest period. This study's topic demanded that time was spent carefully looking through the material accounting for the BBC's early explorations of television's feasibility, much of it years ahead of official transmissions and experiments conducted by the corporation themselves. This book demonstrates exactly how enlightening much of this material can be, even if replies to missing memos and contemporaneously collated timelines can serve to highlight how much is unavailable. Nevertheless, the key events are well covered, including the early experiments and demonstrations such as the public radio exhibition Radiolympia in late summer 1936, prior to the official launch. Memoranda detailing suggestions, decisions and misgivings are often present in the files detailing television's overall development. This is alongside the many documents that help to clarify the important details and facts, such as dates or the reasoning behind key decisions.

In addition, the British Postal Museum has its own archive of material that has been consulted. This has been particularly helpful as it understandably encompasses much of the documentation relating to debates prior to the BBC's official involvement. To an extent, the Post Office's involvement was the result of a technicality. As the body in charge of communications including telegraphy its remit was the closest to this new technology; especially true when it was unclear exactly what the technology would be used for.

The emphasis on material found in these archives does not result in an institutional bias, however. In practical terms, it should be remembered that these files consist of original correspondence and documentation, not an official written history. The result of this is that they contain material from those writing to the BBC and Post Office as well as within the institutions themselves. Thus we can witness not only the reactions towards, for example, Baird's request for a licence from the Post Office but also the original letter from Baird Television, outlining its plans and intentions. Additionally, the use of press reports allows an external viewpoint that highlights broader expectations. Television was not a rival to newspapers, with its lack of live news, and such is the range of titles consulted that we can gain an excellent understanding of the overall attitudes towards television. Such reports demonstrate that there could sometimes be quite a difference between the feelings and expectations of those working on the technology, and the way television was perceived and reported in the press.

Indeed, it is this range of attitudes and expectations that makes this period such an interesting one to explore. With no specific aim in mind, television meandered towards a role that now seems inevitable, but was actually the result of a great deal of debate, discussion and innovation. It will become clear that multiple histories, including the technological and legislative concerns, eventually formed the medium of television. This is an opportunity to properly consider this fluid sense of television early in its existence, a time when no-one could be sure exactly how it would develop.

Private Television

1

The Pioneers of Television

While television would ultimately be developed by national and international companies, with dedicated teams of researchers developing new and better technologies, many of the initial ideas that led to television's genesis came from private individuals. Television had been seriously, if intermittently, speculated about by scientists and engineers since the late 19th century. As early as 1879, *English Mechanic and World of Science* covered discussions of possible mechanisms for broadcasting moving pictures over a distance relying on the use of selenium cells.[1] These are highly influenced by light, and the principle was returned to several times over the coming decades, not least by the man whose name was largely synonymous with television during the 1920s and 1930s.

John Logie Baird remains the individual most readily associated with early television in the United Kingdom, and yet the general perception of him in academic histories is often dismissive. This is not unique to him; other individuals who contributed crucial (or ultimately superseded) pieces of technology which contemporaneously allowed television to further develop are often dismissed in favour of an emphasis on institutional developments. Andrew Crisell summed up the widely-held view of Baird amongst television historians when he wrote that:

> [R]omantic tales of lone inventors and brilliant eccentrics should not blind us to the fact that the major developments in television were the result of well-funded and systematic research by the major communication companies such as Marconi and RCA. Indeed, the most romantic of the lone figures, the Scotsman John Logie Baird, pursued his ideas down a dead-end, persisting with the mechanical method of image scanning long after its limitations had become generally apparent. Nevertheless, Baird achieved one or two firsts and several publicity coups.[2]

Conversely, the popular perception is more generous. For example, there have been at least three children's books published within the last decade alone that tell the story of Baird's work. These educational titles variously place him as a 'Super Scientist',[3] one of the 'Scientists Who Made History'[4] or as part of a group of 'Groundbreakers'.[5] As part of his analysis of the changing perceptions of Baird Donald F. McLean points to the 1966 transmission of a BBC documentary about the origins of television,[6] which opened with a selection of members of the public responses to the question 'who invented television?'. With the exception of three schoolboys (who came to the conclusion that Robert Louis Stevenson was the most likely candidate) all replied with the name John Logie Baird. His status is then dismissed by the narrator:

> But was it John Logie Baird? It was he who sent those first flickering pictures in 1923, and it was Baird who first transmitted television programmes on BBC transmitters. But the modern television system contains nothing, not one single piece of equipment or idea originated by John Logie Baird.[7]

This narration is typical of many serious histories of television and broadcasting since the 1950s. Baird is mentioned only in order for him to be dismissed, as if the programme-maker feels that a history of the medium must reference the famous inventor in order to placate public perceptions of television's creation, but that his presence would be deemed a misrepresentation of its 'true' development.

It may be fairest to say that Baird's role in television's early development lies somewhere between these two extremes. Essentially, understanding his role relies on the extent to which the closure of Baird's system in February 1937 influences one's perspective on the part that he and his contemporaries had played in the development of television to this point. Although his technology put him at the forefront of television in the mid-1920s, by the next decade his work was rarely at the cutting edge. Despite this he was already being perceived by many as television's 'inventor', and the reasons for this need consideration in order to understand the popular perception of television and its origins. However, for the purposes of this book, we need to discover what Baird himself was expecting from the system. This question can be applied to the technology, but also to the medium of television as a whole. We also need to consider the attitudes of others towards his work. This section is an opportunity to not only analyse the exact influence of those working privately on television's development, but also uncover their intentions and own predictions for the medium.

On a national level, Baird played a crucial role in convincing others that television could be a workable system even if his technological developments were eventually to have little in common with the system finally adopted. In time this would lead to the BBC's system of transmissions, which had helped to motivate larger companies, such as RCA and EMI, to dedicate more resources to higher quality systems of television, resulting in the technology that would remain in place for seventy years. Baird was far from the only person to be working on the development of television internationally at this time, as we will soon see, but his actions motivated serious discussions about the future of the medium. Baird's influence and skill in keeping television experiments an ongoing concern would extend internationally, even if his own work was to reach a dead end before the official BBC service was up and running. Tony Bridgewater, who in 1928 joined the Baird Television Development Company (which Baird set up the same year following these early experiments) has said that 'Baird used publicity a great deal and he used it recklessly – though I suppose that it was necessary when it came to going to the public for money'.[8] It was essential for Baird to convince the public of his technology's worth, as he initially perceived television as a wholly private enterprise that could only receive funding from the sale of sets. When Baird first came to public view in 1925 the BBC had only operated for three years, and was still running as a private company. As a result, their involvement at this stage would not have been a natural step and Baird decided to go it alone with his venture and attempt to garner as much interest as possible in his work, in order to secure a financial backer. In many ways, the location of his earliest public demonstration would indicate the crux of the problem that many would later have with Baird, in that he was often considered to be more interested in personal gain than scientific advancements.

Early Demonstrations

On 24 March 1925 Selfridge's department store placed an advertisement in *The Times* to highlight a new attraction for those visiting its Oxford Street store. The commercial article bore the headline 'Television: The First Public Demonstration' before informing the newspaper's readers that:

> For the first time in the world's history Television was publicly and successfully demonstrated on the stage in Palm Court at Selfridge's last week. A good deal has been written about Television but here, for the first time, this new wonder was shown in a form which proves scientifically that 'it can be done'.[9]

Britain was experiencing economic prosperity in the midst of the 'roaring twenties', with fashion and commercialism at the forefront of society. Increased spending power had allowed many to indulge in luxuries that would have earlier been perceived as frivolous, and this burgeoning technology could have been added to the ranks of these new items of interest.

Television was offering something new and innovative to the general public, and while the cinema may have offered the spectacle of *The Lost World* (d. Harry Hoyt, US: First National, 1925) and *Ben Hur* (d. Fred Niblo, US: MGM, 1925), this new medium was a markedly different prospect. It was far from a competitor to the cinema, at this point at least, given that it was only at the very beginning of its development. As with early film, the marvel was the technology itself, and the placement of such a series of demonstrations within a department store was less unusual than it may initially seem. Selfridge's had carved itself a reputation for putting on exhibitions and demonstrations that could entice customers into its store ever since its opening in March 1909. Its founder Harry Gordon Selfridge had aimed for the building to be more than simply a faceless department store. He said that he wanted 'to make my shop a civic centre, where friends can meet and buying is only a secondary consideration,'[10] and such exhibitions enabled him to cultivate this exclusive atmosphere. At its opening the store displayed over £1,000,000 worth of diamonds in its windows, while later the same year it housed Louis Blériot's famous monoplane which had been the first powered craft to cross the English Channel.[11] These were just two of several talking pieces that would attract publicity as well as contributing to the uniqueness of the store, a tradition that continues today. The exhibition of this television system sat alongside an array of marvels and achievements and was a guarantee of interest in both the store and the technology.

It was John Logie Baird who had showcased this basic system of television within the department store. Baird had spent much of his life trying to incite interest in his inventions. Born in Scotland in 1888, Baird showed an interest in basic engineering from an early age, including creating his own small telephone exchange as a child.[12] He studied at the University of Glasgow but suffered from many bouts of ill health, which he attempted to alleviate by temporarily moving to the West Indies before eventually relocating to Hastings in Sussex.[13] Most prominent amongst his earlier efforts was his work on the Baird Undersock, which he hoped would eliminate the problem of cold feet being caused by damp socks. Despite his claim that advertising was not 'the key' he publicised his undergarments in any way possible, including women patrolling the streets with sandwich boards.[14] This created some interest in the local press, a device which Baird called 'editorial publicity' that in turn led to 'considerable profit'.[15] This was a precursor to his later emphasis on garnering as much attention as possible for his work on television, and Selfridge's was to become just the first of many times when he courted the press.

Baird's own journey was just beginning. He had first created a mechanical system of television in 1923 and continued to refine it for many years, but Selfridge's was to be its first public demonstration. His television device was to be just one of many items of interest on show at the store that year, and even the flyer, distributed alongside Baird's demonstration at the department store, makes it clear that there were no commercial ties between Baird and Selfridge's. It read:

> We should perhaps explain that we are in no way financially interested in this remarkable invention; the demonstrations are taking place here only because we know that our friends will be interested in something that should rank with the greatest inventions of the century.

Selfridge's was correct in its prediction, but television's dominant role in culture and society in the second half of the twentieth century would not come about through Baird's technology. Selfridge's unambiguous distancing from Baird's work should not be taken as a slight against it, but rather an indication of exactly how early in the process this was. Selfridge's had no financial links with the product, but then few people did. Indeed, had Baird been able to offer television as a commercial concern at this time then it is unlikely that he would have been granted the privilege of publicising his effort in Oxford Street without coming to a financial arrangement with the store. In fact, Selfridge's offered Baird a fee of £20 per week for his time,[16] an indication that the system was being shown as an entertaining curiosity, akin to a sideshow, rather than a presentation of a serious business venture. Despite this seemingly generous offer, Baird's associate Will Day would write to the store on 20 April 1925 in an attempt to hasten payment, while also suggesting that the payment could be increased to 75 guineas.[17] Day himself had earlier bought a one-third interest in the invention for the sum of £200 after he had seen mention of it in the *Daily News* earlier that year.[18] There is nothing to indicate that the amount paid by Selfridge's was increased in accordance with the request, but Baird had made his first profit from the medium. He was not to make much more.

If Baird had anything on his side, then it was the initial timing of his invention. The mid- to late-1920s were a strong period for the British economy as a whole. As A.J.P. Taylor has put it, 'Englishmen drew closer together; class conflicts were dimmed; the curves of production, wages, and the standard of living, which had previously oscillated widely, now moved soberly upwards.'[19] The economic recovery following the 1914–1918 war had been relatively swift, and by the mid-1920s there was prosperity akin to that experienced at the end of the nineteenth century.[20] Indeed, the country actually seemed to be on an upward trajectory in terms of wealth, following the inevitable economic blip of the First World War. For example, it had been reported in 1899 that 15.46% of the working population of the city of York were living in borderline poverty, but thirty years later this had reduced to 6.8%, a figure that was indicative of increasing levels of personal wealth.[21]

Fig. 1.1: *Baird demonstrating his apparatus in Selfridge's in April 1925*
(Courtesy of the Royal Television)

There is a need to be careful when describing television while dealing with these earliest experiments. There are many potential pitfalls of using the word television to refer to both the medium and the technology, especially in a history that considers both elements. The peculiarity of the device operated in Selfridge's in the spring of 1925 only adds to the confusion. Photographs demonstrate the extent to which the system is unlike the technology that is now so familiar.

They show members of the public viewing the image through an apparently cardboard triangular viewfinder, at the end of which is a spinning disc (accompanied by a 'Danger' sign). This is a Nipkow Disc, a circular piece of card that has many holes cut in it, developed by German inventor Paul Gottlieb Nipkow and patented in 1885 (although this had lapsed shortly before the turn of the century).[22] Nipkow discs were a fundamental part of many of the early mechanical systems of television. They were spun at both the transmitting and receiving end of the apparatus, which could be physically connected or communicate through radio waves. Each tiny hole would pick up a small portion of the object being transmitted, although it could only really indicate whether the relevant part of the image was light or dark. The more holes drilled in the discs, the higher the quality of the transmitted image. There were always practical difficulties with the technology, not least the requirement that the discs operated directly in sync with each other. However, at this point in his experiments, Baird had an additional problem. He had not yet managed to produce an image with an appreciable greyscale. Instead, there was only light and dark, resulting in the transmission of shadows. As the scientific journal *Nature* said at the time, 'Mr Baird has overcome many practical difficulties, but we are afraid that there are many more to be surmounted before ideal television is accomplished.'[23]

Other Early Innovators

Baird was not the only person to be working on a system of television. For example, there was the work of Leon Theremin in the Soviet Union, who had worked on developing a mechanical system that would achieve 100 lines of resolution by early 1927, and so was a world leader for the time, albeit one shrouded in secrecy by the government and consequently little acknowledged for many years.[24] More famously, just three months after Baird's first demonstration in Selfridge's, Charles Jenkins of the United States gave a similar demonstration of a moving image (in this case, a toy windmill), with the added advantage of synchronous sound, which Baird had not achieved due to practical limitations.[25] Born in Ohio in 1867, Jenkins had long been fascinated with the technology of moving images, and first published his own theories on television in 1913.[26] Jenkins' system was based around the Nipkow disc in the same manner as Baird's own work. Jenkins had first been able to show moving images on 14 June 1923, but took until this 1925 transmission to make his first public demonstration.[27] Compared to Baird, Jenkins was perhaps more modest in his ambitions as he targeted radio enthusiasts rather than making claims for his technology as a long-term solution to the 'problem' of television, as Baird would. Jenkins' more understated approach has allowed him to largely escape the accusations of vague details and hyperbolic claims that would come to dog Baird. As it was, Jenkins would initially find success for his work, just on a smaller scale than his rival was aiming for.

While Baird was excitedly fine-tuning his mechanical apparatus, work on all-electronic television had reached a breakthrough. As early as 1907, the Russian scientist Boris Rosing had suggested that a television system could exist with a cathode ray tube (CRT) as a receiver for the images.[28] CRTs are vacuum sealed glass tubes, with a screen at one end, utilising electron guns at the opposite end to project an image on to the screen. The principle was easier than the practicalities of constructing such apparatus, but nevertheless the following year saw British scientist Alan Archibald Campbell Swinton offering his own suggestion in the journal *Nature* which expanded the idea into electronically capturing images, as well as receiving them.[29] Various practical limitations stood in the way of work on this theory, including the manufacture of cathode ray tubes to a sufficient standard. However, the work of an apprentice of Rosing, one Vladimir Zworykin, was to change this.

Zworykin's work with Rosing had shown results as early as 1911,[30] when they managed to show what they confessed was a very crude image, but it was one that proved that Rosing's idea that it could reproduce high quality images was more than just a theoretical one as it improved on the results of his earlier work. In 1919, Zworykin moved to the United States where he became a naturalised citizen and by 1925 he had constructed a basic but complete working electronic television system.[31] Unfortunately for him his then employers, the Westinghouse Electric and Manufacturing Company, were unimpressed and elected to move him away from his work on television. This would not be the end of Zworykin's contribution to the medium, but the sidelining of his innovative work on electronic systems of television would allow the lower quality (but more easily constructed) systems to flourish in its stead.

Many of Baird's later problems had their roots in this earliest work. He would find it difficult to move away from the mechanically-based systems of television, as this is where his strengths lay. When high quality all-electronic television developed by Marconi-EMI was slowly unveiled in the mid-1930s it demonstrated the strength of a purely electronic system in contrast to Baird's work. By the time of the 1936 broadcasts Baird Television had started to move towards electronically-based methods in part, but other aspects remained mechanically complex. However, perhaps it is telling that by this point Baird was no longer controlling the technical direction of the company. The journey from this earliest demonstration to the launch of the BBC service over a decade longer was not to be a straightforward one.

From Experiments to Business

While the overall impression of television's development may be that Selfridge's was Baird's breakthrough moment, after which he managed to gradually strengthen his business as a result of the initial publicity, this was not the case. Rather, there was no serious interest expressed in his work. As

Briggs has put it, 'From the glare of publicity, Baird passed yet again into the twilight world of insecurity.'[32] In a move symptomatic of wider views of the feasibility of (and interest in) television Baird was forced to borrow money from his family in order to continue his work.[33] It seemed that television was less desired than Baird had hoped, although he did receive some ex gratia free products from companies to help him further his efforts, including £200 worth of valves from the General Electric Company.[34] While this demonstrates a general sense of goodwill towards his efforts, it also indicates that he was not particularly seen as a serious businessman – nor, perhaps, television as a serious business concern. Instead, this seems to be an example of Britain's love affair with the principle of a lone inventor working on bizarre inventions, a relationship that has continued with individuals such as Clive Sinclair and his C5 electric scooter/car hybrid. Baird had already attracted some private investors, however. In 1925 he had been joined by Captain O.G. Hutchinson as a business partner alongside another friend Captain Broderip; together, the three men had bought back Will Day's share in the company.[35]

On 2 October 1925 Baird had managed to substantially improve upon the shadow images that he had earlier demonstrated at Selfridge's. The head of a ventriloquist's dummy, called Stookie Bill (sometimes spelt Stooky Bill), was the first object to be seen with proper variation of greyscale and as a moving image, although initially it was only five frames per second,[36] which was far too low for a convincing illusion of movement.

By early the next year Baird's system had advanced to the point where it allowed the viewer to clearly make out objects, movement and half tones. On 26 January 1926 he showed this system to the Royal Institution and the press, keen that the new developments were widely seen and known about.[37] This was not simply because of interest in personal acclaim, but some savvy

Fig. 1.2: *Baird and 'Stookie Bill'*

(Courtesy of the Royal Television Society)

business thought. Hutchinson and Baird realised that publicity was the only way to attract financial interest, making such demonstrations to the press of paramount importance.

International Developments in Television

While Baird was sometimes at the forefront of the technology across the globe, during this period international developments occurred so rapidly that pole position in the quest for a high quality practical system continually changed. Additionally, some of those working in the field were playing the long game of steady investment, the exact opposite of Baird's approach of gaining investment for new innovations, rather than producing a stable solution to the problem of television. For example, across the channel Édouard Belin and Fernand Holweck demonstrated CRTs to French officials on 26 July 1926.[38] Although the demonstration could only show outlines and operated at a mere ten frames per second with screen resolution of 33 lines, it was a rudimentary step in the eventual direction taken by television.[39] The short term results may not have been particularly impressive, but Belin and others felt that further refinement would show it as the way forward for television. Just two weeks after Belin and Holweck's demonstration, on 2 August 1926, Dr Alexandre Dauvillier (also of France) demonstrated a superior CRT system showing 40 lines of resolution, once more at ten frames per second.[40] Later that year, on 25 December, Kenjiro Takayanagi of Japan independently demonstrated the electronic display of a symbol on a CRT, captured using a Nipkow disc mechanism.[41]

Work on mechanical television was not entirely abandoned, however. For example, the Hungarian Denys von Mihaly would demonstrate a system akin to Baird's at the Berlin Radio Exhibition in 1929, with a 30-line resolution.[42] Mihaly would later try to introduce his system to the UK, including discussion with the BBC, but his attempts were met with disdain similar to that encountered by Baird.[43] Germany showed some interest, but actually ended up collaborating with Baird for a time, as Baird Television was invited to help form a company that was essentially a consortium of those working in the field, which was named Fernseh AG.[44] Their work continued until 1935, when Hitler instructed the removal of Baird Television from the company.[45]

Such work on mechanical television would eventually be superseded by all-electronic systems, work on which was beginning to show results, and would eventually dominate the technology of television.

One of the best indications of Baird's and Hutchinson's personal hopes for the system lies in their approach to one of the biggest problems that needed tackling before television would be able to launch. This was not an issue related to television content, or even to necessary advancements in the technology, but to the question of infrastructure. It would not be fair to say that Baird was naive to overlook the role of the BBC at this point considering its youth and then status as a private company. However, a letter written to the Post Office by Hutchinson on 4 January 1926 indicates that they certainly hoped for a more straightforward process of setting up a system of television than was to be the case. In the end, Hutchinson's letter would begin a series of correspondence that would last for several years, such were the problems presented by it. It read:

Sir,

Having completed and patented a machine with which vision can be transmitted instantaneously by wireless. [sic] We beg to apply for a licence to broadcast same from London, Glasgow, Manchester and Belfast.

We have been informed that there is no necessity for a licence to transmit vision, but before going to the expense of opening these stations we submit the above application to keep ourselves in order.

Should there be any restriction, of which we are at present unaware we would be pleased if you could acquaint us with the same at the earliest moment.[46]

This letter appears to have created a degree of confusion at the Post Office, with the request coming as something of a surprise as there had been no decision regarding the technical specifications for broadcasts of television over the air. It may be that Baird and Hutchinson hoped that such an application would simply be approved by a junior official as a matter of course, such is the tone of the letter in its attempts to underplay the question. However, the letter manages to contradict itself when, following a request for a licence, it also states that 'We have been informed that there is no necessity for a licence to transmit vision'.[47] Had the company genuinely believed this then it is rather more likely that such correspondence would never have been entered into.

It is also significant that while Baird had perfected some form of moving image, the practical implementation of the system was little considered, with Baird and his colleagues expressing little interest in issues of content. The most ambitious claims of possible uses for the principle of seeing live images from a distance could hardly be satisfied by Baird's groundbreaking but primitive receiver. Baird had made what was then an important technical leap, but it needed considerable refinement and development before it could be used as anything other than a novelty, as had been seen in Selfridge's the previous year.

Fig. 1.3: *Captain O.G. Hutchinson*
(Courtesy of the Royal Television Society)

As it stood, television was an unknown quantity, and Hutchinson's expectation that the Post Office would be in charge of licensing any transmissions (should a licence be required at all) was not necessarily shared by the organisation. The request prompted a degree of correspondence within the Post Office as, for the first time, the crucial question of what television was expected to be was asked by a public body. Such discussions highlight the extent to which Baird's role in television's development was an unwitting one. Hutchinson's dogged persistence in presenting a fully functioning official television system, with the resulting opportunities for making money, forced considerations of how television was to be dealt with. At the Post Office, staff members internally pointed out that the body held responsibility for any messages or other communication by telegraphy, with 'communication' being the key point of discussion. 'The material question is, therefore, whether the transmission of "Vision" by etheric waves amounts to the transmission of a message or other communication,' reads one message. It goes on to say:

> I assume that by the transmission of "Vision" the company means the transmission of a photograph that is, the reproduction at the receiving end. If this be so, then, in my opinion the transmission of "Vision" by itself cannot be regarded as the transmission of a message or communication. But it would appear to be quite impracticable for the company to transmit "Vision" by itself; they would, I should imagine, be compelled to send some kind of signal to the person receiving the "Vision" indicating either some step in the process, or the time when the process was about to commence, or the nature of kind of "Vision" which was being sent, e.g., the name of the person whose photograph was transmitted.[48]

For the first time, a fixed definition of television was being sought. It is telling from Hutchinson's original letter that no specific use of the system was offered, and it may be this that caused the most confusion at the Post Office. Without being clear exactly what the licence was to be used for, and precisely what the accompanying technical requirements were, the Post Office was circumspect of the request. When it requested clarification, Baird and Hutchinson seemed once more to sidestep the issue of television usage, instead sending a clipping from the *Daily Telegraph* detailing the successful transmission of a doll's head in his experiments earlier that year. It seems unlikely that they were being coy. Rather, Baird and Hutchinson do not seem to have formulated their own idea of what their technology could be used for. Certainly Baird gives no concrete indication in the press reports around this time, other than to vaguely compare the system to radio. This comparison appears to be a technical one, however, regarding the transmission over the air, and the question of content is not touched upon. Considering the low resolution of the pictures when compared to the transmissions ten years later, the possibilities would certainly have been limited, but it is clear that few knew what uses would be found for Baird's work. What were to become elementary aspects of the medium are unclear to the Post Office at this point. Most strikingly, we can see from the above letter that the first expectations of television do not even touch on the use of sound alongside moving images. Additionally, it fails to consider the underlying issue of programming, with its expectation of content being limited to static images and preceding messages, potentially an indication that personal communication may be its principal use. Much of television's development in the next thirteen years would not only be technical, but also related to expected uses of the system itself once established.

Despite this lack of focus regarding the possible uses of the technology, Baird and Hutchinson not only claimed to be ready to set up these four transmitting stations but issued a follow-up letter outlining their business intentions more clearly. Written just seven days after the earlier letter, this missive implored the Post Office to give its permission for broadcasts as soon as possible so that a planned 500 sets could be manufactured, stating that 'At the moment we are held up awaiting your reply'.[49] That this letter is also signed by Hutchinson, doubtless a man keen to recoup some of his investment in Baird's work, is unlikely to be a coincidence. However, it is representative of Baird's attitude that as soon as he achieved the absolute basics of a television service, the transmission of a doll's head with sufficient clarity to be identifiable, he felt it should be rushed into mass production.

The Post Office eventually decided to be cautious in its response to Hutchinson, but not dismissive. After a demonstration to one of their engineers, it decided that Baird and Hutchinson's venture was small scale but required permission to use radio wavelengths in order to improve its current 'rudimentary' wireless aspect.[50] The Post Office's official reply trod a careful line between condoning such a service and denying Baird any prospect of

Fig. 1.4: *Baird looking into a Nipkow disc in 1925*

(Courtesy of the Royal Television Society)

television transmissions. After first clarifying the technicalities, the Post Office agreed to licence no more than two transmitting stations at a specified wavelength of between 150 and 200 metres, outside normal radio broadcasting hours. 'It would be a condition of such licences that the stations should be established on private premises and be used for experimental purposes only,'[51] said the letter to Hutchinson, sent on 28 January 1926. This was an important clarification, as the original request had made no indication of the experimental nature of any broadcasts; instead, there was an implication that such broadcasts would be a fully fledged, independent television system. The Post Office appeared to be unsure of its own power over this new technology, stating that the permission would only be granted 'with the concurrences of other Government departments concerned,' although it is not made clear which departments this was referring to.[52]

The main reasoning behind the Post Office's unwillingness to assign any wavelengths to Baird on a more permanent basis would have had its roots in the problem it faced in 1922. When radio became a service that utilised transmissions to a wider audience, rather than as a form of communication between two persons, several companies lobbied for licences to broadcast. However, the spectrum of wavelengths was finite, and so broadcasters would need to be either limited or conglomerated. In the end, the latter option was taken, with the six major wireless manufacturers joining forces to create the British Broadcasting Company. Indeed, Paddy Scannell highlights the limited wavelength available for such transmissions as a reason for the emergence of radio as a public service.[53] Undoubtedly aware of these problems, Baird's company (at this point simply called Television Ltd.) agreed to the letter's terms and requested two licences, call signs 2TV and 2TW, each costing £3 a year. However, their technology undoubtedly limited what they would be able to show, resulting in marked differences to the system that eventually launched a decade later.

The Technology of Baird's Early Television

Much of the internal correspondence regarding television at this time relates to the question of how its broadcasts could be accommodated within the existing bandwidth allocated for radio transmissions, but there was a more pertinent question to be asked of the technology. Later in this book there is an examination of early television programming and in part this is because the programming was often very different from later television content. By the same principle, the early technology of television transmissions was very different from that later adopted. The Nipkow Disc formed the basis of the technology, which initially did not use a television screen as we might know it, but a small hole through which the image could be viewed. Existing photographs of Hutchinson's face as transmitted by Baird's system in early 1926 also demonstrate the poor clarity of the image, with individual lines of resolution highly visible and no fine detail. However, we should consider exactly what Baird's system was at this point. It was a mechanical, thirty-line system of broadcast at five frames per second. Baird points out in his memoirs *Television and Me* that the image as seen by a user of television would be of higher quality than the existing photographs,[54] but it was still a system that required modification in order to be assured of public acceptance and investment.

It is difficult to assess exactly what television could be used for from such scant, and sometimes contradictory, evidence of its overall quality and usefulness. In actual fact, except for the brief press reports and Baird and Hutchinson's own claims, it is not easy to get a sense of exactly how usable Baird's system was at this point. Certainly it is the basic principles rather than the real effects that Baird and Hutchinson understandably focused on. That is to say, the achievement of a moving image at a distance, rather than the usefulness of such an image when the camera was static, the resolution low, and the viewing area small.

If we are to understand the reasoning behind the perception of television from those viewing Baird's apparatus then we need to gain a better impression

Fig. 1.5: *The first photograph of a television image, showing the system as it operated in 1926. The face is O.G. Hutchinson's.*

(Courtesy of the National Media Museum/Science and Society Picture Library)

of exactly what they were presented with. We are fortunate that an engineer with no vested interest in the project on either side was to view the experiments and later provide a detailed demonstration of both his own views of the technology but also, crucially for this study, a recollection of Baird and Hutchinson's privately discussed plans for the system, where they were rather more forthcoming than in their carefully written formal letters.

The origin of this written account is somewhat unusual in itself. In 1948, the Gas Light and Coke Company, later to become part of British Gas following the nationalisation of the industry in 1949, sent the BBC a typed appraisal of one of Baird's 1926 demonstrations that one of their employees, E.G. Stewart, had recently re-discovered. 'It might prove useful for some coming of age programme!'[55] said the covering letter, and it is certainly extremely valuable as an independent person's view of the system. Following his meeting with Baird and Hutchinson, Stewart defines television by saying that 'It is claimed that such an invention will have a public appeal in that pictures may be shown of subjects in movement at the time of their occurrence, either in public, as in a cinema, or in the home as an attached supplementary to a broadcast receiver.'[56] The potential of television sets in public would be one explored by other countries, such as Germany, as well as by Baird, but it was broadly seen as something that could complement a domestic service rather than the principal use of the technology.

Mention of television as a supplementary device for the radio receiver indicates that close parallels were starting to be drawn between the systems; indeed, later there would often be clarification of the placement of television as a potential alternative to radio rather than a system designed to supplant it. In the early years of broadcasts there was even an option from some manufacturers for a 'vision only' television set which could be connected to a radio receiver in order to provide sound, an attempt to reduce the cost for the potential purchaser. It may be telling that it was not the involvement of the BBC that invited comparisons with radio, and that some time before their involvement this connection was already being made.

Stewart goes on to point out another potential use that was referred to by Baird's company during the demonstration. 'Further, that pictures may be sent by telephone and photographed at the arrival end for newspaper work with less risk of being spoilt by electrical faults than is the case with existing picture transmission methods.'[57] This is such a specific use that it surely must have been suggested by Baird or Hutchinson, and it has similarities to many of the ideas in the magazine for enthusiasts of the new medium, *Television*. In that periodical, those who had taken an interest in television would fill the pages with more than just technical news and developments. They would also speculate on potential uses, from televising plays to its potential as a spying device.

Considering that picture definition was the most significant concern with Baird's television system, it is curious that the transmission of static images was being touted as a potential use for a system that, as he acknowledged above in reference to the photograph of Hutchinson through his receiver, only becomes poorer in quality when photographed. However, this suggestion is just one of many that Baird used in order to give a wider range of potential uses of his new invention so as to attract interest and investment. Baird frequently did this, tailoring the uses and advantages of his technology to appeal to those currently viewing it or expressing an interest. Certainly there is no evidence of this claimed use being based on any of the work undertaken by Baird for a moving picture system. Nevertheless, the Fultograph system, developed by German scientist Otto Fulton, has similarities, being a primitive precursor to the fax machine in its method of transmitting still images across a distance. This system was in the later stages of its development at this time and was even trialled by the BBC, to the ire of Baird.[58]

Stewart also highlights one aspect that was to come to dog Baird's work, that of the usability of his undoubtedly innovative technology. 'I found it possible to distinguish between two images I had previously seen in the life,' he wrote, before pointing out that 'At the same time it would be very difficult to recognise an individual previously unknown from the television representation.'[59] Not only were the images unclear, but the experience of watching the apparatus at work was far from a comfortable one, as he goes on to say: 'I found that after about half an hour's watching of the screen that ocular distress was noticeable.'[60] Such 'ocular distress' is likely to be the result of the very low framerate of five frames per second (which would exhibit considerable flicker) rather than the low resolution. While Baird speculates on ways of increasing the quality of the images, this is an example of his non-lateral appreciation of the problem. It would simply be impossible to gain a high quality system using this method of transmission, but Baird suggested quadrupling the detail by splitting the image into four separate squares, although Stewart remained unconvinced. 'I believe the apparatus will be considerably complicated by this idea and I am of [the] opinion that four wavebands instead of one will be required for wireless transmission which in view of the already congested stated [sic] of the ether is not likely to be practicable.'[61] It was not, and such a usage never came to pass.

The underlying impression of Stewart's assessment is that he found the demonstration to be of interest, but he also clearly believed that there were limitations to the fundamental approach of Baird to the question of television. Stewart could not perceive how the approach taken by Baird could be furthered so as to be appealing to the public at large. This is a problem that would fatally affect Baird's company in the coming years, but at this point he was still at the forefront of the field of television. However, the refining of the technology itself was just one of the problems faced by Baird at this time. His company was in an unstable financial state, in dire need of continual ongoing investment in order to continue its work. With private backing increasingly difficult to obtain, there was only one option left open.

2

From Experiments to Business

In the United Kingdom, the transition of television from a private concern funded by individuals and businesses to one that that was perceived as a public product was to be a complicated one. The principle of what could be meant by television as a 'public service' had been notably absent from John Logie Baird's considerations to this point. Although the notion of Public Service Broadcasting was to be a central facet of the official service a decade later, there was little mention of this amongst Baird's publicity. At this juncture the emphasis was on the technology rather than content and given the state of the BBC at this point the lack of clarification should come as little surprise. It is unclear why Baird and Hutchinson ignored the specifics of television broadcasts so entirely, when Hutchinson in particular was so keen to recoup his investment. It may well be that they perceived programming content to be a long-term problem, with the novelty of the technology enough to carry it through the short term. Certainly they could cite precedent, with early film actualities relying on audiences paying to witness technology that allowed the very principle of moving images on screen to be a reality, rather than innate interest in the viewing of workers leaving a factory or trains leaving station platforms. Baird and Hutchinson little considered the considerable obstacle of extra cost, however. It may well be that they also realised that Baird's technology was likely to be usurped, and needed to capitalise on their short-lived leading of the field.

In 1926 the BBC was still a private company in just its fifth year of operation, a far cry from the huge broadcaster that it now is. It operated a monopoly out of expediency, and it was not unreasonable to imagine that it could occupy itself solely with radio broadcasts. After all, the BBC took no role in distribution of telegrams or telephone calls. It would be nearly a year before the company became a public corporation and so it remained a private company at this point, but the Baird company had little serious idea as to how to form a sister company for television broadcasts. Their use of the 'public service' phrase in official communications was cynical, used so as to encourage 'a

LIVERPOOL JOHN MOORES UNIVERSITY
LEARNING SERVICES

concession' from the Post Office.[1] Hutchinson in particular seemed to lack tact, and made his desires for monetary recompense so blatant that internal correspondence indicates that Baird and his company were eyed with a suspicion that better behaved rivals, such as Marconi-EMI, would avoid.[2] Hutchinson's decision to effectively treat the early development of television as a battle with authorities rather than a co-operative process sealed Baird's fate when his technology became disposable once it was overtaken by better-performing rivals.

Retrospectively we can see that Baird only had a small window of opportunity to successfully launch his own private system of television, essentially between 1926 and 1929. The latter date would give rise not only to the most significant involvement of the BBC to that point, but also to the Wall Street Crash, which would affect the country's economy to the extent that any consideration of investment in television would be somewhat peripheral to any private investor or company's wider concerns. Nevertheless, the BBC was not a rival in a commercial sense. Indeed, its monopoly formed a central aspect of its public service obligations for radio. It was believed that any rival would necessarily engage in programming designed to appeal to the largest audience possible at all times, and such an environment would force the BBC to compete on a commercial level in order to retain an audience. This did not prevent Baird Television from attempting to secure public investment for their product, hoping that television might be operated entirely or partially separately from the institutionalised form of radio, something that would have seemed possible considering the lack of a firm guiding hand for television's development at this point, even if it did not come to pass.

Following a telephone call from Hutchinson on 4 February 1926 a Post Office memorandum revealed that '[Hutchinson] and Mr Baird are short of money for further development and desire to raise capital on the prospects of their invention'.[3] The request almost coincided with a key moment in broadcasting history, as just one month later the Crawford Committee would report its recommendations for the future of the BBC to parliament. A licence fee was already in place so as to negate the need for advertisements, but the Committee would recommend the placement of the BBC as a public corporation. From 1 January 1927 there would be a more explicit public service remit behind the country's radio broadcasts. Baird appears to have seen this investigation into the merits of public service radio as justification for state assistance with his work. '[Baird and Hutchinson] were anxious, therefore, that we should give them some kind of concession for a public service, or at any rate a promise of such a concession,'[4] the memo continued. This usage of 'public service' seems to be quite different from how it has generally been perceived. Rather, Hutchinson and Baird appear to use the phrase feeling that it would place television as a utility alongside electricity, water and gas, or simply a service to which the public could gain access, a concept that Paddy Scannell has also highlighted as a potential reading of what can be meant by 'public service' broadcasting.[5]

There is no real question at this point of their system operating because of anything other than a desire to make money out of a perceived public demand. The very technology of television seems to be understood as a 'public service' by Hutchinson and Baird, overlooking issues of content, because it was felt that this would facilitate some sort of financial bursary. Further, it had been envisaged that the technology of television could form the basis for many different types of services, an implication of the extent to which Baird was considering only the technical aspects of the medium. This is despite the fact that Baird's largest problem was not a lack of interest in the system more generally, but a widespread appreciation that despite his achievements there would need to be quite some advancement to make the system a convincing proposition. As Stewart had concluded, 'at the present time the image resulting is appreciably lacking in detail and so can have but little practical application,'[6] even though he viewed Baird's work just two months before Hutchinson claimed to the Post Office that it was 'practically out of the experimental stage'.[7] This fundamental difference of opinions about the intangible issue of acceptable quality for television broadcasts was to be irreconcilable. What is enlightening is that Baird's diaries express little dissatisfaction with his early technology. Written a significant time after his involvement in television, there is scant acknowledgment that his technology was unusable as a practical proposition, whatever its merits as a new development in the field of television. Baird was blinkered by his excitement at having produced a notable first; Hutchinson was blinkered by the its financial implications.

Hutchinson's pleas for a concession fell on deaf ears however, with his claims for the public service value inherent in the medium being viewed with some cynicism. The Post Office memorandum goes on to claim that he seemed to have 'a very vague idea as to what kind of public service would be given,'[8] indicating again that this was just a phrase that Baird and Hutchinson hoped would give positive connotations that would be to their financial benefit. In terms of content, Baird Television had just made vague suggestions of being able to see what was being broadcast on the radio or, as in this conversation with the Post Office, the notion of viewing a play in Paris from across the channel. Hutchinson was attempting to echo the then-current debate about radio's own public service role by applying some of the same terminology to television, although the meaning was muddled.

Over the next two years Baird would start experimenting with additional types of television, including a form of colour broadcasts. However, these developments were once more based on his mechanical method based around the spinning disc or mirror drum. While this was certainly an impressive start, substantial refinement would be required in order for the system to serve a practical purpose. The company's financial situation was precarious at this point and Baird's memoirs demonstrate the extent to which he relied upon the uniqueness of his invention. 'In 1927 we had a complete monopoly of television,'[9] he wrote. 'We shouted it loud and we shouted it long and it was our main prop and argument with the rather nervous underwriters [of his company].'[10]

Early Television Stations in the United States

Baird had not been alone in developing television and as far as public demonstrations were concerned, this was the year that his monopoly was well and truly broken. In the United States, the company AT&T (American Telephone and Telegraph) made a television transmission over telephone lines on 7 April 1927 using a system akin to Baird's spinning disc method.[11] Just one year later the aforementioned Charles Jenkins would be granted America's first television licence for his station W3XK, which transmitted from 2 July 1928.[12] Crucially, however, the United States lacked the onus of accountability for television stations that operated in the United Kingdom. Jenkins' station was a private concern that had few restrictions beyond the technical. This is not to say that it was simply a cynical venture, but it highlights the difference in obstacles between the two nations. On 11 September 1928 Jenkins' television station achieved a notable first in its broadcast of the play *The Queen's Messenger*, which was the first dramatic broadcast on television.[13] This perhaps signposts more clearly than anything that the idea that television's core programming is authored programming was not present from the beginning of television. Jenkins' station broadcast five times a week for over two months before their first work of fiction. The emphasis was very much on the technology, while the speculation over television's uses emphasised its 'liveness'.

In the United States concerns over whether the medium should become a public service (with the vague set of definitions that this would entail) were entirely secondary to the consideration that private enterprise should have the freedom to develop television, and (initially at least) licences were granted more freely, as had happened with radio.[14] This did not mean complete freedom over the airwaves, however. By 1934, when television was still in its experimental stages, the Federal Radio Commission was dictating that licensees were free to experiment with television broadcasts, subject to certain regulations, but that they could not sell advertising time.[15] This may be read as an early attempt to assert at least some control over the types of broadcasts being shown, and establish them as experimental rather than permanent (with no established national standard for television by this point) or purely commercial. A more cynical, but compelling, argument is that fully fledged commercial television stations might have been expected to pay more for their licences than experimental ones.

Baird was riled by international developments such as the work undertaken by Charles Jenkins in the United States, whose apparatus was based on the same principle as Baird's and so could not be rightfully considered an advancement. Indeed, companies as large as Bell Telephone Laboratories in the United States were continuing to work on mechanical television, with two of their engineers demonstrating both small screen and large screen television systems, with the images transmitted by cable and across the airwaves, in April 1927.[16] However, he did directly respond to the work of Bell Laboratories by transmitting a signal across telephone cable between London and Glasgow using just two engineers, as well as transmitting across the Atlantic.[17] Nevertheless, the increased rivalry only compounded Baird's fear that he would be usurped, and he would later ask, 'Oh! Why did I not cash in when the going was good?'[18] Nevertheless, Baird had continued work on a series of 'firsts'. These included his Phonovision discs, which were recordings of his television broadcasts onto gramophone records. There is no evidence that Baird was able to actually replay these discs, however. Decades later, Donald F. McLean created computer software that could decode the recordings and the brief, silent and low-resolution images have now been recovered – proving, if nothing else, that Baird's concept was basically sound.[19]

To an extent, then, Baird did in fact 'cash in when the going was good', as he put it. If there seems to be a lack of direction from Baird regarding television's future over the next two years then this was because he did not continue to refine the basics of his own technology in order to placate those less convinced of its long-term merits and achieve his aim of an independent television service. Instead, he worked on new aspects of the presentation of images that utilised the same basic technology, including successful experiments in 'stereoscopic' (3D) television.[20] Although such work demonstrated that he could advance in some areas, he was failing to exploit his 'monopoly' and launch his own service to the public. This is once more a result of the Post Office's misgivings concerning the infrastructure of the service, and underlying concerns surrounding the quality of Baird's transmissions. These would only become more apparent as work continued on all-electronic systems of television elsewhere in the world. On 7 September 1927 Philo Farnsworth of the United States transmitted the first image using his electronic picture dissector camera tube.[21] There were significant problems with the technology, including the need for very high luminance when capturing images, but this was advancement towards television's eventual all-electronic future.

In light of these international developments, it should come as little surprise that concerns about Baird's work were also raised separately from the Post Office discussions. While some engineers and private hobbyists were impressed with Baird's work others were less convinced. A.A. Campbell Swinton, proponent of using CRTs for reproduction of television images, was so concerned by Baird's publicity and ongoing insistence to the press that television was an immediate concern that in 1928 he wrote to *The Times* regarding the issue. The letter was published, but not in its entirety. Even the published portion was unequivocal in its stance, with Campbell Swinton attempting to counter the prognostications which he called 'at times, very absurd,'[22] and pointing to the inherent mechanical nature as the biggest flaw. Part of the unpublished section expressed his view that he feared that 'Baird and Hutchinson are rogues, clever rogues, and quite unscrupulous, who are fleecing the ignorant public, and should be shown up.'[23]

Campbell Swinton's letter followed what was to be the first element of co-operation between Baird and the BBC. A letter from Hutchinson to the Post Office on 17 August 1927 indicated that the BBC had in fact granted its consent to the use of its stronger transmitters for Baird's test broadcasts although they were not colluding on the future of television.[24] Baird's work and the BBC were entirely separate, and it was only the corporation's transmission infrastructure that brought the two together at all. This early co-operation did not last, with the Post Office ordering that the transmissions were too strong for the agreed stipulations of the current licence held by Baird. He was encouraged to apply for a new licence in order for his transmissions to continue. A Post Office internal memo the next month said of Baird Television that 'these people are not acting very well,' and advised caution in allowing the use of BBC facilities.[25] However, it also stipulated that 'We should not lay ourselves open to the charge of being obstructive or of failing to give reasonable facilities for the development of what may be an important invention'.[26] Baird's own reliance on external assistance had signalled the requirement for further investigation of the long-term feasibility of television, and indicated the likelihood of collaboration for any system of television.

Baird himself would later assert that 'We might have developed completely independently of the BBC; we had already broken their monopoly.'[27] He points out in his memoirs that his company had its own series of low powered, private transmitters, stating that 'In effect we had a separate broadcasting system independent of the BBC.'[28] But circumstances changed once more, and Baird and the BBC were forced to become allies. We should not presume that this co-operation amounted to Baird handing over his technology for the corporation's own use. Far from it, rather it was the case that the BBC simply had to provide assistance as the only body with the broadcasting infrastructure to help further development of the technology. We will see in the next section that the corporation was not particularly suspicious of television itself, although it hardly took a particular interest. It did, however, find that its personnel would have something of a personal battle with Baird and Hutchinson.

The BBC was undoubtedly obstructive when, following incidents outside his control, Baird was forced to request their assistance. Baird had transmitted some material for those with the necessary equipment to view, including a production of the play *Box and Cox*, from a small studio and transmitter situated on Long Acre, a street near Covent Garden.[29]

However, the transmissions were forced to close down when they interfered with other broadcasts, and so Baird requested the use of the BBC's 2LO transmitter which, ironically, was situated above Selfridge's. The BBC's Chief Engineer Peter Eckersley was amongst those who viewed the demonstrations that were arranged to show the service. He was not convinced of its

Fig. 2.1: *The Long Acre studio in 1928*
(Courtesy of the Royal Television Society)

merit, and his personal reservations would create tensions between Baird and the corporation from this point on as opinions of what could and should constitute a television service differed.[30]

Collaborating with the BBC

By early 1929 the phrase 'public service' was still being used by Baird Television as a justification for launching an official form of television, despite the BBC's own protestations following demonstrations in late 1928. A 'Terms of Reference' document for internal BBC use from early 1929 indicates the extent of the fundamental disagreement between the BBC and the company, with an already fractious relationship worsening. Written by Gladstone Murray, the BBC's Assistant Controller in charge of Public Relations, it claimed that 'the advisers of the Baird Television Company believe that their apparatus is sufficiently developed to have a public service value. They contend that the attitude of the BBC is obstructive and irrational.'[31] Further, it emphasised Eckersley's opinion that the system had already 'reached the limit of its development owing to the basic technical limitations of the method employed'.[32] In time, Eckersley was to be proven right, but whatever the motivation behind use of the 'public service' term, Baird and Hutchinson were also correct. Eckersley's opinions on the workability of the Baird technology clouded BBC perspectives on the principle of television as a whole. The intervention of Hutchinson was the main reason the BBC was considering television at all. They certainly were not spending time considering television outside specific communications. As a corporation that was made up of a conglomeration of telecommunication companies it might seem that the BBC was in a perfect position to develop work on television technology themselves. Instead, the medium was left up to others to work on. If the BBC could have formally separated themselves from discussions about television at this point then there is little doubt that they would have.

The BBC had not been the only ones to be unimpressed with the current state of affairs regarding television technology, however. 'It appears that both Hutchinson and Baird were the targets for a considerable knife throwing display by the RMA [Radio Manufacturers' Association] exhibition council when they gave their demonstration of television,'[33] stated a BBC memo written by J.H. Whitehouse for Murray's benefit a few months earlier on 25 September 1928. 'The council wished to ensure that the public were not being sold "a pup",'[34] continued the report, indicating the extent to which those in the technical community were suspicious of the private company's motivation. Nevertheless, the memo acknowledges that Hutchinson ('who was continuously evasive') had claimed that the limitations of the service should be made clear when and if sets were sold. Also worthy of note is the comment in the memo that 'I heard one of the stand assistants being subjected to rapid fire by what appeared to be an American Journalist. The leading question was headed off by a reference to the directors, Xmas being given vaguely as a date of commencement'.[35] Similarly, Whitehouse had his own reservations:

> The Baird machine may be said to give a recognisable human head. It is curiously unlike any particular face. I suspect that the eyebrows were heavily made up. Only very slow movements are possible, anything of even normal speed producing a wild blurr. [*sic*] The impression is of a curiously ape like head, decapitated at the chin, swaying up and down in a streaky stream of yellowy light. I was reminded of those shrunken human heads favoured by such persons as Mr. M. Hedges. Not even the collar or tie were visible, the effect being more grotesque than impressive.[36]

Although Baird's system had likely moved to the more effective small flying spot scanners by this point rather than the large Nipkow discs, and advanced to 12.5 frames per second at around this time, the comments indicate that from the BBC's perspective fundamental flaws remained present. The principle of television that Baird explored was simply not capable of high quality broadcasts, while Baird did not have either the resources or the technical skill to develop alternative systems. Years of refinements were only advancing Baird's early technology slightly further towards a final dead end.

However, perhaps more interesting are Whitehouse's observations relating to the general public who had seen this demonstration. 'The faces of those leaving the show showed neither excitement or (*sic*) interest. Rather like a Fair crowd who had sported 6d. to see if the fat lady was really as fat as she was made out to be.'[37] Whatever Baird's achievements, he was still being seen by some as working on a technology that was little more than a one-off attraction rather than something that would benefit from a long-term financial investment; his work was seen as a sideshow attraction, just as it had been in Selfridge's some three years earlier. In fact, some were even less kind, with Eckersley following Campbell Swinton's lead when he said in a 10 October 1928 memo that Baird's system was either 'intentional fraud or a hopeless mechanical failure'.[38]

If the attitude towards Baird had become a little more antagonistic, then this was perhaps inevitable given the frank exchange of views between Baird and the Post Office in the summer of 1928. On 4 August, Baird Television had placed an advertisement in *The Times* declaring that 'Practical Television is Here!' while other newspapers, including the *Daily Mail* on 3 August, quoted Baird as saying that the service was imminent and televisors would be on sale from September costing £25 each. Baird later claimed that he had both been misquoted by some reports, and also that the advertisement should have been read as an indication that experimental broadcasts were imminent from his own Long Acre transmission headquarters.[39] The Post Office was unconvinced, while Baird Television was damaging its own reputation by making such claims, as they only proved that those running it could not be relied upon to keep a level head. Baird's own keenness had always been beyond question, but here was the clearest indication yet that he and his associates were more interested in his personal gain from selling receivers than the best future for the medium. As a Post Office memo, dated 29 August 1928, would say regarding their defence: 'The company's letter seems to be an attempt to explain plausibly a statement in the advertisement which cannot really be justified.'[40]

It had not all been bad news for Baird, however. On 1 August 1928 he had first met the journalist Sydney Moseley, who specialised in writing about radio, a man who would go on to figure as something of a guard dog figure for Baird and his work.[41] Ostensibly independent (although he would replace Hutchinson as Baird's business manager by 1930), Moseley would often communicate with the BBC in matters relating to Baird's invention, urging the corporation to assist as much as possible in its development and implementation. His background as a journalist allowed him to speak without concerning himself with diplomacy, but this also gave him less credibility. As Briggs has said of Moseley's attitude toward what he saw as a David and Goliath type battle, 'This kind of fight is a favourite British pastime, hallowed by the popular press, but it does not necessarily achieve results.'[42] Although Hutchinson had been a difficult person for the Post Office and BBC to deal with, his replacement was even more openly hostile.

Indeed, Moseley only served to antagonise Gladstone Murray (who had previously been perceived as amiable towards television), eventually resulting in the latter seemingly trying to wash his hands of the entire system. He has been quoted as saying that 'I am not sure whether broadcasting as it is now established should ever absorb television even in a state of development that would justify general application. It is more probable that television will evolve into a new art form in its own way and for its own public.'[43] Such a dismissal, and grand claim, would not be built upon but at least emphasises the fluid nature of television's use at this time. Television would eventually establish itself as distinct from the other form of broadcasting, radio, but would also share several elements. Here, however, Murray seems to be washing his hands of the medium, as if to indicate that it would be developed and implemented outside the BBC, with the corporation taking no role in it. In principle, Baird, Hutchinson and Moseley would approve of the obstacle of the BBC being removed; in practice, without concerted funding and support from anyone else, they needed the corporation's facilities.

To add to the Baird Company's strife, too much time had passed without significant advancements for Eckersley to believe that Baird was developing more impressive technology. The system had effectively remained unchanged save for minor refinements for nearly three years. Much of the blame for the disappointment in the current work can be placed squarely at the door of Baird and Hutchinson themselves. When Hutchinson had told the Post Office that television was 'practically out of the experimental stage' in 1926 it indicated either very low hopes for the medium or deliberate misdirection so as to secure a licence.[44] It would therefore not be unreasonable to expect statements such as this to indicate that the basic clarity and quality of television was on an upward curve. Instead, representatives of the BBC and the Post Office were faced with effectively the same technology that had met with such suspicion and confusion in early 1926. The point should be reiterated here that we are not discussing a system of television that was simply inferior to that which is now so familiar. While it was to some extent a technical marvel for its time, the image was widely considered to be of insufficient quality to support a service of any kind. This was the basis of Eckersley's misgiving; the personal clashes would come later.

We cannot avoid the impression that Baird had no particular vision for television once he had created his apparatus. It is understandable that a scientist should not necessarily envisage all of the potential artistic or cultural uses of his invention, and his attempts to conglomerate programming, transmissions and television set manufacture were doomed to failure without substantial investment. A discussion about Baird's request for support in September 1929 led to the Post Office's suggestion that:

[A] clear understanding [should] be reached that the grant of facilities for experiments would in no way imply that a public service would be permitted and would in no way affect the complete liberty of action of the Post Office and the BBC in regard to the question of a public service when the time is ripe to deal with that question.[45]

The 'public service' here was apparently literal, merely discussing the possibility of a television system accessible to all, rather than touching on the issue of Public Service Broadcasting. However, Baird was not the only individual in conversation with the BBC. We will later see that Thomas Thorne Baker had met with a more gracious response when he requested the use of BBC facilities to transmit still images over the air.

What Baird had done, however, was to present television as a working system of technology and continually reaffirm its potential to the press and interested parties. This role should not be underemphasised. He forced consideration of how television in any form may operate, something that had

Fig. 2.2: *Baird television demonstrations at the National Radio Exhibition of 1929*

(Courtesy of the Royal Television Society)

not been even superficially considered by the relevant authorities to this point. While history has not been kind to his achievements, he was not short of supporters, even if they were generally located outside influential circles. The Television Society had been formed in 1927 as a means of keeping fellow enthusiasts in contact with each other. It even launched its own magazine, *Television*, the next year, which was effectively a vehicle for the Baird company in its early years. Baird claimed that the circulation was 150,000, although Robert W. Burns puts it at 10,000 for earlier issues.[46] Whichever is true, the readership was substantial enough for the title to continue, with the title continuing ever since in various forms. He claimed to have sold almost a thousand sets, although this seems to be a rather generous figure. The early systems were basic enough for sets to be constructed in the home, and so Baird estimated an even higher uptake from these enthusiasts. It was not, then, unreasonable from Baird's perspective to suppose that his system of television had a real future.

Certainly, an article by The Television Society's Vice President and Chairman, Dr C. Tierney, called 'The Future of Television' gave a rather better impression of the system. Published in *Television*, it reports on recent experiments by Baird, following which Tierney keenly describes what he perceives to be marked increases in the scope of what can be broadcast:

The image of the head and shoulders of the subject is received with complete satisfaction to all, and more recently he has transmitted *a whole stage scene* showing two athletes giving an exhibition boxing-bout to demonstrate the practical application of his system to larger scenes. [...] The scene, received in another room of the same building, clearly depicted the small but recognisable images of the combatants and their every movement, which at times were particularly rapid.[47]

In the event, experimental broadcasts (with the 'experimental' aspect being made explicit by the BBC) were transmitted during the night, when radio was not being broadcast, later that year. This followed the conclusion of the Postmaster General, William Mitchell-Thompson, who had attempted to resolve the impasse between the corporation and Baird's company. It was stated in a letter to the Baird Television Company on 27 March 1929 that:

In the Postmaster-General's opinion the system represents a noteworthy scientific achievement; but he does not consider that at the present stage of development television could be included in the broadcasting programmes within the broadcasting hours. He bases this view not so much upon the quality of the reproduction which further experiments may be expected to improve as upon the present limited scope of the objects which can be reproduced. The Postmaster-General is however, anxious that facilities should be afforded, so far as is practicable without impairing the broadcasting service, for continued and progressive experiments with the Baird apparatus, and he would assent to a situation of the British Broadcasting Corporation being utilised for this purpose outside broadcasting hours. He understands that the corporation would agree in principle to this course, provided satisfactory terms were negotiated between the corporation and the Baird Company.[48]

So it was that Baird's 30 line system began experimental broadcasts from 30 September that year, even though the relationship between the BBC and his own company was still less than friendly. Moseley in particular had criticised the personal stance of Eckersley, who he felt had impeded the progress of Baird's work and the overall attitude of the BBC towards television. The BBC had also grown more suspicious towards Baird Television when leaks about supposedly secret demonstrations (which eventually took place in March 1929, along the same lines as those seen in late 1928, and towards the same end – to push the Post Office and BBC for more regular experimental broadcasts) were reported in the press; Baird Television denied any responsibility.[49]

The grudging co-operation between Baird and the BBC achieved one notable clarification of the imminent plans for television, however. As

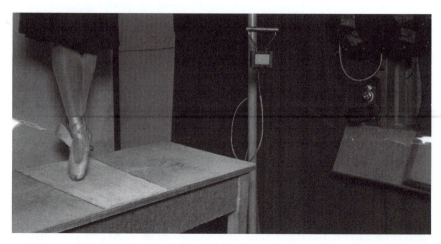

Fig. 2.3: *The televising of ballet from Long Acre. The cameras were largely immovable and so the dancing had to take place on a raised platform. It would be broadcast entirely as a close up of the dancer's feet.*

(*Courtesy the Royal Television Society*)

Hutchinson wrote in a letter to Eckersley on 15 May 1929, 'The broadcasting of music, singing and speech has already been brought to a highly developed stage [on the radio] and can at any convenient time be used in conjunction with television to afford to the receiver of the broadcast programmes an additional form of entertainment.'[50] In time this would become one of the key uses of television, but this was far from being the only use of television speculated on by Baird and his contemporaries.

While Baird may have been excited by the prospect of an ongoing series of television broadcasts, dark clouds were brewing on the horizon. Philo Farnsworth's work on electronic television had advanced to the point that by 3 September 1928 he was able to show off his system to members of the press. Similarly, Vladimir Zworykin had seen a demonstration of the cathode ray tube created by Édouard Belin and Fernand Holweck which demonstrated a crucial advancement in the way that images were displayed which Zworykin felt he could adapt to create a solution to the mystery of high quality all-electronic television. All that was needed was proper and ongoing investment in developing these possibilities, something that would soon be forthcoming.

Baird's Future at the BBC

Baird's experimental broadcasts with the BBC would continue for six years, until 1935, but this time spent on experimental 30 line broadcasts saw no material improvement to the system and little emphasis placed on the programmes being broadcast. A 1967 reconstruction of one of the most ambitious programmes, a 1930 adaptation of Luigi Pirandello's play *The Man with the Flower in His Mouth* (originally co-produced by Moseley), indicates the extent to which the service would have been difficult to view for extended periods, with its static nature and necessary use of a black and white checked board placed immediately in front of the camera whenever there was a need for the camera to capture an entirely different image in order to minimise picture disturbance.[51]

Murray had forbidden the use of the production to back any publicity drive by Baird and his associates, no doubt mindful of previous experiences. Instead, the company achieved a further 'first' with an outside broadcast of the Epsom Derby on 3 June 1931, which attracted fleeting press interest. Earlier in the year, the BBC Director-General John Reith had told Baird that there was 'maximum good will' towards him at the corporation, while Moseley had continued to attempt to drum up publicity for television.[52] However, from late 1931, an already precarious relationship between Baird and the BBC started to disintegrate even further, and Baird even wrote to the Prime Minister, Ramsay MacDonald, as he started to feel threatened by the American systems of television that the BBC was beginning to investigate. He was right to have misgivings. In the late 1920s, RCA (Radio Corporation of America) invested in the development of a system based around the receiver earlier championed by Campbell Swinton and developed by Zworykin, the cathode ray tube.[53] It was looking increasingly likely that Baird would have a serious rival, although details of RCA's advancements would not be publicly announced until 1933. Additionally, a unique selling point of television, the combination of sound and vision (subject to the availability of the required wavelengths), had been usurped by the now widespread practice of talking films. Such use of sound had been unfeasible in the earliest experiments, when bandwidth restrictions disallowed sound and vision from being transmitted simultaneously, but this was no longer an issue.[54] Baird's technology was looking increasingly outdated at a time when he would need to make a considerable impact to ensure any further investment due to the economic downturn. Given that, as Briggs wrote, 'Two sets of financial considerations were clashing. At the very moment that Reith was arguing with the government about the BBC's contribution to national solvency, Baird was pleading with MacDonald to give financial help to save television from falling "into American hands"'.[55]

Indeed, Baird was aggrieved that the BBC should be considering any system other than his own and his company would spend a great deal of effort imploring the BBC to stay 'British' with their invention. The tone of his argument

Fig. 2.4: *The control room at Long Acre*

(Courtesy of the Alexandra Palace Television Society)

attempted to suggest that his own financial considerations were secondary. Writing on the 24 September 1931, Baird had informed MacDonald that 'It is only the gravity of the situation that compels me to point out that unless the government takes some action with regard to television, a big British industry and invention will inevitably fall into American hands. [...] America is going right ahead without restriction whereas we are being hopelessly impeded through entirely inadequate broadcasting facilities.'[56] The letter was simply referred to the Post Office while Baird was requested to restrict such communication to the Postmaster General.

In actual fact, while the Radio Corporation of America had owned some shares in EMI, Marconi-EMI was a British company. Baird's concern was simply that he would be usurped, with a resulting attempt to place himself as the 'British' option compared to the 'foreign' efforts of Marconi-EMI, with the implication that RCA had effectively created the Emitron camera tube. His appeals fell on deaf ears, however. If the involvement of the BBC signalled that Baird's dominance of television was becoming less monopolistic, then the BBC's talks with Marconi-EMI signalled the beginning of the end of his overall involvement. Although in need of refinement, the quality and potential of Marconi-EMI's rival television technology meant that granting Baird any exclusivity would not be in the public interest. Even before television was officially placed as part of Public Service Broadcasting, it was the general audience's interests that were being taken to heart.

The BBC's acknowledgement of Baird's rivals meant that by the time that the corporation took charge of the content of the test broadcasts in 1932, the medium had effectively moved out of his control. By involving the BBC in the development of television Baird could no longer be considered the single person behind television's development. Despite the fact that the BBC was initially just allowing use of their facilities, this associated the respected corporation with the medium. Although it was external circumstances that had eventually dictated this co-operation, it was far from being a predetermined route for television. Had Baird offered a higher quality system of television then his bargaining power with the Post Office would have been stronger, but this was not the case. Baird did not get left behind because of any personal disputes but because he does not seem to have contemplated any other way to tackle the problem of television than the use of spinning discs, while later advancements by others in his company similarly failed to impress. This opened the way for rivals to capitalise on other theories of television transmission and reception.

This was made explicit in a meeting between Baird and the BBC on 17 August 1931, where it was emphasised that the corporation's view was that 'It is no part of the function of the BBC to concern itself directly with the development of commercial inventions, or allow itself to be used by outside concerns as an instrument of research, unless the invention appears likely to become applicable to the service after a reasonable period of research.'[57] The stance was unequivocal; there had to be a clear and practicable end in sight to the experimentation, and this was not the case with Baird. The tension remained and was only exacerbated when, in early 1933, news reached Baird that Noel Ashbridge (Eckersley's replacement as Chief Engineer of the BBC) had viewed a demonstration from Marconi-EMI. Baird cried foul, claiming that this devalued a co-operative agreement which he considered to be exclusive; the BBC disagreed. Television was being removed from Baird's grasp; suddenly the BBC was becoming the entity most synonymous with the medium. Baird retrospectively understood that the corporation's involvement had resulted in the end of his private broadcasting system, writing that:

> In the old days we had, in Long Acre, our own studio and our own broadcasting and had, in effect, a rival broadcasting system to the BBC, with our own independent production being received by the public. This came to an end when the BBC took us over and I often regretted this and thought that we would have been better to have continued operating independently.[58]

It is telling that Baird sees his work with the BBC as the corporation 'taking over' his work on television, rather than it simply taking some responsibility for television as a whole, which Baird was only a part of. Such was the guarded jealousy he exerted over his technology that it was clear that he knew rival developments had real potential to replace his work. As such, he must surely have known that he was to only be one player in the development of television unless he could assert absolute independence. He was never able to do this, and the BBC's involvement ensured that television's future would be a collaborative process. Baird's romantic vision of his technology being 'taken over', and the potential for independent broadcasts, ignore the facts. Perhaps he found it more palatable to put the blame at the door of the BBC rather than his own limited technical know-how. In doing this, he actually does himself a disservice. Baird was a visionary in terms of television's potential, and helped to initiate widespread recognition of the principle.

That the BBC could exert such control is the clearest indication that television's future would operate alongside the corporation's public service commitments. It had been a gradual movement, but the public corporation was now taking control, fuelled by the imminent arrival of another manufacturer's technology. A letter from Baird of 31 January 1933, protesting about the viewing of such a rival demonstration, indicates the importance he placed on the BBC making such a gesture.[59] Television was no longer his, and nor was he an equal part of an amicable system of co-operation. The principle of Marconi-EMI's electronic approach was superior to his, if it could be properly refined and implemented. The theory had been known for some time, but it was long considered unfeasible with the current level of engineering. However, as D.C. Birkinshaw, BBC television's first Chief Engineer, said following the next year's demonstration by Marconi-EMI, this was:

A picture not produced by mechanical means. No whizzing discs, no mechanical drums, silence, lightness, portability. It showed the way things were going. It was quite easy to see, even then, that the Baird system couldn't eventually lead anywhere because television would have to follow the lead of sound radio and do outside broadcasts and there was no way that I could see anything so far invented or projected by Baird could ever do an outside broadcast. And to my mind that had always been the chief stumbling block of his system.[60]

Despite all Baird's excitable predictions for the multiple uses of television it was still primarily being viewed as a system likely to be similar to radio in many respects, an expectation only exacerbated by the BBC taking control. Indeed, while the official assignation of the BBC as television's overseer came in 1935 we have seen that this was informally true even earlier. This year also saw an unfortunate irony for Baird, as other companies started to show an interest in selling sets to view his test 30-line transmissions even though they were expected to end relatively soon (although they actually continued until September 1935). To the surprise of both Baird and the BBC advertisements started appearing from the Plew company, trying to encourage sales of their own televisor.[61] In reality little more than a footnote in television history, it clearly demonstrates that another company believed that there was merit in the television market. Baird was not a lone advocate of television in the UK, and indeed the manufacturers Bush were to release their own televisors, without success as they coincided with the announcement of the curtailment of the service.[62]

The Plew company's overblown sales pitch ('The strangest dream that man has ever dreamed') and the generally hyperbolic nature of the advertisements evoke memories of Baird's earlier publicity coups. Certainly, television was being touted as a technological marvel, even if the indication of content was rather misleading. 'The BBC [...] are out to do big things in the way of [television] programmes, encourage them by buying a Plew set,' the flyer claimed. Rather more problematic was its note that 'you'll never again be content just to listen to your radio,' and that the televisor just needed to be plugged into the user's existing wireless set. While true, it was not made clear that the programming was infrequent and experimental, while standard radio programmes certainly could not be viewed. As a result, there was little positivity surrounding these advertisements within Baird's company and the BBC. Rather, there was concern surrounding the increasingly complicated nature of television. The general public would have struggled to differentiate one system from another, or even understand whether television, whose arrival was imminently announced so many times, was in fact currently a broadcasting reality or not. The situation would only become more complex in the short term, but the increased attention being paid to television meant that definite steps were being taken to ensure that a fully fledged, technically viable and high quality system was to be seriously considered. The difficulty was in deciding the exact nature of it.

3

Television's Power Struggle

Ownership of 'television', an intangible object based on many different sets of principles, was a complicated matter in the early days of the medium. Baird's work had attracted many private radio enthusiasts who had seen television as the natural next step of technology, and had a vested private interest in its future, albeit not a financial one. The nature of radio sets at this time allowed for interested amateurs to construct their own receivers, which became a hobby for many. Television's own mechanical basis during the late 1920s allowed this interest to extend to Baird's apparatus. The formation of the Television Society and the magazine *Television* created an outlet for their own interests. The members were not meekly following television's progress, however; they vociferously campaigned for its progress to be hastened by the authorities. In December 1928, for example, *Television* criticised the BBC's perceived cautiousness in its approach to the medium. They believed that this was demonstrated by the BBC's investigation of the Fultograph process, which transmitted still images across the airwaves. 'Has the BBC vision?' asked the strapline of their cartoon, depicting the BBC operating a Fultograph machine in front of a John Bull-type character trying to remove his blindfold.[1] The implication is that the United Kingdom was failing to have the same ambitions for public transmissions of a full television service. Considerably troubling to them, and to Baird, was the United States' contrasting openness towards such experiments.

Clearly, it was not just Baird who was frustrated by the BBC's lack of vision for his system of television. In fact, the corporation's co-operation with Thorne Baker for his Fultograph system was used as a reason why it could not ignore Baird's requests for assistance (something highlighted by Moseley). Retrospectively, it is ironic that the magazine should criticise the BBC for giving too much consideration to items that were perceived to have been superseded (although the Fultograph did have limited success in its own right)[2] shortly before it became public knowledge that Baird's own work had been bettered elsewhere, particularly by Marconi-EMI. *Television* is explored in more detail later, but it was clear to the BBC that they could not satisfy this relatively small band of amateurs at all costs. Because of their status as a public corporation, they were obliged to work for the long-term longevity of broadcasting generally.

Baird Television Internationally

During the late 1920s and early 1930s Baird was often finding his work more appreciated across the channel, in continental Europe. While the BBC operated a softly-softly approach to television broadcasts, Baird had been encouraged by discussions with parties in France, Belgium and Germany. In November 1929, Baird launched his collaboration with the film director Bernard Natan in France. 1929 was an ambitious year for Natan as he had also acquired the French film company Pathé. However, when the first official broadcasts from France were transmitted from the Eiffel Tower in 1935 neither Baird nor Natan were involved. Instead, television was broadcast by the Ministry of Telecommunication (PTT), indicating that France had followed Britain's lead in maintaining governmental control over broadcasts, rather than the more relaxed series of experimental stations seen in the United States.[3]

In Germany, Baird was invited over in a formal capacity for discussions with Chancellor Brüning, and even found himself in the same room as Hitler.[4] The extent of Baird's role in television development in Germany is debatable, but the country's initial use of the intermediate film system, which would later be used by the Baird company, indicates a degree of co-operation. Germany's use of television was notable for its differences rather than similarities, however. Initially there was a degree of private enterprise, with several test broadcasts in the early 1930s, and the company Telefunken showing a degree of success.[5] However, under the Nazis television was to be brought under state control and used for propaganda purposes, something that was curtailed when war broke out in 1939.[6] Television was used as a public service system, in the sense of relaying events of special interest, especially patriotic material. This would be most prominent when it came to the 1936 Berlin Olympics. The difference between the German system and the principles explored elsewhere in the world was that it placed receivers in public areas, for communal viewing. This could perhaps be put down to the keenness of the Nazi government to allow as much access to the broadcasts as possible; it was not in their interest to allow slow growth of private purchases. What it does demonstrate is that television was not strictly established as being a domestic product, even as late as the 1930s. There are echoes of other attempts to broadcast big-screen television, including Baird's showing of the Derby in cinemas earlier in the decade, but these were touted as alternatives to domestic television sets, not replacements.

Baird had also operated in New York during 1931, but this was a 'very expensive affair' that met with limited success.[7] Baird's own personal involvement included a three month trip to the city, and followed demonstrations featuring the Mayor which took place in late 1929.[8] Baird's interest was no doubt moderated by the fact that his station was one of 22 experimental services then licensed in the United States.[9] His later extended visit was one which his company's board took some umbrage at; this was the beginnings of the unease that would end with his ousting from the company.

Although Baird was trying to find an outlet for his technology, attention had begun to be paid to assessing how television was likely to function in the long term. There were some serious scholarly and technical publications

Fig. 3.1: *A Baird International Television sales stand*
(Courtesy of the Royal Television Society)

about television up to this point and its potential future long before its launch as a public service medium. Internationally there would be a total of a dozen or so books on the subject prior to 1936. 1926 saw the publication of Alfred Dinsdale's *Television – Seeing by Wireless*,[10] the first book to be devoted to the medium; the fact that it was revised for a second edition in 1928[11] and then reworked once more for 1932's *First Principles of Television*[12] gives some idea of the speed at which developments were now occurring and the level of interest attracted. There were also other titles from further afield, including H. Horton Sheldon and Edgar Norman Grisewood's *Television – Present Methods of Picture Transmission* published in 1929[13] and initially subtitled 'The first American book on television', which works as an interesting comparison piece to the very similar Dinsdale volumes. There is also Edgar H. Felix's American-published 1931 volume *Television – Its Methods and Uses*,[14] which is a fascinating mixture of analyses of the technology to that date and speculative chapters discussing television content, which is unusual for a largely technical book in this period.

All of these volumes were published before a purely electronic system of television had been properly developed, and so they rely on examinations of largely mechanical apparatus. This is likely to have been of interest to its readership, undoubtedly made up of those with an interest in the practicalities of television at the time. With the exception of Felix's book, there is no real exploration in these titles of television content beyond some oblique references to the potential for it to be used in a range of situations. As one might expect, the work of Baird was at the forefront of this ultimately doomed system in the UK at this time, a fact reflected by Dinsdale from the first edition of his book. 'A most remarkable thing about Television is that its successful development has been a one-man job. From the very beginning Baird has worked alone, and even to-day he has no technical assistants.'[15] It is intriguing that here Dinsdale indicates that Baird was almost entirely synonymous with television when he also dedicates chapters to the earlier work of others. Regardless, his appreciation of Baird was not to last. By the time of Dinsdale's 1932 publication, just six years later, Baird had been demoted to the sixth chapter of the volume, sandwiched between a history of early television experiments and an analysis of the American 'Bell' system. Experiments in cathode ray tube technology had proven to be rather more successful than Baird's system of mechanical televisors, and so they were given greater prominence than his work by being placed early in the book.[16]

Dinsdale had edited the magazine *Television* since its first issue in March 1928, to be succeeded by Moseley the next year. The periodical was very much in the manner of similar publications for the wireless enthusiasts, including *Popular Wireless*, first published in 1922, which featured news items on advances in radio technology, suggestions for building one's own set and other feature articles. *Television*'s articles often speculated on the content and uses of television, and it was quite common for the periodical to run an article dedicated to a single, often rather outlandish, proposition demonstrating television's potential. The second issue speculates on using the medium to 'copy' an actor into a transatlantic performance in ways that this author confesses not to understand, so convoluted was the proposed system. Of course, no-one would have known exactly how television was to develop and, in turn, know what would be an inherent part of television and what would either be experimented with or dismissed. For example, there are similarities in the form of what might be considered a natural progression, between colour and 3D for example, the former of which is now the standard while the latter is no more than a rarely used gimmick, and yet both could conceivably be seen as the potential next step for television once high quality monochrome broadcasts began (as evidenced by Baird's work on them).

But most importantly for Baird, the magazine (and by implication Dinsdale) had been a clear supporter of his work, often championing his ongoing developments in spite of perceived lack of interest from the BBC and government. Baird had played a role in the formation of the Television Society that spawned the publication, but had no ownership over it. As Baird was the only person publicly working on television it is unsurprising that he should be discussed sympathetically. Baird even allowed readers of the magazine to write to request permission to construct their own televisor based on his patent. In fact, early issues of the magazine very much feel like the newsletter of an oppressed society, with Baird being hailed as a beacon of light in the days when recognition of television's potential was minimal. By 1932 he starts to be sidelined as it becomes clear that Baird, a man who had filed nearly one hundred patents related to television (most of which were refinements to his basic system), was no longer at the forefront of the most exciting developments and articles on his work become less and less frequent.[17]

One notable factor in the books on television is the extent to which they advise caution regarding expectations of its development. As Edgar H. Felix puts it in his 1931 book:

> [I feel] that a conservative attitude is particularly helpful at this time, because television has been treated to an excess of premature and unwarrantedly hopeful publicity. The author, of course, realises that an exacting analysis of television as it exists today may be significantly altered by a development of tomorrow.[18]

This is somewhat different from the relentlessly enthusiastic attitudes of the contributors to *Television* magazine, who like Baird generally fail to understand the reasoning behind a conservative approach. Just one example of the positive perspective of the magazine can be seen in its November 1928 claim that 'There is real, definite entertainment value in television as it is to-day'.[19] It is understandable that those interested in the system to begin with would want to believe that television was already a fully functioning system that simply needed proper implementation. The magazine itself would have little reason to counter this, not just for cynical reasons of circulation, but because the contributors were enthusiasts themselves.

The uncredited writer of this November 1928 article (possibly Moseley himself) is vitriolic in his condemnation of what he perceives to be some sort of bureaucratic impasse whenever attempts to create a universal system of broadcast for television were undertaken. However, once more, there is no proper sense of what television would be for or how such a sudden introduction could secure its long-term future. Until an official decision was reached enthusiasts would have to satisfy themselves with sporadic test transmissions. The author did little to disguise his contempt for 'The dear old so-called "authorities",' who he claimed 'have used up so much ink during past months to the Press damning television'.[20] It seems that the author is referring to the rebuttals that the government and BBC were occasionally forced to issue whenever the question of television's ongoing development was put to them. As has been demonstrated in the previous section, it is clear that while television was never a priority for the BBC it was also not overlooked, with systematic and ongoing research taking place at this time. Judging by this article, the enthusiasts seem to care little for developing a different system (which was the eventual outcome), instead feeling that the present Baird technology was satisfactory as the basis for a new medium.

If it seems that the articles within *Television* were unrealistically positive then this is not necessarily because of naivety. It is tempting to wonder whether a reason behind the founding of the Television Society and, in turn, *Television* magazine was something of a deliberate attempt at a self-fulfilling prophecy. By forming the society and demonstrating through the periodical that there was an aggressively enthusiastic group of people who were embracing television those involved, including Baird in an advisory capacity, may have felt that more pressure could be put on the government and the BBC to expedite the development of an official system of broadcast. Ostensibly the society was set up 'to form a common meeting ground for the assistance of amateurs, and for lectures, also for professional research workers and others interested in the progress of television', a mission statement that does not explicitly mention promotion of the service itself, but the society would inevitably have an interest in pushing for further state development of the medium.[21] Perhaps the content of the magazine was largely secondary to this concern. Certainly it seems that there were few developments that could be covered in each issue, with much of the bulk being taken up with highly speculative pieces that had little link with the available technology, a fact that at least highlights that such enthusiasts were considering more than just the technology of television.

High-Definition Television and the Official Launch

The Television Committee headed by Lord Selsdon dictated that when television launched it would alternate between Baird Television's 240-line system and Marconi-EMI's 405-line system. By the time this occurred in November 1936 Baird had stepped back from the day-to-day running of his own company following a boardroom coup in the summer of 1933,[22] while Hutchinson had been forced out in 1930 to be replaced by Moseley, who himself resigned, also in 1933.[23] This followed the takeover of the company by the Gaumont-British Picture Corporation in 1932, after which Baird was relegated to privately working on his own inventions, separate from the work on television, only to be called upon for publicity. Although the company would launch a limited independent test service for its new 180-line technology, transmitting from Crystal Palace, by the time it reported to the Television Committee it was already working on 240-line systems.[24]

Transmitting between February and June 1935, the 180-line transmissions at least showed that television could still operate independently from the BBC, although not for long. In terms of the technology, from late 1935 Baird Television's system now alternated between a spotlight method, where a completely static close-up could be transmitted in reasonable quality, and the intermediate film system, for wider shots and slightly increased flexibility. Both were problematic. The former could only be used for linking material or talks and was both noisy and bulky, incorporating a disc spinning at 3000 revolutions per minute, while the second was an inherently complex solution to the problems of low definition previously encountered by Baird. The intermediate film process was already in use in Germany, where work on it had begun in 1932. The image would be recorded on film (with the sound on its optical soundtrack), which was rapidly processed in a somewhat dangerous system that included water and cyanide baths. The 'near instantaneous' system took a little under a minute, with the finished result being scanned for television transmission, but it was prone to mechanical breakdowns.

Compared to the sleek and silent Marconi-EMI process, it was clear that Baird was doomed. Baird was no longer spearheading the technical developments of the company, with Captain A.G.D. West (formerly of the BBC) now resident as Technical Director, but the legacy of his work was apparent. As early as 1933 there were signs that Baird was being allowed to continue in the spirit of fair play rather than because of any innate confidence in the abilities of him or his company. A meeting on 21 April 1933 between the BBC and the Post Office followed a demonstration of both the prospective systems of television, whereby the Marconi-EMI system was judged to be considerably superior.[25] The Post Office claimed that it was 'afraid that if the Baird Co. were prevented from installing high definition equipment, questions would be asked in parliament and in the press which would be difficult to answer, and the Post Office mainly, and the BBC to a lesser extent, would be blamed for the inevitable bankruptcy of Baird Co.'[26] It is unlikely that this was down to any protectionist agenda for the company, but rather derived from a real concern that Baird's placement in the public eye had resulted in a stay of execution for the company that took his name.

On 6 December 1934 Baird Television gave a demonstration of the intermediate film system to the government's Television Committee so as to demonstrate its quality, later sending a selection of clippings from the actual developed film. The system seems to have reasonably satisfied those who had seen it at the time, but there were misgivings relating to both of Baird Television's systems shortly prior to the launch. 'The Committee have unanimously decided that the spotlight system of transmission is inadequate and undesirable for employment at the opening ceremony on 2 November,'[27] read a letter to Baird from the Television Advisory Committee in October 1936, before going on to point out the underlying problems of his alternative method. 'Moreover, the Intermediate Film method of transmission is understood to be proving not altogether reliable and it seems to be doubtful at present whether it would be safe to rely upon it for the opening ceremony.'[28] In a period of ten years television had moved from being a private concern, the chief aim of which was to transmit a picture of whatever quality, to one where the long-term future and inherent quality of the medium were the main concerns. Albert Abramson has said that television 'is probably the first invention by committee, in the sense of resulting from the efforts of hundreds of individuals widely separated in time and space, all prompted by the urge to produce a system of "seeing over the horizon",'[29] but this implies a system of co-operation. Instead there was a whittling down of ideas and private advancements until a system deemed workable arrived, so it is not difficult to understand Baird's angst at having his 'invention' taken away from him.

The Overall Role of Baird

In November 1936 fire destroyed Crystal Palace, the place where the Baird Company had installed their laboratories, and many of the spare components were lost, creating a significant problem for the ongoing broadcasts. Resultantly, in February 1937, the Baird television transmissions ceased.

However, had the fire not occurred, Baird's system would have lasted little longer due to an overall lack of confidence in the usability and quality of his technology compared to his rival's.[30] For Baird as a person, this was not the setback that one might presume. Ever since his ousting from the company Baird had been little more than an observer of their work with the BBC, while he continued his own separate experiments. In many respects, the initial exploration of his own ideas was his preferred working environment. As Briggs wrote, 'Baird was always exploring the fringes of his imperfect medium, taking up one experiment after another, more with the passion of an artist than the prudence of a scientist.'[31] For example, a diagram of a potential system of colour television was designed by Baird in 1938, and was used for some experimental broadcasts in the cinema with mixed results. Even by this time, the diagram shows that Baird was still advocating a system with a mechanical basis, indicating once more the extent to which he struggled to consider alternative approaches to the problem of television. That is not to say that such experiments should be dismissed, especially when this analysis is striving to discover precisely what was meant by television at this time. Baird and Marconi-EMI were the two main competing systems, the only ones to be seriously considered, but not the only ones to be acknowledged. As early as 1926, Alfred Dinsdale refers to several different systems that had been theorised for television to that point in his book *Television – Seeing By Wireless*, including principles from Mihaly, Belin and Holweck, and Jenkins. In the 1930s alternative systems continued to be developed, including an advancement of Mihaly's system and, perhaps most notably, a system developed by Scophony, who initially developed another mechanical receiver, before working on a 405-line system that could be used as large-screen receiver in public areas.[32] Sets were installed from 1938, but as would happen in Germany (where a similar system was better established), the coming of war meant that television was forced to take a back seat.

Without a firm guiding hand there was no clear direction for television. Even companies such as Baird Television did not have a coherent vision for the technology. They would have adapted their apparatus for the eventual domestic system, as indeed they did, just as easily as they would have for any other means of distribution or content. Had a private investor wished to purchase Baird's system of television exclusively for their own use, perhaps as an early form of closed circuit television, then there can be little doubt that Baird would have happily agreed. For all of the company's attempts at ensuring that 'television', in whatever form, was under their jurisdiction they were rarely rewarded for their endeavours. Baird certainly had shortcomings as a scientist, with his own engineer J.D. Percy later describing him as 'not a very practical man,'[33] while Briggs claims that he possessed 'abundant vision even if his techniques were limited'.[34] Had he owned the patent to the only technology capable of high quality television transmissions then it is plausible that Baird Television could have operated as an official broadcasting company (although the Post Office would have had to agree).

As it was, Baird was kept in check not only by the Post Office's insistence on slowly considering what was the most appropriate course of action, but also by the inherent limitations in the technology that he had devised. Despite his repeated protestations that an army of enthusiasts were waiting to pay £40 for his new receivers, such a low quality system could never have achieved mass appeal simply because of the poor range of entertainment suitable for the small, low-resolution screens, coupled with the high price. However, by making an issue over what he perceived to be the slow development of the medium through machinations outside of his control, Baird did force the establishment into considering the medium rather sooner than they would have without such pressure. Baird knew the power of publicity, and he is widely credited with bringing knowledge of the very concept of television as a practical reality to the masses. That the system eventually adopted was not his is almost immaterial for the development of television itself, even if it was undoubtedly a crushing blow for Baird, although he did not see it as the end for his work on the medium. He later wrote in his memoirs that 'It seemed to me that we should now concentrate on television for the cinema,'[35] perhaps underlining that even when television broadcasts actually commenced there was not necessarily a sense of finality, and that the role of television had not been clearly and absolutely set. His widow, Margaret, later commented on Baird's state of mind following the cancellation of service when interviewed by the BBC in 1968:

> He took this blow philosophically; I mean what else could he do? I don't think perhaps he expected anything else although the pictures compared very well they were very good pictures [from] both companies; you know very similar pictures but it was a different system you see, which everyone knows now.[36]

J.D. Percy was rather more forthright when describing the last day of Baird transmissions, acknowledging the superiority of the Marconi-EMI system:

> Everyone at Alexandra Palace was very kind when we were fighting and losing Baird's last battle. However there was no stopping the advance of the flicker-less, tireless, inertia-less electron camera so sadly we pulled out the Baird circuit breakers for the last time, turned off the taps on the old film, carefully disposed of the chemicals and went home.[37]

Although Baird Television exhibited some strengths, such as the quality of transmitted films, the cameras were to be their downfall; they simply weren't able to compete with Marconi-EMI's system. Baird Television continued to fall behind even after Baird himself he was no longer part of their day-to-day experimental work. R. W. Burns politely puts it that 'Essentially, Baird was a man of ideas, of imagination,'[38] but even if he was not taken seriously as a scientist by his peers he achieved a great deal in his demonstration of television as a desirable technology. His drive and enthusiasm ensured the medium was seen as inevitable even when it was more like science fiction given its development to that stage. Nevertheless, Baird's enthusiasm could not make up for his system's technical deficiencies, and what television actually needed was an external body who could take a less emotional stance on its development and future. Baird's rush to have a fully fledged system available as soon as possible was a great coup for those who wished to emphasise the potential of the medium, but could never have worked without serious financial backing and a rather more reliable and high quality system of transmission. By entering into the fray late, the BBC undoubtedly found itself stepping on the toes of Baird and his contemporaries who had been working privately on the system. If Baird had got his initial wish for a private licence, what would he have been broadcasting, and how would it have been paid for? There was no infrastructure for such a bold step, and the only body that had any sort of experience in similar fields was the BBC, making it likely that there would be

Fig. 3.2: *Baird alongside a display of his apparatus at the Science Museum*
(Courtesy of the Royal Television Society)

collaboration at some stage unless Baird's company could find a serious financial backer.

It says a great deal that so much of this book can discuss the work and influence of just one man. Much of this is down to the attention that Baird garnered, but there is also the amount of time and effort that Baird then dedicated to furthering the system. The BBC Written Archive holds eight files specifically relating to Baird, including correspondence and minutes of meetings related to him. It holds just one for Marconi-EMI in the pre-war period. Perhaps Baird's work accelerated the efforts of his rivals, and perhaps he forced the BBC to consider the role that television would eventually play in its role as broadcaster, it is not possible to be certain. One element of his legacy that is clearer is that we can be sure that Baird raised awareness of the medium to such a point that extended procrastination would not be tolerated; the experimental transmissions were a token gesture, but at least they were a gesture. Television as a mass medium was slowly becoming a reality, and Baird had helped to force a proper analysis of its future. Unfortunately for Baird, despite the fact that he would go on to be readily associated with the medium by the general public, he was not to be part of that future; for all of his efforts, the decision regarding whose system to use was made as a result of the technology, and nothing else.

This should not be used as an excuse to downplay his role in the earliest years of television. The publicity that he attracted was crucial, but just as important was his the impetus behind the institutional adoption of television that he provided. This may not have been his initial aim, with his hopes for independence or at least co-dependence, but he did the development of television in the United Kingdom a great service in doing so. He swiftly fell out of favour within the BBC, especially after Marconi-EMI's efforts were judged superior, but had not been held in much esteem in the first place. Although Baird and Eckersley were later to become friendly, the reputation of Baird within the BBC was wounded by the Chief Engineer's feelings. Despite Baird's claims that the two technologies were broadly equal, independent observers tended not to agree. Indeed, by the time of television's opening ceremony in November 1936, Baird was not even invited to give a speech alongside the others who had worked on television, a snub that he understandably took personally. He may no longer have been a dominant figure in television, but it was his work a decade earlier that had opened the minds of many to the possibilities of such a technology. The public never forgot him, however. As far as the public at large were concerned, Baird was the first to show television in public and then continued to work on the medium for the next decade. There was enough publicity circulated to this effect that his name was readily associated with the medium. When Marconi-EMI's system was the one eventually adopted, not many would have made the distinction. Few would know, or care, that the system exclusively in use after February 1937 was not the same as that developed by Baird Television.

Baird would later regret that he failed to collaborate with Marconi-EMI early in his endeavours, but the decision was not his to make as his rival had no interest in working with him. Whether an earlier collaboration with another contemporary research company would have benefited Baird is difficult to judge, but as it stood he desired financial assistance rather than technical know-how. Perhaps this was his greatest downfall. As he was later to say, 'Our policy of facing the world singlehandedly was sheer insanity.'[39]

Points to Consider

1) Why was the early development of television so often undertaken by private individuals, rather than large companies?

2) Why was publicity so important to Baird and Hutchinson, and what was the effect of it?

3) To what extent were those working on television development operating entirely independently?

4) How was the social and cultural landscape in the 1920s and 30s likely to either encourage, or discourage, the development of television?

5) Can we define the work on mechanical systems to be 'television' in the sense that we know it today?

6) How have technical limitations affected the types of programmes suitable for television, from this earliest period onwards?

7) Why were the mechanical systems of television not more widely adopted, both in the UK and abroad?

8) What can you judge was being understood as 'television' in this early period? How does it seem to have been defined?

9) Was there any scenario where Baird television might have existed alongside, or instead of, BBC transmissions?

10) With the power of retrospect, was the pre-BBC period at all important to television's eventual development, or was it simply an irrelevant dead-end before all-electronic television was a practical reality?

Public Television

4

Attitudes towards Television

The previous section of this book was an exploration of private individuals who saw potential in the basic concept of television and strove to develop their own systems that would allow this 'seeing at a distance'. This section, however, is concerned with developments on a larger scale. On the whole, this takes the form of looking at the *infrastructure* of television, including the large companies and public bodies that worked together to make television a fully formed system of broadcasting. The development of the technology went hand-in-hand with a demonstration of at least some wider interest from the public; or, perhaps more significantly, a wide expectation that television was in some way inevitable and expected. As part of this, there are some segues into discussion of the larger multi-national companies whose resources facilitated the dissemination of television broadcasts to the home, but largely this is a discussion of how television was brought to the masses, using the first public, permanent, high-definition system in the world as its basis – the BBC in the United Kingdom.

In discussing the emergence of television as a brand new medium, it would be easy to lose sight of the broadcasting context into which it was born. It is tempting to imply that television was the youthful invader on to radio's territory, but it should be remembered that the first major experimental broadcasts of television using BBC facilities took place just seven years after the corporation had first been set up as an independent company. Radio was still establishing itself, and television could easily be viewed as an unnecessary complication at this point. The various bodies who concerned themselves with radio, most notably the Post Office and the BBC, were still trying to discover the best way forward for public radio broadcasts. As with television, the issue of radio was more complicated than purely technical concerns. For example, the corporation had to decide its policy when it came to the reporting of political developments, something that required careful consideration and took some time to formalise. In 1926, the BBC was led by the government in its reporting of that year's general strike, although they also attempted to present more rounded coverage. At the time the BBC was in fear of governmental takeover or their licence not being renewed, and so the corporation played it safe, doing their best not to rile the government at a time of national instability.[1] This is a contrast to their later unequivocal aim of impartiality; the extent to which the reporting of the strike was partial is still debatable, some claiming that the BBC simply broadcast what the government wanted, while others claim that there was little in the way of suppression of information and twisting of facts.[2] The formulation of policy about complicated issues such as political reportage would be just as important to radio's development as most technical advancements.

Such concerns and questions about public broadcasts followed decades of private uses of wireless technology, however. Radio had been developed throughout the second half of the nineteenth century by various engineers, but it was Guglielmo Marconi of Italy's conglomeration of the various advancements from 1894 onwards that led to him being christened the father of radio.[3] Initially, the technology was used for communicative purposes, especially for the military, but in a foreshadowing of similar concerns from the television enthusiasts, those who had an interest in this new medium found themselves with an interesting piece of technology that had little actual use as it currently stood. As Andrew Crisell has said, 'The enthusiasts, many of whom had already built their own receivers, were keen to have something informative or entertaining to listen to on a routine basis, rather than having to eavesdrop on messages for someone else.'[4] It is not hard to see the comparisons with television here, as the enthusiastic discussions in *Television* magazine were initially centred on the technology, before frustration mounted about the lack of content for home-made sets.

The change from being a purely communicative medium to something with wider appeal came about following the end of the First World War in 1918 because of the interest in radio transmissions from these private enthusiasts and the resultant willingness of manufacturers of wireless sets to fulfil this demand.[5] What was to become a public service had its origins in the manufacturers' aims for the service to appeal to as many potential set-owners as possible, but the final solution would come about because of more practical necessities. For radio, the companies exerting pressure were multi-nationals with considerable wealth and expertise. For television, the manufacturer pushing for official broadcasts was effectively a two-man band. Had Marconi-EMI's television system been the first to be presented, rather than the premature demonstrations of Baird's early apparatus, then it may well have been that the medium would have been taken more seriously.

When the possibility of public radio transmissions was raised, the Post Office pointed out that any such broadcasts could only operate on spare wavelengths, and the quantity of these was finite.[6] Should each manufacturer require its own broadcasting station operating from each transmitter, then this would be impossible to maintain once the number of manufacturers inevitably grew. Such problems were not particular to the United Kingdom, but there were some other areas of the globe that did not face the same obstacles. In the United States, for example, the geography of the country dictated that individual radio stations were sufficiently thinly spread that strict licences could be granted more freely. However, the dense population of the relatively small British Isles meant that separate broadcasters in neighbouring districts or cities would be impossible, unlike in the United States where most population centres are some distance from each other, and so frequencies were not at such a premium. The fact that matters as seemingly unrelated as geography and intrinsic constitutional approaches to the freedom of businesses fundamentally affected the way that television was able to operate in different countries indicates the extent to which the medium's development has been driven by external concerns rather than a concerted ideological desire for a particular type of television.

Marconi-EMI's Work in Television

It would be Marconi-EMI whose system of television would lead the way from the service's launch in 1936, but they were still some way from developing a serious rival to Baird's system even by this stage. The company's development in the field of television is perhaps best traceable through the career development of Isaac Shoenberg, a Russian who was to oversee the company's key developments in television. Shoenberg had moved to the United Kingdom in 1914, where he joined the Marconi Company,[7] before moving in 1924 to the Columbia Graphophone Company, a British gramophone business.[8] In March 1931, Columbia Graphophone and the simply titled Gramophone Company, which included the HMV record label, merged to create The Electric and Musical Industries Ltd., better known as EMI. When combined, these companies were an extremely strong presence in their field, both domestically and internationally. Shoenberg was made Director of Research and Patents and made it his personal aim to push for development of television.[9] By this stage, Baird's primitive offerings were being broadcast and television was starting to be seen as having mainstream potential, perfect for a new company with ambition to work on. EMI presented a system for transmitting films to the BBC on 11 November 1932, to only mild interest, the main issue being that the system could not show live broadcasts.[10] After this disappointment, Shoenberg and his team worked on developing an electronic camera from 1932 with less success than they had hoped for, while two of

EMI's research engineers, W.F. Tedham and J.D. McGee, surreptitiously worked on an improved cathode ray tube for capturing images.[11] Following this, on 22 May 1934 there was a further merger as EMI joined forces with Marconi to develop this television system.[12] Just ten days earlier, EMI had patented their Super-Emitron camera, which produced a notably superior picture when compared with earlier attempts by the company.[13] The group of engineers now working on television was formidable, and included Alan Blumlein, whose various technical innovations would substantially increase the quality of electronic television. As Tony Currie has put it, 'Blumlein and his colleagues created the detailed design and specifications of the system that was to survive for some 50 years'.[14]

There has always been some debate about the extent to which Marconi-EMI perfected an all-electronic system themselves. Certainly there were often links between the companies working on television. RCA in America held shares in EMI, and had developed an electronic camera that was substantially more successful than any other efforts to that point. However, in his detailed technical history of television, R.W. Burns denies that there is any evidence of collusion or detailed information sharing, instead pointing out that the companies were simply operating on parallel, but separate, lines.[15] If true (and there is some debate on this point) then it indicates that all-electronic systems along the lines developed by RCA were being widely seen as a more likely basis for any eventual permanent high-definition television system than the oft-seen mechanical apparatus. Such systems were starting to move out of the laboratory, with Philo Farnsworth finally demonstrating his all-electronic system to the public on 25 August 1934 in Philadelphia, some six years after it had first been demonstrated in private.

In the United Kingdom, the suggested solution to the problem of limited frequencies was that a single broadcasting company should operate, established as a consortium of the major players in the radio manufacturers' marketplace – something that was also an administrative convenience.[16] The result was the formation of the British Broadcasting Company in 1922, a private broadcaster that would make its money in three ways. The first would be the sale of its initial stock; the second source of revenue came from a royalty levied on the sale of wireless sets themselves (those who had constructed their own were required to pay an 'experimenter's licence'); and the final portion was part of the money collected by the Post Office from those with the statutory radio licence.[17] The company returned any profit or excess revenue to the manufacturers, although in reality this was a relatively small amount.[18] Although it was initially privately owned, the BBC was never a truly commercial entity in the way that commercial broadcasting was to develop later, with no advertising present on the service. It operated a system of public service broadcasts from the very beginning, and just a month after the company's first broadcast its first General Manager was appointed, a day before the BBC was formally registered as a company on 15 December 1922.[19] This man was John Reith, a person who would be the personification of BBC values for decades and come to be widely referenced in later developments of public service broadcasting, so influential were his views on what it should constitute. His overall strategy that broadcasts should inform, educate and entertain has often been cited, but this was a simplistic summation of a complex problem: the question of programming and content. The company found itself broadcasting a large quantity of music, as well as plays that were sometimes specially adapted and written for the medium alongside outside broadcasts of significant events.

So popular was radio, with two and a quarter million licences sold in 1926,[20] that its future needed careful consideration, and it was generally felt that a private monopoly was not a fair basis for the medium. This resulted in the setting up of the Crawford Committee to establish its future. The committee's report was published on 5 March 1926, and it rejected the possibility of adopting the system that had proven successful across the Atlantic, feeling that the United States system was 'unsuited' to Britain, and that a monopoly should remain.[21] The conclusion was that the BBC should operate as a public corporation rather than a private company and retain its monopoly. Its Royal Charter came into effect on 1 January 1927. To put this in context, this is more than a year after Baird's demonstrations at Selfridge's and twelve months after his display of a more detailed television picture for members of the press and the Royal Institution. If television can be said to be in its infancy at this point, then public radio was not much more advanced. Nevertheless, radio had taken over twenty years to become a source of entertainment, whereas Baird had requested a licence for broadcasting within days of his 1926 demonstration.

Few at the time could have seen the BBC's role in television as a foregone conclusion. The practical difference in the government simply choosing not to licence another radio broadcaster may have been negligible, but it signalled that the BBC was not necessarily expected to be the only company that would ever be permitted a licence. Resultantly, this indicates an understanding that the broadcasting environment remained liable to change. This created a much more stable broadcasting environment than was implemented in many other countries, but it also made for a strong central broadcaster that would be difficult to rival. It was felt that in order for the corporation to fulfil its Public

Service obligations it would need to be free from commercial rivalry, with a presumption that commercial radio would problematise the establishment of the worthy credentials of the new medium.[22] However, the early television experiments, such as they were, were distinct from radio at this point; their close relationship in the United Kingdom had yet to form.

The BBC's Concerns

The scenario of a new system of broadcasts immediately raised the fundamental questions of whether there was a need (or desire) for television and how it should operate. The BBC itself was not a leader in the development of television for much of the pre-war period, but the existence of its broadcasting infrastructure sometimes made it a central focus for developments outside its control. Once it was definitively assigned the task of running television along similar lines to its radio work, the system came into operation after a relatively short period of time (a little under two years). The difficulty was in reaching this point, following the decision that television was both workable and desirable. The BBC conglomerated the work of others and followed the direction given by the government and the Post Office; it was not in the business of developing its own television technology at this point, rather it allowed the developments of others to be put to use. It accepted its eventual emergence as the most likely candidate for a permanent broadcasting system, but the corporation had little power in its own right.

The final clarification that Public Service Broadcasting would form the basis for television transmissions was essentially straightforward, with the publication of the report of the 1935 Television Committee headed by Lord Selsdon, but this followed years of debate between the various parties involved. Baird lobbied extensively for independent transmissions until he started regular experimental broadcasts in 1929,[23] but the eventual agreement of the BBC to allow the use of its own facilities for these signposted the beginning of what was to be an ongoing involvement in the medium. The partnership would weigh even more heavily in favour of the BBC when the corporation took control over the creation of content in 1932. This co-operation would not necessarily fulfil the vision of Baird Television, however, which by this point was hoping to dominate the manufacturing market, built on the adoption of its technology. While Moseley acted as producer for the test transmissions from 1930 to 1932,[24] this was largely because they were not official BBC broadcasts rather than because of any particular desire from Baird Television to create content. More problematic were the issues of technological development and the broader question of how desirable television broadcasting in itself was to be, and what exactly would be offered by the service. These were the questions that the government and the BBC would have to consider. The government's role was crucial in assigning the BBC the job of developing the system, but it offered little in the way of specifics. The issue of the eventual content would provoke much debate, but it is clear that there were more general questions of programming that needed consideration first, as the corporation found itself ruminating on what should constitute a service. This section, therefore, analyses the key developments and traces how attitudes towards, and expectations of, television altered, principally from the perspective of the BBC, but also with reference to the views of the government and the Post Office.

It was certainly the case that the BBC's infrastructure allowed for expansion to cover television, but the medium did not arrive fully formed. Indeed, there was the question of whether television would come to exist at all. The watchword of the BBC was caution, with its efforts to curb the publicity-seeking antics of Baird being symptomatic of a desire to downplay expectations of the system wherever possible. There were particular issues with Reith and Eckersley in the early years of television. Reith expressed little interest in the system, although he did meet Baird on at least three occasions and personally drafted at least one reply to a piece of the Baird company's ongoing correspondence about the future of the medium.[25] At the very least, he understood that there was significant potential in the development. The issue with Eckersley was somewhat different, and came down to fundamentally different opinions from Baird, the man who was most publicly petitioning for a fully fledged television service as soon as possible. Eckersley's low opinion of the 30-line technology meant that he also felt that it was not of sufficient quality to be the basis of an entire system of official broadcasts. Indeed, much of the 'work' of the BBC in the late 1920s and 1930s in relation to television was confined to refuting claims made in the press about the medium's imminent arrival or 'miraculous' advancements. This gave the impression of the corporation having an antagonistic approach that was somewhat unfair; in fact, the frequency of Eckersley's and Ashbridge's memos relating to the system indicate that it was far from being overlooked, simply perceived as unworkable in its then-current form, despite publicity sometimes claiming otherwise.

It will become clear that it was the Post Office's more sympathetic stance that resulted in the test transmissions of Baird's 30-line system, but Eckersley, and as a result the BBC, had never considered this to be a system with any practical future. The corporation understood that this left them open to criticism, as stated in a Control Board meeting of 15 April 1928, where Eckersley 'mentioned the sporadic attacks made on us for doing nothing about television, and suggested some form of cover for the public eye, such as the appointment of a committee to investigate the matter (he already being thoroughly in touch, and being satisfied that there was nothing to be given to the

Fig. 4.1: *Baird pictured in 1928*

(Courtesy of the Royal Television Society)

public at this moment). It was decided finally that the matter should be covered by a series of three articles in the *Radio Times* by experts.'[26] Had the relationship between the Baird company and the BBC been more cordial then such test broadcasts might have been embraced more readily by those at the corporation. There was no reason why the broadcasts could not have been a badge of honour for the corporation, one that they could have proudly announced as a significant development in the advancement of television, and simply made their limited and experimental nature clear. As it was, Baird and Hutchinson could not be trusted to play down the merits of their system and properly engage with the transmissions as the test broadcasts that they truly were. Instead, they viewed them as a platform for permanent and official television transmissions in the UK, meaning that mentions of the experimental system were low-key and tentative. The rationale for this attitude can be explained by Baird's own actions; his repeated public experiments and publicity coups gave the impression of a fully developed system which many expected to see implemented. So it was that one of the BBC's first major acts in relation to television was not proactive development, but the establishment of a defensive strategy.

In the event, the *Radio Times* did not publish such an article, although Eckersley had approached scientists Professor L.B. Turner, Dr W.H. Eccles and Professor E.V. Appleton with the intention of their writing an article each, either as a series or for one to be selected. Only Turner was to submit a draft, but this was considered to be too technical for the likely *Radio Times* readership. Significantly, the articles were not commissioned to explore the potential or likely uses of any eventual television system, but rather commissioned to outline the technology to that point. It is clear that this was a concerted attempt to counter the more outlandish claims of Baird Television. The BBC was not actively pursuing the question of television content or other practical issues relating to any prospective service because of the objections raised by Eckersley. The corporation was passive rather than proactive in the way that it dealt with television, batting away more outlandish claims while acceding only to formal orders for co-operation. When Eckersley initially wrote to Turner on 11 June 1928 he had outlined his own concerns in order to explain the need to publish such an article. 'The world is apt to go mad and it is the duty of experts to restrain enthusiasm which is based on insecure foundations,'[27] he began. 'My private feeling has been for a long time that the public is being somewhat deceived as to the immediate possibilities of television,'[28] and certainly the issue throughout this point seems to be that of the 'immediate possibilities'. There is no indication of widespread feelings within the BBC that the system would never be workable – quite the opposite, in fact. Nevertheless, Eckersley in particular had an issue with the way in which Baird was publicising his endeavours. Television was being widely seen as a nuisance, as the BBC failed to make the distinction between the more troublesome aspects of Baird television and the potential of the principle as a whole.

This exchange foreshadowed the culmination of these concerns when Baird Television placed an advertisement for Baird televisors in *The Times* on 22 June 1928. R.W. Burns points out the implications of it. 'According to this the Baird televisor would be purchasable either as a separate instrument or in combination with a listening in set; and so at "one and the same moment" the owner would be able "both to hear and see" a performer at the broadcasting station.'[29] Reith was concerned that this implied that BBC television was imminent, and it reinforced Eckersley's other stated concern in the letter to Turner that he envisaged people making 'speculative investments and considerable companies are being formed with this idea in view.'[30]

The BBC's Initial Expectations

While the BBC did not initially concern itself with developing the technology of television, it did survey the possible results, but wished to do so discreetly. However, there was no concerted effort or plan in place before the technology had reached a sufficiently advanced stage to justify the provision of a complete service. So paranoid was the corporation about the release of information related to television that an internal memorandum dated 18 September 1928 dictated that 'The greatest possible caution should be observed in making any reference in public, either in speech or writing, to the forthcoming picture transmissions,'[31] while Eckersley continued to emphasise that the imminent test transmissions could not constitute a full service. 'If it is thought by the control board that what they see demonstrated, i.e. what has been done by Baird, justifies in itself a service, then let us go ahead, but I warn everyone that in my opinion, it is the end of their development, not the beginning, and that we shall be forever sending heads and shoulders,'[32] he stated in

October the same year. He was certainly prescient in his adjudication; there was to be relatively little advancement for the 30-line service despite a further seven years of test broadcasts of low definition services. The system was restricted by the existing broadcasting infrastructure which Baird had chosen to use for his transmissions (the same technology used for audio on medium wave); by using this, higher resolutions were not possible. While there was potential for greater quality with mechanical systems, it would eventually become clear that the advantages of the silent sleekness of later all-electronic developments were impossible to ignore.

Eckersley's concerns can probably be put down to his own misgivings about the way in which the Baird publicity machine would interpret such broadcasts. Significantly, Eckersley does start to engage with issues of content and appeal, as he asks: 'Are heads and shoulders a service? Has it any artistic value? Is it in fact simply a stunt?'[33] This is one of the earliest instances of the BBC actually considering television in more than an abstract sense. Briggs claims that Eckersley 'had more ideas about broadcasting than any other man in the country,'[34] and he was certainly passionate about new developments, whether it was in a positive or negative sense. In this case, now that television transmissions (albeit experimental ones) were imminent there was a sudden importance attached to considering what should actually be shown in such broadcasts. This was less important for the limited experimental broadcasts, but it was not a question that could be avoided forever. Baird Television had spent little time considering issues of content, but the BBC realised that it would be key to the success of any eventual official service.

Indeed, it was becoming increasingly clear that television would not simply go away, or be the subject of low-key research. Private meetings indicated that the BBC was under pressure from the Post Office to monitor developments and, more particularly, keep the fantastical claims of Baird in check with a series of official clarifications, with Eckersley pointing out the deficiencies of the technology prior to a special demonstration for the BBC (including Reith) on 9 October 1928.[35] It was not a success, with Murray proclaiming that the prospect of a service would be 'ludicrous if the financial implications did not make it so sinister.'[36] The BBC was not being paranoid in its constant attempts to underplay television in the public eye; rather there was a real danger of the public being misled by the drip-feeding of such suggestions by Baird Television, and as a result a notice was issued to newspapers later that month which implored editors to ignore any claims made by Baird about a television service. The BBC had no better idea than anyone else regarding where television's future would lie, but it found itself having to protect its own interests due to the inevitable backlash if the grand suggestions made elsewhere did not materialise. While Baird remained synonymous with television, the BBC was now involved alongside him, which meant that it was now subject to more scrutiny regarding its action (or non-action) towards television from all quarters.

On 21 November 1928, Hutchinson assured Murray that he 'accepted [Murray's] repeated assurances that there are no extraneous or hidden motives behind any action of the BBC,'[37] and it is certainly true that the corporation was not attempting to entirely discredit the operations of Baird Television, but once again this highlights the different aims of the two organisations. At this point establishing television as a public service required that an attempt be made to form the highest quality service practicable, with the long-term success of the medium being the primary concern. The fact that the BBC could not see a tenable future for the technology as it then stood indicates a fundamental difference of opinion regarding what would be an acceptable technical basis for television. This can be simply summarised as Baird feeling that his technology was of sufficient quality to operate as a system of public television, while the BBC did not. This clash was the fundamental issue for the breakdown in the relationship between the two.

In an effort to clarify the answers to various questions relating to television in advance of these transmissions there was an internal document circulated on 3 November 1928 that set out the BBC's current stance, essentially amounting to an admission that no-one was clear what the future would bring for the medium and that there could be no concrete plans at that stage. This document, entitled 'The Truth about Television', opened by asking 'What is television, as it is popularly understood? There is so much in the idea of television to appeal to the imagination that it is not surprising that wrong conceptions of it are current. Some people think of television as the direct and natural counterpart of [radio] broadcasting. They imagine, for instance, that it is now possible, by combining play with broadcasting, to transmit visual images with plays, ceremonials and great events as and when they happen.'[38] In many ways, television was to become a 'direct and natural counterpart' of radio, but the distinction here was necessary to make it clear to the general public that this was not a simple case of being able to see what was being broadcast on the radio. As previously stated, there were occasions when the BBC found itself forced to make a statement to the effect that television and radio were distinct entities, especially when some listeners worried that the emergence of television would signify the end of the present sound-only wireless service. In actual fact, there was never any serious consideration within the BBC that television would replace radio.[39] Even ignoring the fact that the media have inherently different advantages over each other, radio was enough of a success that there would be no consideration of terminating the service in favour of a new technology.

It is worth keeping in mind the extent to which the BBC's operations were wholly focused on radio. When this book discusses the machinations of 'the

BBC' in relation to the developments of television, it is important to remember that such important decisions were actually the actions of only a handful of people. For example, it is notable the extent to which the quoted internal correspondence covering the early years of television development tends to be written by one of a core group of people, generally engineers (such was the necessary preoccupation at the time with the technical issues of any eventual service) and Gladstone Murray. There was no institutional stance towards television; this would develop over time. The new medium was very much a peripheral concern and the cost of the BBC's broadcasts of television prior to the official 1936 launch was low: £2,225 in 1932, £7,129 the next year and finally £6,617 in 1934.[40] That is not to say that television was not taken seriously, but nor was it a dominant aspect of the BBC's ongoing affairs at this point. It could easily have been overlooked, or indeed quietly forgotten, were it not for the vocal arguments in its favour from the more rabid enthusiasts, including Baird Television.

Early 1929 was a period that indicated to the BBC exactly what the weight of expectation was for a supposedly imminent television service. What is particularly curious is that even those who were advocating the immediate launch of television rarely gave any indication of exactly what would be

Fig. 4.2: *Baird employees gather around a large Baird television receiver in 1929*

(Courtesy of the Royal Television Society)

expected from such a service. As it was, the corporation was instead facing a sudden rush of publicity around its explicitly unpublicised imminent experiments. Articles appeared in several publications, including the *Manchester Guardian*, the *Daily Telegraph* and the *Sunday People*, the latter of which was particularly vociferous in its stance towards the BBC when it came to supporting and developing television. The article claimed that 'the attitude of the BBC in regard to this amazing British invention is incomprehensible,'[41] with the provenance of the technology being emphasised in a manner similar to many of Baird's own proclamations and later press reports. It was widely felt within the BBC that Baird had fed this information to the newspapers himself, despite the fact that this went against the agreement that he had with the corporation; he denied the claims.[42]

Perhaps as a result of these newspaper reports, Cyril Andrew Craygy, a member of the public, wrote to the BBC enquiring about the future of television, and received a reply dated 30 January 1929. 'The BBC is fully alive to the importance of encouraging and adopting inventions calculated to improve and widen the broadcasting service,'[43] read the letter from the corporation. 'You will readily understand, however, that the corporation owes it to its listeners to be particularly careful to avoid arousing expectations which are likely to be unfulfilled. New ideas and inventions are constantly under review; as and when they reach a stage capable of general operation, without dislocating the existing service, they are adopted. This is the rule which is applied to systems of television.'[44] It should be noted here how television is described as a development of broadcasting (usually used as a synonym for *radio* transmissions in this era), rather than an entirely new innovation in its own right, despite earlier attempts to explicitly separate the two. It is not possible to reach any definite conclusion about this muddled usage other than to use it to emphasise the extent to which there was no single concerted aim or expectation for television.

The 'Terms of Reference' document, noted previously in relation to the stance of the Baird company that the BBC was being 'obstructive and irrational', gives a more detailed impression of the BBC's own expectations in the late 1920s. The document points out that television at this time could 'be done in a limited way but, in its present stage of development, it requires either laboratory conditions or such elaborate and expensive apparatus that its range of application is necessarily limited.'[45] A nine-point breakdown of the system's problems followed, ranging from the method of viewing (at this point, it was only through a small viewing hole rather than on a larger screen), through to practical concerns of what would be possible to transmit, with football matches or most public events impossible to relay, and concerns regarding the placement of the transmissions within the available radio wavelengths. All were valid, but most pertinent was a simple question relating to the medium more generally. 'Has it, in effect, as shown, the permanent service value and a permanent artistic value to the general public?'[46] On the evidence that the BBC had seen, it would seem not. Television was not perceived as a fixed entity. Indeed, the document specifically refers to television as it then stood. There was an expectation that the technology would improve, and even a stated feeling that Baird's system was working towards a dead end. This is likely to be at least partially a result of the BBC's investigations into different systems, as will later be touched upon, which did not specifically highlight any superior methods of television transmissions, but did demonstrate that there were multiple approaches being investigated by other interested parties.

This document finishes with a series of questions that would require positive answers in order for the technology to be used as a basis of a service. The first question is whether the system could transmit significant events as an outside broadcast, including football matches. This was a crucial concern in these early years, as such a live relay would be an advantage unique to television. Early public demonstrations of television would result in somewhat muted reactions from some members of the public regarding the transmission of films on early television experiments; it was felt by some that all of television should be live by its very nature.[47] The second touches on the cost and asks if the viewer would pay £50 for the apparatus required. The third question touches on the more moralistic implications of such a service, asking if it would be right to encourage the general public to spend money on the system at this point in its development. Finally, the document asks whether private experiments should continue until the previous conditions were met.[48] There was nothing to gain for the BBC from stalling the development of television, but there was the potential for a great deal of criticism should it have handled the situation badly. Although it faced a great deal of criticism from some corners because of its cautiousness, it is reasonable to presume that this was minor compared to the problems it would have faced had it encouraged the general public to buy ultimately useless receivers simply because it was a form of television. Television could not stay in limbo forever, and there were serious signs of movement towards a concerted decision about television's future.

5

Deciding on Television's Future

John Logie Baird's largest contribution to television may well not be any practical contribution to technological development, or even publicity, but that the results of his own endeavours in each of those fields led to the operation of a system that was authorised by, and received co-operation from, the appropriate authorities. Although it was the case that the Baird company's technology had been superseded before the first programme was shown (albeit in the private laboratories of engineers and scientists), the broadcasts whetted the appetite. Perhaps there was limited excitement from the general public, who nevertheless remained bemused but mildly interested, but more the case for the dedicated band of enthusiasts who were keen to ensure that television did not slip back into a coma now it had finally been brought to life.

Chief villain in the eyes of many of these enthusiasts was Peter Eckersley. In order to clarify his generally negative stance, the BBC's Chief Engineer was interviewed for *Popular Wireless* magazine's 14 July 1929 issue, while the periodical ran its own editorial, entitled 'Television – The Position Today'. *Popular Wireless* had been less enthusiastic than the periodical *Television* about the prospects for Baird's technology. The editorial touches on the 'over enthusiastic' press reports and general publicity, and explicitly denounces the notion of Baird as the inventor of television. 'It has been claimed by innumerable writers of the press that television is the invention of Mr J.L. Baird. We say that this is untrue and that television – like the wireless – is the particular invention of nobody, but is due to the work of many people,'[1] it read. 'Mr Baird has his system and, we are the first to admit, it has its merits but, unfortunately, owing to over enthusiastic press publicity and to the claims made by those associated with Mr Baird, we have been forced, much against our will, to adopt an attitude which many people seem to consider as antagonistic to Mr Baird.'[2] The statement is unequivocal, and highlights that the actions of Baird Television did not always result in a positive presence in the specialist press. It does, however, highlight the influence of Baird's publicity, in response to which the BBC could only clarify its own involvement. The quality of Baird Television's apparatus was open to wider debate. In his interview, Eckersley reveals his conclusion, also stated within internal BBC documentation, that television needed a radical discovery or advancement in order to become a practicable system. 'Now if television were perfected,' he is quoted as saying, 'that would be a different proposition. There would be, I believe, a very popular demand for the BBC to take it up. But in its present form it would be useless for us to do anything.'[3] Television as a concept was of interest to the BBC, then, but Baird's apparatus was less appealing. This distinction was often lost on the more vocal supporters of Baird Television. However, this also underlines the extent to which the BBC declined to be proactive in its pursuit of a high quality television service. Eckersley's open acknowledgment that there was 'a very popular demand' for television could be seen as a significant development in the BBC's stance were it not for the immediate clarification that the BBC would prefer to 'do nothing' rather than actively seek out a technical solution. This is not necessarily a criticism of the BBC, who had little relevant expertise in the available resources to pursue television (certainly when compared to large companies such as RCA and EMI), but indicates the extent to which television had to be perfected in the private sphere, regardless of any public interest in the system.

However, if the BBC had initially felt that it could simply operate as it saw fit when it came to television, it soon became clear that there would have to be some middle ground. Its dismissive view of Baird's apparatus was deemed unacceptable by the Post Office, which held the view that there was a duty to at least investigate the possibilities offered by his company. 'The Postmaster General declared that he was finding it difficult politically to defend an entirely negative attitude towards television,'[4] said an undated private BBC précis of events. 'He did not suggest that the BBC was wrong, but he felt that it was necessary to arrange a further test under stringent conditions.'[5] The eventual result of this was an ongoing series of test transmissions from 1929, which at least pacified Baird. They commenced in August 1929, and despite the request for no publicity these experiments were even noted in the *Radio Times* alongside their medium wave frequency, covered in the main listings pages:

11.0 – 11.30
(261.3 *m. only*)
Experimental Television Transmission by the Baird Process.

As Tony Currie, author of *The Radio Times Story*, has put it, '30-line pictures transmitted mid-morning without any sound [which did not arrive until the next year] certainly didn't merit more than three lines of highly sought-after space in the programme pages. However, those three lines established *The Radio Times* as the world's first television listings magazine. There was much more to follow!'[6] It is unsurprising that television coverage was to be somewhat sporadic over the next seven years considering the highly experimental nature of the broadcasts, but it is worth pointing out that the *Radio Times* continued to list the experimental broadcasts, sometimes giving detail on the content of the transmissions. Indeed, overall, the transmissions did contribute to the sense that television was a real proposition rather than simply a theory, while also cementing the relationship between the medium and the BBC itself. However, television was not in a state that would be acceptable to most of its potential audience, and no end of experimental broadcasts utilising the same basic technology throughout would alter this fact.

The BBC Takes Control

The next significant development within the corporation towards television would seem to be good news for all parties involved in the medium, although this would not be the case in the long run for the Baird company. Murray considered that the current situation regarding television was untenable and felt that the transmissions needed either to progress or to cease. On 12 August 1931, he wrote to Moseley, pointing out that the BBC was 'anxious that British television should retain and increase its margin of superiority,' a statement that already signified more commitment to the service than had previously been expressed.[7] 'The experimental transmissions by the Baird process have been going on now for nearly two years,' wrote Murray, who went on to say that they needed 'some variation'.[8] No specifics were mentioned, but it was indicated that the BBC wished to help the private company in some manner, or at least assist in the ongoing development of television. This would eventually result in the BBC taking on most of the transmission side of television, but not before Murray and Moseley once more crossed swords, this time about the details of financing and exclusivity, both of which were crucial to the company. Moseley took this as an example of the negative attitude of the BBC, and wrote to Murray on 5 October 1931.

'Despite your personal assurance to the contrary, there is no doubt at all that the BBC regards television as a nuisance,' Moseley's letter stated, 'and would be glad to see it "fade-out", but we have no intention of obliging in this way. The venomous hostility of the former Chief Engineer has crystallised into a kind of cynical indifference.'[9] Eckersley had left the corporation by this point, but his successor Noel Ashbridge was little more enamoured with Baird's system than his predecessor. In any case, the letter seems to miss the point regarding the apparent hostility of the corporation to television. It should be emphasised that this was never the case; what there had been was an ongoing issue with the tactics of Baird Television, a somewhat separate problem. Indeed, the BBC had not found it difficult to separate Baird from television more generally when considering the future of the medium, even if Baird and Moseley were obviously less keen to make any distinction. A little over a week later, on 14 October, Ashbridge said that 'television was bound to take part in broadcasting eventually,'[10] indicating that there was no real issue with the medium itself, merely the present implementation of it. If the tone from Moseley was more antagonistic than usual, this was the result of Baird Television's own rather more pressing concerns. It was shown in the previous section that earlier in the year Baird's company had approached the Post Office and, indirectly, the BBC regarding the issue of funding. Its financial state was precarious, resulting in the suggestion of some form of subsidy to justify its ongoing work. This was dismissed by both the BBC and the Post Office, but the financial concerns remained. A BBC board meeting of 27 October 1931 touched on the fact that a decision would need to be made, an opposing view to an earlier stated desire in an undated memo to Ashbridge, likely to be from mid-1931, which stated that, 'The agreed policy is to keep the pace as slow as is compatible with the maintenance of decent relations.'[11] The board stated that:

> Their feeling was that television, though still non-commercial, had got to a stage where we should make up our minds either to co-operate wholeheartedly with the Baird system or see it disappear for lack of funds and opportunity, with the possibility of replacement by an American development at a later date. They were in favour of co-operation. Public reaction against the BBC might occur on both lines of action. We should probably be accused of obstructing progress if we did not co-operate at all, and similarly if we did co-operate and there was commercial failure the extent of our co-operation would be questioned by shareholders and attempt made to place the blame on the BBC.[12]

This concern over the perception of the BBC's attitude to Baird's work was to formulate later policy and the launch of the medium itself. Baird's publicity made it impossible to quietly dispose of him, with the result that this set him up for the humiliation of direct competition with the superior Marconi-EMI system three years later. This point is unequivocal: the eventual alternating placement of the two rival systems was not designed in order for the systems to be compared and the stronger one adopted, as may be presumed. There was no doubt that Baird's system was inferior in every way, but there had to be the perception of giving him a fair chance to prove himself.

Fig. 5.1: *The Marconi-EMI technology allowed for greater flexibility than that offered by the Baird company, allowing for outside broadcasts, such as this 1939 transmission from London Zoo for the programme* **From the Zoo.**

(Courtesy of the Alexandra Palace Television Society)

Television was the centre of a personal squabble, and the Selsdon Committee's report was bound by the efforts of these experimental broadcasts and Baird's involvement.

The result in the short term was that, despite the disagreements, it was decided to press ahead with a new era of television transmissions.[13] Ashbridge had been instrumental in this, viewing Baird Television's most recent apparatus and judging it to be of sufficient merit for the transmissions to take place.[14] This time, however, the broadcasts would come from the basement of the BBC's own Broadcasting House rather than Baird's Long Acre studios, where the earlier test broadcasts had originated. Most significantly, with the exception of maintenance by the Baird Television Company, the BBC would undertake all costs for the transmission side of this service.[15] Given their financial difficulties, Baird and Moseley agreed to what superficially appeared to be an arrangement to their advantage. Burns points out that the BBC was 'to be responsible for the programmes and television transmission while [Baird

Television] would be responsible for technical development and the commercial exploitation of their receiving apparatus.'[16] While this satisfied the company, whose interests had always been more squarely focused on the technology than issues of content, it also meant that it relinquished the only aspect which would remain relatively consistent no matter what technology was used, the programming itself. The company was in danger of being usurped by a rival, should a superior system arrive, which it did. Their requests for subsidies had continually been refused, the most recent request being made of Postmaster General Kingsley Wood in April 1932, when Baird suggested that his company should receive one penny of the ten shilling licence fee; R.W. Burns calculates that this would have amounted to £20,000 a year for the company.[17] Reith had actually supported Baird's requests, but to no avail.[18]

The new BBC-run television service launched on 22 August 1932, opening with a short speech from Baird himself.[19] Programming was broadcast for two hours a week, specifically in the half hour from 11pm on a Monday, Tuesday, Wednesday and Friday.[20] The BBC appointed Eustace Robb to the position of the corporation's first television producer, while Douglas Birkinshaw was the inaugural research engineer. Television was slipping further out of Baird's grasp, something only compounded by the discussions that the BBC had been having with HMV (later EMI, and to become part of Marconi-EMI) about its own apparatus. Baird's was not yet a full service, and it was still the low-resolution 30-line system. However, the BBC was taking control of the medium and making it a point of policy to continue working on television.

The success of television would depend on more than just BBC backing, however. The British public had started to change their social habits, embracing domesticity, with the home now being a place where a person could be entertained. The percentage of British homes connected to the mains electricity increased sharply during the 1930s, highlighting this increased emphasis on the home as a place of modern comforts. Whereas just 31.84% were connected to the supply in 1932 this would more than double to 65.39% by 1938.[21] Domestic developments such as these started to give greater opportunities for entertainment based in the home environment. Radio is a strong example of this new found domestic environment for entertainment as the number of wireless sets in use grew sharply over the years following the BBC's formation in 1922. In 1924, a wireless licence was held by ten percent of households, reaching seventy-one percent by 1939.[22] Over the same period the number of telephone rentals for private use increased from 176,000 to 882,000, a figure that topped one million just the next year.[23] These statistics demonstrate that, despite the economic downturn of the early 1930s, there was still interest from the general public when it came to embracing the benefits that technology could now offer, and with over sixty-five percent of households having mains power by the end of the 1930s access was not limited to the elite. The emergence of a strong domestic model would be essential if television was ever to become a mainstream concern.

The appeal of these new sources of mass communication led the British culture towards the home rather than communal environments. Historian Andrew Thorpe has highlighted that the thirties 'saw a society whose leisure was increasingly private, with the decline of pub and chapel, and the growth of home-based pursuits'.[24] Radio, and later television, would prove to be the devices that ensured the paradox of both integration and disintegration, as Thorpe goes on to describe the social changes. 'Domesticity and its accompanying materialism had arrived,'[25] he says. Television's domesticity has always been a crucial factor behind the content of its broadcasts, with programming being specifically formulated to bring the medium's entertainment or information into the home, and so the medium as we know it relied upon a general public using their domestic space more.

Television was starting to assert itself as a potentially popular medium, but there was still evidence of unrest amongst some at the BBC, who disliked the allocation of funds for a service that was still used by so few. Resultantly, in September 1933, Baird Television was given notice that the service would terminate on 31 March 1934.[26] In the event the transmissions would actually continue until 11 September 1935,[27] but this was the beginning of the end for the 30-line broadcasts. More importantly for the expectations of how a system of television could operate, the broadcasts demonstrated the likelihood that it would be a public system, centrally funded from the licence fee. This relied on official confirmation that the BBC would take control of the system and an improvement in picture quality, but the infrastructure of television had been removed from the grasp of private investors. Whether the system would have reached this stage without this private investment is questionable.

Alternatives to Baird

Even when Baird was providing the principal form of television transmissions, the corporation had been open to the consideration of other systems. In addition to its occasional discussions with HMV (and, later, Marconi-EMI), as early as 1928, the BBC had internally acknowledged Eckersley's report that Marconi and British Thomson-Houston were rumoured to be embarking on television development, although the latter company did not go on to demonstrate any television technology during this pre-war period.[28] The corporation actually conducted tests in transmitting still pictures by the Fultograph method in late 1928, this being the action that resulted in

Television magazine's 'Has the BBC Vision' cartoon. It is unclear exactly why the BBC felt the need to allow the use of their facilities to conduct such experiments considering that, as Briggs points out, the corporation's willingness to co-operate with the private company Wireless Pictures Ltd. in this manner made it difficult for it to then refuse Baird similar co-operation, even if it did resist this for a further year.[29] Nevertheless, the experiments indicate a broad-mindedness when it came to an understanding of what 'television' should be. This was earlier indicated on 14 February of the same year, when an internal document 'For Information' was circulated, which highlighted the different methods of picture transmission that might be referred to. This was the document mentioned in my introduction, which mentioned the varying types of television-like systems. These included the still picture transmissions of the Fultograph and Telephotography, where the corporation claimed that it was 'co-operating [...] in experiments on the Thorne-Baker system,'[30] although it is unclear where this co-operation led, other than to say that such a system of transmission of still pictures was never officially launched. Television is the next system mentioned, touching on the fact that the corporation was 'not at present co-operating' with the discussions between the Post Office and Baird. Radioscope is then described as a system of 'follow up' whereby the audience would be supplied with pictures 'for cinematographic or magic lantern use,'[31] a magic lantern being the name for a simple projector of static slides. 'It is NOT transmission of pictures,'[32] the document makes clear. Finally, 'Vienna Lamps' are mentioned as an alternative name for a similar system to the Radioscope principle. What this document really enables us to understand is that the television system as finally established was the most complex of all these prospective types of picture transmissions, and that despite the ridicule of *Television* magazine, the BBC seemed to investigate these systems out of a sense of duty rather than through any heady expectations of their long-term futures. Indeed, it is important to remember the extent to which the BBC was operating as a pioneer in its subsequent experimental transmissions, even if its work was not completely unique.

It is not, then, fair to say that the interest taken in Marconi-EMI's technology, or the ultimate abandonment of Baird's system, was simple treachery. Although Marconi-EMI had technically only existed since early 1934, they had undertaken a great deal of research and had a long history in the field. For their part, the BBC had always been open to investigating other potential types of television, both in the fundamental sense of what television could be (for example, through the potential transmission of still pictures in whatever form) and had never given an indication to Baird or anyone else that it considered its system to be the eventual destination of television; quite the opposite, in fact. The seriousness with which the corporation undertook its role as a public body underpins the developments of television throughout its history, but this is especially true during this period. Decisions were literally made by committee, with every position having to be justified. Even the Post Office, itself a public body, did not particularly serve as an ally. In terms of the government, the BBC had been left to its own devices in respect of television. Until the BBC felt that there was a demonstrable system of television that had real entertainment value, the government paid little attention to the system and simply referred any of the infrequent queries to the corporation or Post Office. There was no active petitioning for the service internally, the government only stepping in when aggravated by external factors to put pressure on the corporation to consider television more seriously. The main extent of the government's influence was the influence of the Postmaster General himself. While six people held this position between 1925 and 1936, their personal influences were less significant than that of Murray or Eckersley, instead tending to mediate between bodies or approve technical matters.[33]

Television was perceived as having great potential importance, but it was also understood that this was a future possibility, not an overnight revolution. Even if the experimental broadcasts had achieved little in the way of technical advancement, they had at least ensured that the corporation was aware that television was an issue that was not going to go away even if left unattended. Indeed, by 1933 the BBC had seen advancements from both Baird Television and EMI, and was stating internally that, 'It is probable that television will become a practical proposition within the next few years, and will take its part in the daily programmes.'[34] This internal memorandum also emphasised the likely limited nature of any programming, however, while also stating the expected future position of the medium in relation to radio broadcasting. 'For the present it should be looked forward to more as a possible addition or aid to what we are doing now rather than as a feature which will revolutionise the whole art.'[35]

Deciding on Television's Future

In 1934 Reith consulted with the Postmaster General of the time, Kingsley Wood, regarding the possibility of a committee to definitively fix the future of the medium.[36] Wood agreed, and set up the Television Committee, headed by Lord Selsdon with Sir John Cadman as the vice-chairman. Two members of the Post Office also formed part of the Committee; assistant engineer-in-chief A.S. Angwin and assistant secretary F.W. Phillips. From the BBC were Ashbridge and the corporation's controller Charles Carpendale. The final member was O. F. Brown, from the Department of Scientific and Industrial Research, while the secretary was J. Varley Roberts, again of the Post Office.[37] The Committee was meticulous in its approach, calling 38 witnesses to discuss television and its likely uses and effects. As Briggs has put it, 'The Selsdon Committee had to examine both the technical merits of the rival television systems and future finance and organisation of a television service.'[38] There was, in fact, little in the way of controversy regarding the conclusions drawn. The consensus was for a BBC-run television service, once again operating as a monopoly in the manner of radio. The most difficult issue may be seen to have been the decision to allow the alternate usage of both prospective systems of television, but as highlighted in the previous section, this was also deemed necessary so as to give the appearance of being fair to Baird. The Committee published its report in January 1935 and its findings were accepted by Wood and the BBC. The report set out technical issues, including the provision of both services and the official curtailment of the low-definition service, while settling on the wavelength to be used. It was also stated that the system should start as soon as was possible (within eighteen months), and should initially be available in the London area 'with the planning of additional stations, until a network is gradually built up.'[39] Such forward thinking indicates the extent to which television was now being considered as a fully-fledged, permanent service rather than something that required more experimentation. However, provision was made for the potential emergence of a superior system of technology. In such a case it was proposed that notice of no less than two years should be given to areas with an existing service, while any new transmitting stations should adopt any improved service.[40] In the event, the 405-line Marconi-EMI system would continue to be exclusively broadcast until the 1964 launch of BBC2, which adopted a superior 625-line method, with BBC1 and ITV phasing out 405-line transmissions from 1969 at the same time that they adopted colour broadcasting technology.

The Committee also claimed that the question of content and programming was 'scarcely' theirs, and devoted only two paragraphs of their findings to this issue. It pointed out that:

> To what extent those programmes should consist of direct transmissions of studio or outdoor scenes, or televised reproduction of films, must be determined largely by experience, technical progress and public support, as well as by financial considerations. No doubt the televising of sport and other public events will have a wide appeal, and will add considerably to the attractiveness of the service.[41]

The question of original programming does not feature at all, indicating the extent to which television's principal aim appeared to be the relaying or adaption of pre-existing events or material. While this remains true today to some extent, with sports programming and events of national interest being televised live, the majority of the schedule consists of original material. The inevitability of trial and error would be raised once more immediately prior to the official launch, but this could only be the case because there was no precise requirement for programming. The emphasis on the visual, for example, was left unexplored. Should programmes be considered more 'worthy' if they included more content that could only be enjoyed by television viewers, or was this secondary to the issue of arranging for a balanced schedule that informs and entertains, assuming that these two requirements were not mutually exclusive?

Television had been given a future but what the Selsdon Committee had decided was little more than the question of overall responsibility, with the BBC officially being entrusted with the service, and technical considerations, while ensuring that the finance for the system was in place. The estimated £180,000 (for the period to 31 December 1936) would be drawn from the existing radio licence fee.[42] For the first time, the BBC had to consider what to do with the service as a permanent feature of its broadcasting in the London area. The next section of this book will show what the corporation settled upon in these first months and years of official broadcasts. However, their initial high-definition broadcasts to the general public came a few months earlier than the November 1936 launch, and met with rather less interest than had been hoped for. Had television, in fact, been of only passing interest some ten years earlier, with the corporation missing out on the initial wave of excitement and interest?

6

Television Faces the Public

With the official launch imminent, the BBC started to feel the need to encourage public interest and understanding of the still new technology, perhaps in part due to concerns that the earlier low-definition broadcasts might confuse both the press and the public when it came to the launch of the new high-definition system. So it was that television was still not in operation when, suddenly, plans were made for a series of public demonstrations at that year's Radiolympia, a show for radio manufacturers and enthusiasts to share their wares. The Radio Manufacturers' Association (RMA) had invited the inaugural Director of Television at the BBC, Gerald Cock, to a dinner on 11 June 1936, where its members took the opportunity to express their concerns. Intriguingly, the RMA had seen television as a hostile rival to radio broadcasts, rather than a complementary technology. It is not difficult to understand why BBC statements and press reports aimed at the general public felt the need to clarify that television was not intended to replace radio, but it is more surprising that professional bodies such as the RMA clearly saw television as a threat. Such concerns also indicate the extent to which television was now being taken seriously.

Cock was happy to gently fob off their concerns, although it seems that he did not dispel them. 'My personal relations with its individual members were extremely pleasant,' he wrote 'but it was quite obvious that, led by their president Mr Rosen [...] there was a majority with the firm intention to slow down on television as far as they can, and get us to stop all publicity about it.'[1] Cock did not appear to take their stance seriously, but the apparent hostility towards television from the RMA, however politely expressed ('they continually assured me that they were only too anxious to work hand-in-glove with us and help all they could'[2]), indicates that they were a body with a genuine fear of television becoming a replacement for radio, despite the assurances in the previous Selsdon Committee report indicating otherwise, along with repeated notices to the same effect from the BBC over the course of the previous decade. Cock goes as far as to mock the Association's apparent concerns in his memo ('Rosen actually stated that the press and Parliamentary visits might, through publicity result in endangering the employment of thousands of workers and the future of a good many manufacturers!'[3]). Perhaps the RMA's might be seen as more reasonable when considering that radio was still in its relative infancy, although it is curious that they should be so diametrically opposed to the increasingly positive BBC views on television's potential development. Of course, the RMA's sole concerns were the wellbeing of, and ongoing available work for, its members and their employees, but this appears to have held little sway with Cock. The RMA's reasoning for their attempts to delay the launch of television 'was expressed by them as the necessity for "the right kind of publicity"!'[4] states Cock, clearly incredulous at the suggestion. Publicity was an ongoing issue for television, inasmuch as it needed to be the *correct* publicity, ever since its earliest days of 'wildcat theories', and the wish for it to be explicitly stated to be a medium that did not supersede or replace radio was clearly not a completely ridiculous suggestion, despite the repeated assurances. Nevertheless, this at least demonstrates that there was some expectation that television could be a mainstream success able to rival the popularity of radio broadcasts.

At around this point it was suggested that the BBC might wish to publicise its imminent television service at the event, as it was expected to officially launch before the end of the year, in light of the Selsdon Committee's report. Initially the corporation's reaction to the event was lukewarm but, perhaps at odds with Cock's experience, the RMA was keen to have television demonstrated at the exhibition.[5] This may have been because it was not keen on alleged plans to demonstrate the system to the press and certain members of parliament privately, when Radiolympia could certainly benefit from the added publicity that television would bring instead. Possibly to this end, the minutes of a liaison meeting between the BBC and the RMA just a few days after Cock's encounter, paints a rather more positive picture. 'Mr Rosen, on behalf of the RMA said that they now wanted to see television put over at the earliest practicable time to the public, in the best possible way and with the fullest measure of co-operation between the BBC and themselves,'[6] opened the minutes, which went on to apparently dismiss any misgivings of the RMA towards the new medium. They go on to state: 'There was an impression that the RMA were softpedalling [on the issue of television] because of Radiolympia. This was not true.'[7] The timing was certainly a coincidence considering that there was a problem with selling stands for the show.[8] Whatever the reasoning, the situation led to an alliance of sorts between the two bodies, and the difficult question of what should be shown in such a demonstration needed to be resolved.

After years of secretive and low-key developments and tests, suddenly thousands of members of the general public were to see high-definition television for the first time. The experimental transmissions had previously only reached those with a particular interest in the service, by dint of its covert nature and expense. It is perhaps ironic, and indeed potentially problematic, that the future of the medium was assured some time before the reaction of the general public to these two methods of broadcasting was assessed. So much time had been spent on the long-term potential of the medium, and the short-term practical difficulties to be overcome, that little attention had been paid to the medium-term prospect of constructing entirely new programming for an entirely new medium with limited resources and a host of technical issues to consider. The experimental transmissions had largely used self-contained entertainment acts which might also be seen in vaudeville or end-of-the-pier shows, and this template was to be utilised throughout television's early period. For Radiolympia, however, more care was taken to show off the service's potential rather than simply broadcast anything that was available and required little in the way of resources. These transmissions are a useful demonstration of how the general public reacted to a system that was by then inevitable, and what they perceived it to be, alongside the question of what was shown as being deemed either representative or of interest. After a decade of intermittent publicity and almost six years of experimental broadcasts, how much did the public even care about television, and how did it measure up to their expectations?

In line with the forthcoming service, both the Baird and Marconi-EMI services were utilised for the transmissions, performing on alternate days from 31 August 1936.[9] The schedule for each was largely similar, and was cautious rather than being particularly ambitious through a reluctance to highlight the limits of the medium. The programme running order featured several film excerpts, covering newsreels as well as feature films. Also featured was the variety programme *Here's Looking At You*, and a handful of singers interspersed with the aforementioned films.[10] Additionally, the Marconi-EMI system featured 'Picture of Alexandra Park with commentary by Cecil Lewis,'[11] something that would have been impossible for the rather less portable Baird system. And so, with the words 'Hullo Radiolympia! This is a BBC experimental demonstration,'[12] the first public view of high definition television was demonstrated.

The Radiolympia attendees were not particularly enthusiastic about these test broadcasts, but nor were they overtly critical. The oft-criticised BBC trait of general lack of interest towards the medium was shared by many of those viewing the stands at Radiolympia, perhaps indicating that the enthusiastic approaches to television seen elsewhere were in fact less representative of wider attitudes than the BBC's earlier general disdain for it. Perhaps most pertinent was a point made within a report made of the first demonstrations as sent to J. Varley Roberts, now of the Television Advisory Committee that had been set up following the publication of the Selsdon report to supervise aspects of the medium's implementation. 'The first transmission was technically quite good but, of necessity, it had to consist of a lot of films, and I think the public would have liked more direct material,'[13] the report stated. When making his own general conclusions from Radiolympia in a document dated 7 September, Cock struck upon an important point for our consideration of the way in which television would develop. Apart from his conclusion that shorter programmes were more effective (he believed that ten minutes could be a maximum), the point of most interest is in his feelings regarding the importance of television programming. He wrote: 'The theory that "anything" will do in the early days of television, due to curiosity about the medium as a scientific achievement, is mistaken. It is almost certain that television will be judged entirely on its programme value in competition with other available entertainment.'[14]

Following years of technical developments and extensive debates surrounding the different potential systems, this problem would finally take a back seat as Cock realised that the technology alone did not excite the general public enough to encourage them to invest in an expensive receiver. His previous experience as an outside broadcast producer for radio certainly indicated that the relaying of live events was considered to be an essential part of the new medium. Moreover, the BBC would not be justified in running a system consisting largely of film material as a public service, even if limitations meant that the medium would have to rely on it to some extent for some years to come. Noel Ashbridge highlighted the public's expectations of a different form of entertainment or information from television, as he remarks in his report of 7 September that he heard one person leaving the demonstration complaining that, 'oh; that's not television, that's pictures,'[15] while Cock also corroborates that there was general lack of interest in the transmission of films. This had been the belief of the corporation for some time, as it had expressed some reservations towards the Marconi-EMI system two years previously, when the company had only demonstrated transmission of films. 'Direct' television had been judged by the company to be of lower quality and to lack the advantage of film's less ephemeral nature.[16] This was no longer the case, however, when Marconi-EMI's subsequent development of the wholly electronic Emitron camera showed a considerable leap in quality. Ashbridge also points out that the wider scope of broadcasting offered by the Marconi-EMI system, including shots of the grounds and the sets of the variety performances, was received more positively.[17]

It might be surprising that even before the official service had begun the general public seemed to have high expectations for the system. It was looking for relatively sophisticated programming, perhaps at least in part due to the advancement of synchronised sound in the cinema since the first television

LIVERPOOL JOHN MOORES UNIVERSITY
LEARNING SERVICES

demonstrations. The excitable reports of 1926 do not quite tally with the rather cooler, perhaps even cynical, reaction of the Radiolympia crowds ten years later, despite the fact that the event showcased a considerably improved television system. Certainly one comment in Ashbridge's report may well have been enough to worry even the most optimistic of those working on television. 'On the whole one can say that the general reaction was that the demonstrations were a very remarkable technical achievement but that it was not certain that the pictures had permanent programming value.'[18] Ashbridge outlined three stated reasons for these feelings. The first was the small size of the picture, screen sizes generally being around seven to ten inches at this point. The second issue was the lack of definition, while the third was the effort required to view the flickering picture as compared to films in a cinema setting.[19] These statements tie in with Cock's own statement that, 'Television is still a strain on the attention.'[20] It seems likely that these earlier experiments would lay the foundations for future attitudes towards television. Whether or not the crowds at a specialised radio event would be representative of the public at large, the comments that were recorded seem to have been taken as gospel when it came to planning the permanent service. Certainly, early programming would rely upon brief specific points of interest for some time, such as variety shows and short interviews, in order to reduce the potential for eyestrain inherent in viewing a small, flickering screen for extended periods of time. It is clear from many contemporary

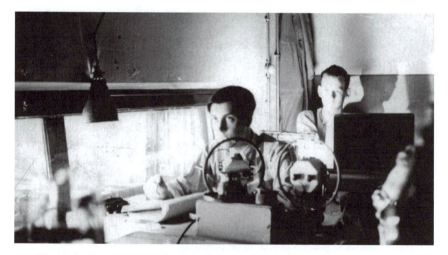

Fig. 6.1: *Royston Morley, producer of* **Picture Page** *amongst other programmes, in the control room above Studio A of Alexandra Palace (which the windows on the left overlooked).*

(Courtesy of the Alexandra Palace Television Society)

reports that this affected much of early broadcasting. Pleasingly for television's future, these were all technical issues that were already slowly being addressed, rather than fundamental problems with the concept of watching such programming domestically.

A little over two months later and television would be transformed from experimental broadcasting to a fully fledged official service operating, as the Radiolympia tests had done, out of studios within Alexandra Palace. A toss of the coin determined that Baird's system would be used first,[21] from 2 November (although on the opening day Marconi-EMI's broadcasts would immediately follow in the next hour), this time using the intermediate film system that had been so unreliable as to be unusable for the Radiolympia tests alongside the flying spot method for close-ups. Marconi-EMI's broadcasts followed in full the next week; Tony Currie has described the range of programming as a matter of expediency rather than reflecting any deep-seated aims for the medium. 'The programmes were as varied as the technology would allow,'[22] he says, 'anything and everything that could be persuaded up the hill to Ally Pally [Alexandra Palace] was paraded in front of the cameras.' Television, in some form, had arrived.

The Launch of Television Internationally

While the BBC won the race for the first public, high-definition, regular television service, it did not have the monopoly on international broadcasting efforts. There had been experimental and low-definition broadcasts throughout the world, most notably in the United States, France and Germany. The United States was still home to many experimental and low-definition television channels, with 31 experimental stations in 1931[23] and 32 fully-fledged commercial stations by 1941.[24] However, radio was still king and doubts were beginning to emerge about the feasibility of television broadcasts being available to the entire nation. Proposals to solve this problem included the erection of a 300 mile high transmitting tower and a network of 33 aeroplanes remaining in the air in order to cover the entire United States.[25] This problem would eventually be solved, at least in part, by the use of UHF (Ultra High Frequencies) in place of the more commonly used VHF (Very High Frequencies) for transmissions. UHF was less prone to interference problems when there was no line of sight between the transmitter and the receiving television set. It has been pointed out that the United States' relatively free commercial market for television was initially seen as an advantage in its lack of governmental interference, but made it difficult for the required investment to encourage viewers to purchase sets.[26] Without viewers there was little reason for commercial investment, and without commercial investment in programming there was little incentive for the public to purchase sets.

However, television was not simply left to stagnate. Experiments in higher-definition electronic broadcasting were regularly taking place by the late 1930s, and during the 1940s the majority of States had a television channel, although the number of sets was still relatively low; estimates vary, but generally place the number in the tens of thousands. Larger companies such as General Electric and RCA were still supplying backing to television, in the form of financing channels as well as manufacture of sets and development of technologies. Indeed, General Electric still has a foothold in television broadcasting with its co-ownership of the NBC network (and approximately 200 local affiliates), which had originally been owned by RCA.[27] In 1941 the National Television Standards Committee agreed on a universal standard for the country; 525 lines of resolution operating at 30 frames per second (interlaced).[28] This not only bettered the UK system of 405 lines but was successful enough to remain in place as the default broadcasting standard in North America some 70 years later, and will remain so until uptake of (the new) High Definition is universal. By the mid-1950s television had entered the mainstream in the United States, and colour broadcasting could operate with just a slight tweaking of the NTSC standards which allowed existing sets to simply view the programming in black and white.[29] In the United Kingdom, colour broadcasting began in the 1960s and would require entirely new sets as colour broadcasts (and the fledgling BBC2) were only available on 625 line sets with UHF tuners (rather than the VHF previously used for 405 line broadcasts).[30] The foresight of the United States is therefore to be commended. In terms of broadcasting content, the Federal Communications Commission (FCC) retained power to grant and revoke licences, and within this to stipulate a degree of public service broadcasting including regionalisation. Over time, not-for-profit networks emerged, including National Education Television, later Public Broadcasting Service (PBS), the formation of which was encouraged by governmental legislation.[31] Fundamentally, the formation of the corporation of Public Broadcasting by the government in 1967 indicated an ongoing desire for public service television to exist in the United States with a degree of government subsidy, if not actual control.

In Germany, as previously indicated, the Nazi regime had initially welcomed television, using it to broadcast the Berlin Olympics amongst other events.[32] By February 1937 German television became all-electronic, operating with 441 lines of resolution. When Germany invaded Paris during the Second World War they took over French television, which had been operating with 455 lines of resolution since 1938, and started their own 441 line transmissions.[33] Such an act should not be overstated; television had been little embraced in France, was still widely regarded as experimental, and the highest estimate is that there were only a thousand sets in operation in Paris.[34] In 1949, four years after the end of the war, France began transmissions using their future standard for television broadcasts. Although the 625 line system had been (or would be) widely embraced elsewhere in Europe, as well as in Russia and Australia, France decided on a superior 819 line system.[35] The broadcasts would remain state controlled, initially by the Minister of Information, for many years. This was somewhat different from the more broad legislative supervision of the government in the United Kingdom, and almost the polar opposite of the United States system. When colour was introduced, it was agreed across Europe that it would operate solely on 625 lines, much to the delight of French television set manufacturers, who had been lobbying for the adoption of the European-wide standard.[36] However, France elected to use a different colour television system from the rest of Europe (albeit still with 625 lines), embracing the home-grown SECAM system rather than the more widely used PAL system adopted elsewhere.[37] Germany, by contrast, did all that it could to avoid the sort of state interference that the Nazis had introduced. Initially their broadcasts were regionalised, with very little co-operation between areas. It took until November 1953 for there to be a single German television channel ('Deutsches Fernsehen', translated as 'First Channel') which, in a not dissimilar fashion to the formation of the British Broadcasting Company back in 1922, had been formed by a group of broadcasting corporations.[38] The system mixed regional programmes with nationally networked broadcasts, with individual productions pooled. It took until 1963 for Germany to legislate for and launch a second television channel, the public service network ZDF. Another two decades would pass before the imminent pressure of cable television to mean that commercial television finally reached Germany in the 1980s.[39]

Elsewhere in the world, television systems tended to follow either colonial or diplomatic lines, with the added influence of geographical relations. For example, Canada's geographical links with the United States and its constitutional relationship with the United Kingdom led to the 1952 launch of an NTSC system that was operated by a public service monopoly, the CBC (Canadian Broadcasting Corporation).

What is perhaps most remarkable is the speed with which television infiltrated most of the world. Some countries took longer to embrace the system; Australia did not launch an official service until 1956, when there were already two stations in the United Kingdom and dozens across the United States, with colour already starting to be introduced in the latter (colour would not arrive in Australia until 1975). However, Australia is a relatively early starter compared to the likes of South Africa, which did not have a television service until 1976. The reasons were not technological or financial, but were based in fears that it would not benefit the government, who liked to maintain control over broadcast media; it is interesting to compare this with Nazi control of German television some forty years earlier.

In time, the cost of television decreased, both in terms of infrastructure and receiving equipment, and so it continued as a mainstream concern. Countries without a service were acutely aware that the technology did exist and was in use elsewhere, increasing local pressure. The BBC's public service system was often used as a template, and while it was not directly compatible with the United States model, the differences were not fundamental. Television was a new and exciting way to disseminate entertainment and information, beamed directly into the homes of the television viewers, whatever the broadcasting policies.

However, television sets were expensive, with most costing between £35 and £80,[40] at a time when the average annual wage was just £134.[41] The broadcasts were also costly although this expense was not initially borne by the television viewer as there was no separate licence fee in the pre-war period, nor an increased cost of the radio licence. This was due to concerns that an increase in the licence fee for all would be unfair on those who could not receive the television service, whereas increasing the cost of receiving the early transmissions would only make it more difficult for the fledgling service to be a success.[42] Nevertheless, funding a full service from the existing ten-shilling licence fee would not be feasible in the long term. Television's existence, not just its success, depended upon a degree of widespread economic prosperity even if it did not need to rely on advertising and other commercial concerns to specifically fund its programming at this time.

Television was also born into an environment where cinema was becoming the dominant form of entertainment, with its low cost and relatively high production values offering the general public considerably more impressive visuals than television would be able to for some time. Although the economy struggled in the early part of the 1930s following the Wall Street crash, cinema attendances continued to rise and reached over a billion by 1940, up from 903 million in 1934.[43] Paul Johnson cites the aforementioned increasing incomes (in real terms) as the principle reason for this rise, saying that it 'gave people the means to participate in new forms of leisure and recreation … the 1930s Odeon and Gaumont cinemas were contemporary dream worlds where the harsher realities of life could be laughed at or forgotten.'[44] Indeed, more than eighty percent of visitors to the cinema paid no more than one shilling for their seats, indicating a strong working class bias.[45] Cinema continued to establish itself as the preferred form of entertainment for the mass audience, but it was also free from public service obligations. Television would have no 'cheap seats', and although renting sets was less expensive than purchasing, the possession of a television was still something of a luxury for decades after the service's launch.

The BBC's Publications

Before summarising the BBC's role in the birth and early evolution of television, there is one further element to be considered. Until this point this book has been focused on largely private correspondences and information in order to explore the birth of television, but these internal views of the public and private companies and individuals were often at odds with the perception of developments in television as reported by the press. The next section will explore these more widespread published views, but before an exploration of the wider expectations of television amongst the general public, a brief study of the BBC's own publications will show the corporation's 'official' public stance on the medium. One cannot take many of these articles as strictly accurate, but they do demonstrate the BBC's public stance and attitude towards television, which was often at odds with private views expressed within the corporation. Two titles are especially important, the first being the listings magazine *Radio Times*, while the other is the in-house publication *Ariel*, which gave some indication of how the corporation as a whole reacted to the new medium.

The BBC was not without some commitment to the service when it came to publishing, even in the medium's earliest years. Although the *Radio Times*' name may now seem somewhat anomalous, it was actually many years before television's prominence in the magazine matched that of radio. Given the very specific location of the pre-war television broadcasts it is understandable that only the magazines distributed in London featured the television listings, and even then as a distinct 'Television Edition', with a standard radio-only version also available. This was actually the first time that the *Radio Times* had created a separate regional edition, while the first issue to feature television listings was also the first *Radio Times* to have more than one cover – the London magazine showcased announcer Elizabeth Cowell in Alexandra Palace studio, while the edition for the rest of the country featured a Guy Fawkes dummy. It is difficult to judge whether this decision was taken so as not to rile those in other regions, who were denied access to television even if they had the interest and finance, or simply because it was not deemed of interest. There was no advertising drive for television and no aggressive cross-marketing with radio, as there has been throughout more recent history, including when supplemental features such as digital-only services were advertised heavily on standard analogue transmissions. Despite the ongoing publicity of the service in the press over the previous decade (little of it propagated by the BBC), television was still a limited market and while officially out of the experimental stage there was nevertheless a great deal to be worked through and either implemented or rejected in order to create a sustainable, ongoing medium.

Coverage of the service on the whole was still limited. Naturally, much of what was published revolved around the programming itself, but there were also articles examining the service more generally. Originally the television section was a double page at the back of the magazine, but this soon changed to a separate supplement. Generally there would be one page, the 'News for Televiewers' in the television guide, along with the week's listings, normally spread so as to be a page per day. Often there would be a single feature, looking at either the making of a particular show or perhaps an article reflecting on the service. These features rarely had any substantial depth, being standard pieces to publicise a programme in particular, rather than the programme in general, but they did often touch on the considerable technical achievement of transmitting television, especially for more elaborate productions or outside broadcasts.

Currie has claimed that, 'The role that *The Radio Times* was to play in the promotion of television was clear right from the start,'[46] a claim substantiated not only by the aforementioned 'Television Edition' and cover for the London issue in the week of the first broadcasts, but also by a special edition in October 1936 entitled *The Television Number*. It highlighted the extent to which television had become important to the BBC (and its reputation) by this stage. This was no quickly put-together attempt to capitalise on the interest around television, however. It included contributions from Sir Charles Carpendale, then the administrative head of the BBC, and Gerald Cock, Director of Television. Cock once again reiterated doubts regarding the ability of television to transmit material originally designed for the cinema, while also claiming that the public might find it more interesting to 'see an actual scene of a rush hour at Oxford Circus directly transmitted to them than the latest in film musicals costing £100,000,'[47] which would certainly be a useful scenario in budgetary terms if true, considering the minimal cost of transmitting live images from a public place compared to the expense of massive specially staged spectacles, or the licensing costs of showing movies. As Caughie points out, such a statement demonstrates exactly how diverse the possibilities for television seemed at this time. 'The view of television which emerges from Cock's predictions can be approached, not as a naively primitive misunderstanding of the medium, but as exemplary of a number of assumptions and uncertainties about the function of television which were formative in the early decades,' he wrote.[48] The appeal of the Oxford Street scene would be in the inherent novelty of live viewing, rather than any specific interest in surveying such a scene. In time, the liveness of television would seem less important as attention focused on overall entertainment value instead, whether live or not. But, as seen at Radiolympia, television was equated with liveness in the minds of many. Domestic viewing of entertainment was a secondary appeal. Carpendale was at pains to emphasise the potential of the new medium, now that it was under the exclusive care of the BBC, and *The Television Number* was a rare excursion into BBC-led publicity for its new service, as otherwise the medium quietly developed in the background.

There was a more general note regarding television in December 1936, the eve of the BBC's tenth anniversary as a corporation. Ronald Norman, the then Chairman of the BBC, celebrated the occasion by writing a full page article in the 18 December issue of *Radio Times*, entitled 'After Ten Years', referring to the anniversary of the BBC's conversion into a corporation. It would be difficult to deny Norman's claim that by this point 'broadcasting has entered fully into the life of people, ceasing to be a novelty or a luxury, becoming something that everyone needs, and on which everyone feels that he can rely.'[49] Radio was resolutely mainstream by this point, but television clearly was not, although it warrants a mention in Norman's article. Calling it 'limited, and frankly experimental, but fit to stand comparison with anything that is being done in any other part of the globe,' he goes on to give a prescient assessment of what he considered television's short-term future to be. 'As for the future, I am not rash enough to commit myself to a prophecy,' he wrote. 'There are too many new factors. Television alone may work considerable changes in broadcasting, not indeed in the next year or two, but in the next ten years.'[50]

Overall, the *Radio Times* was cautiously interested in the new service, and certainly not dismissive, even if it tended not to eulogise and was not always particularly enthusiastic. By contrast, the internal BBC publication *Ariel* was necessarily more introverted in its viewpoint, as it considered the effect of the new service on day-to-day staffing issues as well as in a broader sense of over-arching aims. The magazine shared television's year of launch, having arrived in June 1936, and so there is little to be learnt from it about the overall feeling in the BBC towards the medium until its arrival was imminent. However, there is still some material relevant to understanding the attitudes towards television within the corporation. The same month that Norman had written for the *Radio Times* saw Gerald Cock writing an article called 'Long Shot, Alexandra Palace' for *Ariel*. After opening by saying that the launch of television had 'gone off without a hitch,' Cock then goes on to acknowledge that the launch had been 'a rather terrible day.'[51] He recounts the issues of under-rehearsal and lack of time and facilities, before concluding that 'We need more experience with the apparatus.'[52] It is intriguing that the second half of the article devotes itself to seemingly justifying the work of television to the rest of the BBC. He wrote: 'A.P. [Alexandra Palace] sometimes wonders how those of you at Broadcasting House not immediately concerned, regard television, if indeed you have time to think about it at all. The sixth floor must be reminded of its existence from time to time, when the Alexandra Palace aerial is on the horizon of a clear day. Spare a thought, then, to the turmoil below the mast.'[53] It can be gathered from this that television was widely considered to be a poor relation to radio within the BBC at this time, an attitude that was hardly surprising given its relative youth, but the hints that even senior management had little time for the new medium demonstrate how disheartening it must have been for those working on the broadcasts to have their work go relatively unrewarded and unnoticed. Nevertheless, the following April saw the television department at Alexandra Palace receive the first coverage from *Ariel*'s 'Department by Department' section that introduced staff to each other.

Cock acknowledges that there had been mixed success since the regular high definition tests in October ('I think we have broadcast a mixed bag – a few seem to have been really good; some fair; some terrible,'[54] he says), but also indicates that he could start to see what was, and what was not working as a television broadcast. 'I am convinced that [television broadcasts] will be more and more towards (in broadcasting jargon) topicality and actuality,'[55] he claimed. He made it clear that television was still fluid in its outlook, even after having been on air for three months. 'We are learning every day,' he wrote. 'For more than a year some of us have been thinking of little else but this. What shall we be able to show for it at the end of a year's working? I wish I knew.'[56] If the Director of Television was still unsure about its eventual direction then it seems likely that he was not alone. Television would change gradually over many years, but even modern broadcasts owe a lot to the mixture of programming present from the medium's launch. Cock was skilful in making a forthright acknowledgment that wholly successful television was largely still a mystery and, although technically now an official service, still experimental in practice. It required ongoing attempts at new programming types in order to be able to find the most satisfactory mixture of broadcasts. This took some bravery, but a public corporation was a legitimate testing ground for a public service, not least because it did not require commercial success or rapid public embracement of the service. They could legitimately work towards a long-term goal of television as a mass medium without short-term pressures of finance.

While *Ariel* was a largely informal periodical for widespread distribution within the BBC, another official publication served a slightly different purpose, and is worth consideration. The *BBC Yearbooks* (sometimes titled *Handbooks* or *Annuals*) were, as the name suggests, annual titles that were published in order to provide an overview of the corporation's activities over the previous year. Its remit as a public broadcaster meant that it made itself and its operations more accessible to the public that was funding it, and the *Yearbooks* were a way of it doing this in order to stave off criticism in what Hugh Chignell has called 'a rather defensive action'.[57] It might be expected that the early trials by the BBC in the field of television would have been of enough significance to warrant a mention, but this was not the case initially. With what Asa Briggs has called 'a graceless attitude,'[58] no mention was made of the television trials throughout 1930 in the 1931 *Yearbook*, although this perhaps should not be completely surprising, another result of the BBC's reticence to officially endorse Baird's work. Nevertheless, Andrew Crisell has ventured that the publications needed to strike a slightly awkward balance. 'The handbooks hover uncertainly between objective, factual account and PR document,' he stated when interviewed by Chignell in 2003.[59] It was a no less unusual combination that saw the 1933 Yearbook feature an article, 'Television In 1932', by Baird himself, despite increasingly soured relationships between the man and the corporation. In what was essentially an exercise in self-promotion, Baird claimed that: 'In spite of the large amount of information which has been disseminated on the subject of television, I find that the majority of the general public are still in ignorance of what television means and how the process is effected.'[60] The tone is not a gracious one, and Baird seems to almost chastise the general public for paying such little attention to the intricacies of his invention. Perhaps this is some explanation for his eventual downfall, as the public at large showed little interest in the whys and wherefores of television technology, preferring to consider the content and overall effectiveness of the finished product. Never was this more explicitly shown than in the apparent complete lack of interest amongst audiences when Baird's inferior system was dropped, despite its rich history.

The next few pages of the article are concerned with lengthy descriptions of the process used, which would perhaps be of less interest to many than the potential for programming. A photograph of a seal playing a saxophone in front of a camera perhaps gives a flavour, of sorts, of the potential of television content, but mentions in passing of the cinema transmission of the Derby that had been undertaken as a one-off event in 1932 and the single play shown to that date surely did little to ignite interest or demonstrate much breadth of imagination. After a page dedicated to the progress abroad, and then a section headlined 'Television for the Cinema', which had little to say on the subject except mentioning its potential application, the article appears to have been an opportunity missed. It seems likely that by this stage the public was starting to expect more tangible developments rather than theoretical ones, and while Baird was not the person responsible for delaying the system, his self-appointed status as a figurehead for television development in this country must surely have meant that he could expect to find himself being taken less seriously the longer the official launch was delayed.

1936's annual was the only other pre-launch yearbook to feature television in any substantial way. Starting an article published so close to transmission with the subheading 'The Present Problem', indicates the tone of the article somewhat. Rather than replicating the enthusiasm towards television that was undoubtedly felt in some quarters, the article instead concentrates on extensive technical questions and a brief history of the system and experiments to that point. Some coverage, and a full page photo, were given to the renovation work at Alexandra Palace required in order to make the building a fully working television studio and transmitter. Only at the end of the article were questions of programming addressed, another indication of the technology taking precedence over content. Even then content was only covered in general terms:

> Individual items will be short, to avoid fatigue and eye strain, as considerable concentration will be necessary. Television cannot be a background to other occupations. A wide field of entertainment must be covered, but the more intimate cabaret type is more likely to be successful than the broader music hall material.[61]

Much of this did not come to pass. 'Broader music hall material' was a mainstay of television in its earliest years, whatever its suitability may have been. However it is clear that, even if it was not the main emphasis, some thought as to the content of broadcasts was being given, with attention being paid in the article to the future of television after the novelty of its existence had worn off. 'How far will normal programmes come to consist of both sound and visual elements?' the article asked.[62] In fact, much of the article's discussion of programming is made up of questions. It is clear that, even in the year prior to its official launch, there was much uncertainty surrounding the form that television would take.

The Overall Role of the BBC

This uncertainty continued until the launch and beyond. Although the commencement of television broadcasts was an important point of progress in broadcasting in its own right, it was not a meticulously planned progression, even if it did follow several years of negotiation and numerous debates about how the medium's role was envisaged. Depending on one's viewpoint, either the setting up of the Selsdon Committee came rather late in the process, or the implementation of the official system came about rather quickly following the publication of its report. Until this point there was no discernable future for the medium, making the BBC very much a passive observer for much of this early period, even if it allowed the use of its facilities for experimental work and often found itself speculating on the future of the technology. This indicates that there was no great plan; programming was talked about in vague terms, as a series of concepts (the question of whether it would be possible to televise a football match, for example) but, in the event, such difficulties were rarely insurmountable under the Marconi-EMI system.[63] Nevertheless, much of its contribution to the development of television came about simply because of its status as a public body rather than through any particular internal drive to develop the system.

Indeed, the BBC initially operated very much as an external observer of television; it would infrequently investigate the current status of television's development, almost in the sense that it felt this was something it should be doing just in case it was to become part of its jurisdiction. However, there was little sense of wider interest, and although the television audience can retrospectively be somewhat grateful to Eckersley for his foresight in demanding a high quality technical basis for any television service, his personal issues with Baird Television undoubtedly put the BBC on the back foot regarding the medium. One wonders, in fact, to what extent there would have been benefit in the BBC's conducting its own experimentation earlier in television's development, using experts in the field, rather than relying upon private enterprise. This was apparently not seriously considered, with the corporation instead simply supervising developments and allowing use of its facilities when strictly necessary, but undertaking little more active work in the field. There was no active search for a solution or any sense of urgency except when the situation with Baird seemed untenable due to his publicity-seeking antics. The BBC needed someone with Baird's drive and enthusiasm for any system of television to be seriously considered at all. While advancements abroad would undoubtedly have led to broadcasts in the United Kingdom at some point, the country had the advantage of an infrastructure that was already nationalised both politically and geographically. Certainly, Gladstone Murray's aforementioned hope that Britain could remain at the forefront of television technology and broadcasts indicates a degree of competitiveness that was generally lacking in most of the BBC documentation. More prevalent were concerns that it should be seen to be doing the right thing for the licence fee payers, with the furtherance of the new technology a secondary concern. Once it wholly supported the system, and especially once officially given control of it, the BBC could quickly assign some of its considerable resources to television and have it operating on a reasonably large scale faster than most private enterprises would be able to.

As regards television's placement as a public service within this infrastructure, Paddy Scannell points out that the 'interpretation of that definition, the effort to realise its meaning in the development of a broadcasting service guided by considerations of a national service and the public industry, came from the broadcasters and above all John Reith,'[64] indicating the central role that the BBC played in defining its own requirements as a public service broadcaster. This was certainly to be an issue of importance for the eventual programming for television, but as regards the medium's actual existence such questions of public service were initially largely confined to the previously referenced question of whether transmissions of important public

Fig. 6.2: *Early television tried to escape its studio confines where possible, such as here, where the placing of a scenery flat outside allowed the use of a car in this adaptation of Edgar Wallace's Chicago-based story* **On The Spot,** *which was performed in 1938 and 1939.*

(*Courtesy of Alexandra Palace Television Society*).

events would be feasible, seemingly a central issue for the feasibility of the medium. However, on the whole, the most important aspect of the BBC's involvement with television is the very fact of the involvement itself. The placing of television in the care of one body is significant in itself, but even more so when this one body is a public corporation. The implications of operating as a monopoly are even starker when the monopolising broadcaster has to conform to the requirements of operating as a public service. Such an important role resulted in overall cautiousness rather than dynamism. Given the importance of Marconi-EMI's innovation (it is debatable whether Baird's eventual 240-line system would have been adopted on its own merits), perhaps television could not have launched earlier. It is certainly the case that the BBC did not facilitate a speedy development process for television, but what it did do was ensure that the medium as launched was as stable in terms of a long-term future as possible.

Points to Consider

1) What were the reasons why the mechanical television systems were not widely taken up in the long term?
2) Why might different countries have different attitudes to early television?
3) What were the different understandings of television as a 'public service', both in the UK and abroad?
4) How did the BBC's standing as a public corporation affect television's development?
5) Why was it necessary for a television committee to decide on the medium's future in the UK?
6) How did other countries regulate their television broadcasts, and why?
7) Why was Radiolympia important?
8) What was the significance of the different technical standards of television adopted across the globe?
9) Considering the extracts from BBC publications, can you judge a difference in attitude between the public face of the corporation and the private internal communications?
10) What differences might there be between publicly and privately funded television stations?

Wider Perspectives

7

Views of Television from the Outside

In his book *Restoring Baird's Image*, Donald F. McLean recounts a story of the reaction of the *Daily Express* news editor to Baird's appearance at the newspaper's offices in late 1925. 'The news editor was terrified,' claims McLean, 'he was quoted by one of his staff as saying: "For God's sake, go down to reception and get rid of a lunatic who's down there. He says he's got a machine for seeing by wireless! Watch him – he may have a razor on him."'[1]

The story itself may be apocryphal, but certainly many newspaper reports indicate that the industry was not without its suspicions. This section uses the reports in the press as an indicator of broadly changing attitudes to television from those not directly involved with it, as well as demonstrating the many underlying expectations of the medium. This is the best available way to understand how the developments of television were generally received outside the microcosm of the relationship between Baird and the BBC. For all of their squabbles about the correct way to develop television there is little indication in their correspondence regarding what the public would expect from such a service, or even what the level of interest might have been. By using the press reports it is possible to gain a sense of the perspectives of some of those outside the industry itself. In order to cover the development of attitudes towards television this section will assess the reports of the new medium in the press at two important points in its history, considering the differences between them while also highlighting specific instances of preconceptions regarding television. The first period covers 1926 and 1927, a time of great activity that began with Baird's first proper demonstration of television to the press in January of 1926. The other period spans 1936, when high definition television had finally come to fruition, first through the Radiolympia event in August, and then November's official launch. It should already be clear that many changes occurred in that ten year period, but it was

Fig. 7.1: *Baird with an early version of his television apparatus*
(Courtesy of the Royal Television Society)

more than the technology that changed while television moved from being a privately developed mechanical system to a fully fledged BBC-run public service.

Baird Goes Public: Press Reports in 1926

'How near we are to that achievement [of practical television] cannot be accurately determined from the exaggerated press reports which accompany each step,'[2] wrote Edgar H. Felix in 1931, indicating that the reports of the press were never considered to be a wholly accurate view of television, certainly from the perspective of those with an interest in the medium. While Baird and his associated enthusiasts often saw television as an exciting medium on the cusp of breaking through into mainstream popularity, there was more of a mixed reaction elsewhere. Nowhere is this better demonstrated than in the journalistic reports of early television. These ranged from hyperbolic to uninterested, although they were rarely damning. At times, however, coverage could be non-existent, the worst possible scenario for Baird and his fledgling business. Although 1926 would see something of a flurry of interest in his experiments for the invited members of the press, his earlier demonstrations at Selfridge's had provoked little interest from the press. For a man who thrived on publicity this would not have been particularly palatable. While there was certainly small-scale interest from the public who had seen the demonstrations, this had been fleeting, and there was no real indication of a wider embracement of his basic system of television. When it was refined to the point of demonstrating the transmission of recognisable objects and more subtle tones of grey then there was a new opportunity to show the press his results.

'Possibility of having scenes broadcast – British Invention'[3] read the *Evening Standard*'s report of 8 January 1926 relating to Baird's latest demonstrations. It draws parallels between William Friese-Greene (who had developed an early system of showing moving images using film) and Baird, whose demonstrations took place near to where Friese-Greene had shown off his own work. Indeed, Baird was called 'another British pioneer'.[4] It will become clear that such an emphasis on Baird's nationality would be common in the reports of his work, as it did in Baird's own pleas for institutional assistance. While the intricacies of the technology were beyond the understanding

Fig. 7.2: *Interested customers queue to see Baird's demonstrations in Selfridge's*

(Courtesy of the Royal Television Society)

of the average reporter, or indeed the average reader, the essence of the system coupled with Baird's own emphasis on the British origins of this invention would be a hook on which to hang the story. In this case, the tone of the piece is positive, perhaps unsurprising when it is considered that the *Evening Standard* had been given a special invitation by Baird (alongside the *Daily Express*). The newspaper claimed that the development made the widespread utilisation of such a system now seem possible, indicating that it had seemed an unlikely proposition to this point. Claims were made that 500 sets, at £30 each, were in production. More accurate, however, was the promise that attempts would be made to televise the Epsom Derby; something of a preoccupation of Baird's it seems, given that it was eventually achieved in 1931 (and broadcast to a cinema in 1932). The mention of such an event was clearly devised to make television a more tangible and inviting prospect. Here was a more explicit advertisement for its benefits and the sense is that the public is being told that only those out to hold up Baird's work were preventing them from owning their own televisor.

Certainly it was the prospect of televising the Derby that captured the interest of the *Daily Express* when a different version of the same report of the demonstration was published the same day. Claiming that 'for fifty years television has been the dream of scientists'[5] the horse racing event captured the headlines as, once more, the 'Britishness' of the invention was highlighted. It is difficult to judge whether this emphasis on the home-grown nature of Baird's technology was due to the parochial interests of the newspaper, or Baird's own attempts to instigate national pride in his work so as to attract some form of investment. After all, economic backing could ensure that the country remained at the forefront of developments. Certainly it is worth considering that, while these two titles had been wholly positive in their assessments and had been given something of an exclusive, this was hardly front page news. Both reports were situated some way into the newspaper, within the general news section where many different items of interest fought for space. Despite the press's general positivity, television was not deemed to be of highly significant public interest quite yet, as also demonstrated by the lack of interest in the story from other British newspapers at this point. One exception is a report from the *Daily Telegraph* on 11 January which featured a two paragraph report on 'Wireless Vision'[6] in a very matter-of-fact manner, with an unnamed 'press representative' recounting his vision of a doll's head through Baird's apparatus. Once more, the news was somewhat buried, this time between reports of 'Exploring Maya Mysteries' and an apparent 'Need for Harder Work'.

The *Daily Telegraph* would mention television once more, on 23 January, when reporting on the feelings in the wireless technical press that television would be imminent, with the newspaper agreeing with the views.

Intriguingly, this report highlighted the developments of more than just Baird in this new medium, pointing to the work of Belin in France and Jenkins in America as other innovators, indicating that Baird was not completely synonymous with the invention in the popular press at this point. Three days later the emphasis would once more be focused on the Scottish inventor, with the *Morning Post* now making the most hyperbolic claims yet. The article breathlessly opens by stating that Baird had 'placed Great Britain in such a position that she can control an industry comparable in importance with that of the cinema trade,'[7] once more emphasising the nationality of the inventor so as to create reader interest, or even empathy. This is a long way from the claims of Baird that his invention was rarely taken seriously. While television would eventually be at least equal to the cinema in terms of its international dominance, this statement came only days after the first demonstration of the system. This indicates an expectation that television could be at least as successful as radio, although this report concentrates on the technical aspects of the apparatus, rather than exploring its potential uses. A light-hearted editorial elsewhere in the same issue of the newspaper cites the 'Disadvantages of television' when it amusingly expresses relief that, for the moment, 'involuntary' transmission of television was impossible. 'The television instrument has not yet, I am glad to say, reached the pitch of unobtrusiveness of the tiny microphones that are used in intelligence work, and which enable detectives, spies, and other inconvenient people to overhear one's conversations whether one likes it or not,' the article points out, continuing that 'For a few years more at least I need keep no check on my facial expression when refusing an invitation on the score of "urgent business" in the city.'[8] Television, then, had not been neatly placed as a system for public broadcasts. Instead, the emphasis was on its live nature, and the possibilities that this presented for personal uses alongside those of entertainment and dissemination of information.

Late January 1926 saw the most interest in Baird's work to that point. As the *Yorkshire Post* remarked, 'Mr Baird, the Scottish inventor who claims to have solved the problem of wireless television, is a much sought after man at the moment,'[9] something borne out by the number of articles now commenting on his work, following another series of demonstrations for the press. Articles also appeared in the *Manchester Guardian*, *The Scotsman*, *Westminster Gazette*, *Daily News* and at least half a dozen others, now that the demonstrations were apparently less exclusive. Perhaps this was a result of Baird Television's concurrent attempts to convince the Post Office to allow transmissions, as previously explored. The same *Yorkshire Post* article was less confident of television's immediate uses, however, with the report quoting a Professor A.M. Low's views that the technology needed refinement, but he expected to see it transmitting alongside radio twelve years later; one of the more accurate predictions of this time.[10] Most of the articles simply described the process of the demonstration, and once more reproduced Baird's claims of imminent £30 receivers. Rather more cynical was the *Manchester Guardian*, which intriguingly already linked the invention with the BBC. Pointing out that the public would now be able to 'look in' as well as listen in to singers, the pithy article asked 'Whether in all cases this will be desirable is less clear'.[11] It goes on to say:

> Quite often these songs are sweeter far in which the singers are unseen. One has, indeed, always been doubtful of the wisdom of "Aunts" and "Uncles" whose mellifluous tones had conjured visions of a perfection rare in human form venturing, as they often do now, upon public platforms and revealing themselves as quite ordinary folk. Moreover, as electricity is harnessed to attack one after another of our five senses we shall tend to become steadily more critical; and the BBC, which has enough trouble as it is with our arguments about what we should hear, may well be distraught to cope with more complex tastes. Meanwhile, however, all congratulations to Mr Baird. If this complication to life has to be, at least it is something to have stolen a march on the competitors.[12]

Once more, television's national status is emphasised, with the British lead over international rivals indicated as being of significance to the newsworthiness of Baird's work. While the article is lamenting the very prospect of television, and explicitly not criticising Baird himself, it is at least telling that television was not a prospect welcomed by all. Nor, indeed, was it something that the general public appeared to have an insatiable thirst for. Most news reports are brief, with the tone generally of mild interest rather than awe or excitement. Even acknowledging the more restrained tone of newspapers eighty years ago, there is no evidence of television being a priority of any sort for most of the press. In fact, the sense is very much that it is seen as something unnamed 'other people' must surely be interested in. *The Times*, for example, reports the development in a very matter of fact fashion, remarking that 'It has yet to become seen to what extent further developments will carry Mr Baird's system towards practical use.'[13] This is in marked contrast to the coverage granted by the *Daily News*, which seems to fall more squarely in line with Baird's sometimes rather misleading statements. While opinions may have differed (often within the same newspaper), the level of importance apportioned to television remained consistently low. 'Television Here – Transmissions Next Week'[14] a *Daily News* headline boldly claimed, as had the *Westminster Gazette* the previous day. The report goes on to say that such transmissions would be experimental in nature and suggests that they may feature a 'public man' seated in a chair. Elsewhere, the reporter acknowledges that 'it was apparent that much experiment must take place before television is popularly acceptable,' although it goes on to claim that 'it is only a question of time before a sharpness of definition is obtained to mirror public events with the clarity of the cinematograph.'[15]

It is intriguing that, given the less than complimentary comments from some of those private technicians and engineers who also saw Baird's early work, the reports in the press were largely uncynical, even positive, regarding the potential of television, while unanimously pointing out that a degree of refinement and further experimentation would be necessary. Of course, Baird's work was a significant achievement that deserved recognition, and the reporters were unlikely to be technical men. However, there was no interrogation of Baird's plans, or practical considerations of how such apparatus could be used. The presumption was that this would simply be a starting point for the system. Indeed, it was still a wholly private concern at this point and so issues of finance were of little interest, except to add some colour to the reports akin to the mentions of Baird's nationality. Several of the reports mentioned the financial sacrifices made by Baird and his friends and investors so that his work could continue, with the *Daily Graphic* for example stating 'Belongings pawned to carry on experiments,'[16] as its subheading. Following its launch television would be under more critical scrutiny as it presented itself as a fully-fledged service rather than an experiment. Not only was it new, with its very existence cause for interest, but the weight of expectation on it was alleviated somewhat by the understanding that it was still in the experimental stages. Claims could be made by anyone connected with the demonstrations that would not have to be followed up for some time, because the technology was so new and unrefined. However, the press would become restless over time as the basics of the technology itself managed to lose their appeal.

Such publicity did ensure that television was widely known about by this point, even if it had only just been implemented in a practical form, resulting in one unnamed correspondent of the *Daily Mirror* mentioning the service in a letter designed to congratulate the newspaper on reaching its 7000th edition, wherein he predicted what developments would occur by the time of the 14,000th (then expected in mid-1949). Television, he claimed, would be 'an accomplished fact,'[17] something that was to be quite true (although, to an extent, it was already true at the time of the letter itself, albeit less 'accomplished' than it would become). Another prediction, that Europe would be ravaged by another war, was unfortunately prescient as well.

A week later there were several articles in different newspapers on the same day, none of which seemed to have anything in particular in common except that they all appeared to have been influenced by yet another demonstration by Baird. As time passed so more was expected of the system and questions were asked regarding precisely what the medium could be used for.

Baird did not help his case by making claims such as 'television is not the thing of the future; it is here today,'[18] when he might have been better advised to downplay expectations and emphasise the experimental nature of his work in a bid to advertise for funding or governmental co-operation; at the very least, he could have highlighted how he intended his system to be used. Nevertheless, the reporter for the *Evening News* agreed with his assessment, claiming that his latest demonstrations were 'substantially improved' over his previous one four months earlier, concluding that his claim is 'substantially a fair one'. Publicity for television was already getting ahead of itself, with the *Nottingham Evening Post* printing a report, the origins of which are not stated, claiming that the televising of stage plays was imminent. 'The receiving apparatus will probably cost no more than the one it will be supplementing, and the stay at home will be able to sit by his fire and both see and hear the play,'[19] it stated. *The Birmingham Daily Mail* and the *Daily Telegraph* also covered the new demonstration, although in the *Telegraph* Baird was forced to share the reports with a information about Thorne Baker's method of transmitting still pictures wirelessly; mention of the BBC's co-operation with his scheme was a marked contrast to Baird's characterisation as a wholly independent inventor. Indeed, the small scale of his resources was the central point of many of the reports of the time, with the emphasis being on a single man achieving what so many others were apparently also working on, rather than any excitement about the system itself. Such reports likely contributed to Baird's ongoing reputation as a lone figure. Once established, and repeatedly reaffirmed in reports such as this, it was almost inevitable that he would come to be regarded both as an influential and independent figure. The *Westminster Gazette's* sub-heading of 'Triumph of Soho back-room experimenter'[20] is a good summation of the general balance of emphasis on Baird as a 'small person' making big changes. Meanwhile, the *Daily Mirror* was the latest publication to quip that the public should be asking 'Will television let us see what the operator is up to?', and this light-hearted tone is again indicative of the general approach. There is a degree of speculation that television could be revolutionary, but little sense that this was actually widely believed, emphasised by the less than prominent placing of the news stories safely away from major headlines.

The rest of the year saw a smattering of other reports that offered little new in the way of information but at least showed that television had not been forgotten or written off when the 'imminent' broadcasts failed to appear. Baird was once more claiming broadcasts would soon be seen, this time 'next year'[21] in the *Daily News* of 11 August due to what the newspaper claimed was a 'big advance of the televisor'.[22] Meanwhile, the next month saw a report in the *Daily Telegraph* that Baird's apparatus was to go on public display,[23] something that prompted the *Manchester Guardian* to be the latest to proclaim television to be an 'accomplished fact' although it also clarified that 'No one pretends that perfect transmission of the image has yet been attained'.[24]

The end of the year saw a different aspect of television provoke more interest, with forms of Baird's 'noctovision' system inspiring several press reports. This system of infra-red vision on television sets had been a pet project of Baird's for some time, and would continue to occupy him on an occasional basis over the next decade and more. Indeed, the Baird biography *Vision Warrior* by Tom McArthur and Peter Waddell would concentrate on this work, as well as claimed co-operation between Baird and the government throughout the Second World War on similar night vision and radar related projects. This 'searchlight that cannot be seen' was covered by the *Daily Mail* on 16 December where they also speculated on its possible use in future warfare.[25] Of course, as ever, this was not the simple reporting of news that had emerged through some accident or the newspaper's own investigative journalism. The 'special correspondent' had been specifically invited by Baird to see his latest work. Calling it an 'apparent miracle', the reporter recounted seeing the image of his colleague on the apparatus while he sat in total darkness. The report was correct in predicting its potential use as a military device, but such discussion was almost entirely separated from the issue of standard television, as demonstrated earlier in the year. The next day the *Daily Telegraph* was keener to make a link between the technologies, saying that 'its application to television may have far reaching results.'[26] The report also claimed that tests had already been conducted by the military. An advancement such as this only served to fuel the general sense of wonderment from much of the press regarding both 'noctovision' and television more generally.

Developing Interest: Press Reports in 1927

The People opened 1927 by referring to the advancements in its claim that 'Truly, it may be said that the age of miracles is not yet past,' on 2 January.[27] On the same day *The Observer* agreed, calling television 'a marvel'[28] while intriguingly quoting Baird as calling it a 'telephone for the eye' indicating that it was far from being fixed as a medium for entertainment rather than personal communication at this point. Indeed, as late as 1936 television was often used as a synonym for what would now be called a videophone, as *The Times* reported on German experiments in the installation of cameras in public booths for communication as a form of television.[29]

However, the next week saw *The Observer* drawing parallels with radio rather than telephony as an article entitled 'Television and the BBC' attempted to investigate the links between the new technology and the corporation. The article apologises for drawing attention to the medium's deficiencies as it goes on to say that while television will 'sooner or later become a department of broadcasting,' it is also 'not so far advanced as many folk seem to imagine'.[30] Certainly, judging by the reports in the press to this point, it would not be unreasonable of the general public to have assumed that television was more impressive and accomplished than was the case at this time. This is one of the few articles to have taken a more detached view of the realistic and practical uses of the technology as it then stood, rather than being swept up by any excitement surrounding the very existence of the system. The supposition in the article is largely accurate, as it assumes that the BBC will continue to be the sole body permitted to broadcast entertainment, and that it would not tolerate the system as it then stood. 'At present television is a very young and undeveloped child, though a child of wonderful promise,'[31] it concludes.

The rest of 1927 saw several more general features about television in many newspapers, including many touching on the stories of 'invisible rays', the feature of the 'noctovision' system. Elsewhere reports centred on Baird himself, with the *Glasgow Herald* of 27 May dedicating half a page to Baird's demonstrations of transmission between the newspaper's home city and London, while offering little in the way of objectivity, in favour of emphasising the general 'remarkable achievement' of the Scot. This followed the title's interview with Baird three months earlier, which had understandably emphasised his Scottish roots, but offered little in the way of insight to the envisaged development of television, preferring this discourse on issues of nationalism and local pride.[32]

If 1927 was somewhat quieter for television than the preceding year this should come as no surprise. While the *Daily Chronicle* reported in April that there was 'Hope of television for all this year,'[33] few other newspapers continued to be so optimistic. Although the novelty of television had not quite worn off, there was no imminent sign of practical application and so there was little to report. While 'noctovision' was widely mentioned it was often treated separately from television, with its potential military uses being the understandable emphasis. The frequency of reports was dying down, and would continue to be sporadic over the course of the next few years, largely due to the publicity veto of the BBC and the lack of any substantial technological developments in the public eye.

What, then, can be said of the reports from this period in general? Perhaps the most striking element is the consistency of approach. Criticisms are few and far between, Baird's efforts are generally viewed sympathetically and the medium itself is taken reasonably seriously, even if it is seen as somewhat quirky. However, there are few analyses of what the development of the medium would actually mean, or how it should be conducted. Television was seemingly considered as something that is being developed by 'someone' outside of the public sphere, with little discussion of the role that the BBC might play. It was considered to be a private enterprise that nevertheless holds some interest for those already dependent on their wireless sets. Over the next decade the direction of the medium would become clearer, and with it the beginnings of a change in attitude from the press.

8

A Public Launch

In the period from 1928 to 1935 television continued to garner occasional mentions in the press, especially when advancements were made (or claimed). It began to be considered in terms of its eventual implementation, usually with reference to the BBC following their involvement in the 1929 test broadcasts, rather than as a new scientific innovation. The word 'television', as well as the concept itself, was sinking even further into the public consciousness, with an example being the 1930 British film *Elstree Calling* (d. Alfred Hitchcock et al, UK: British International Pictures). This largely

Fig. 8.1: *Attempts to watch television in* **Elstree Calling** *(1930)*

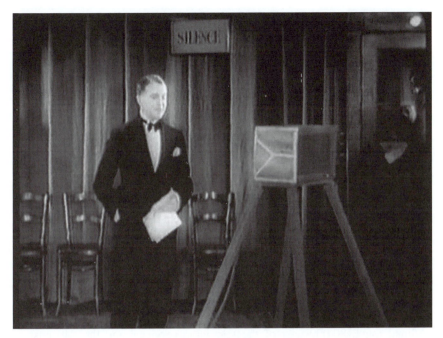

Fig. 8.2: *Tommy Handley being broadcast in* **Elstree Calling** *(1930)*

forgotten production is generally only referenced today because it featured some sequences directed by Alfred Hitchcock. Having something in common with the concept of showcasing different acts that had been seen in the film *Hollywood Revue of 1929* (d. Chuck Riesner, US: MGM, 1929), the film showcases various well known vaudeville stars, framed by the narrative device of a family unsuccessfully attempting to watch the proceedings on television, with the acts introduced by comedian Tommy Handley.

While the experimental 30-line transmissions were operating at this time, this was far from a widespread or even well known service. The sequences are clearly meant to be comical, and should not be read too deeply as a slur on the new medium, but at least may demonstrate public knowledge of what television was (or would be) at this point. Here it is a domestic system show-ing a variety of light entertainment acts on a small screen, something very similar to the eventual system, in its early years at least. The apparatus shown is akin to a modern flat-screen television for those watching at home, albeit connected to a maze of wires, valves and speakers. Meanwhile, Handley delivers his links to a basic box representing a camera, which nevertheless indicates some expectation of direct address.

The emphasis changed over the decade from marvelling at the technical achievement and vague claims of what could be achieved to the search for specifics. The official involvement of the BBC had led to the view that television was now a publicly owned commodity, and while it was still far from front page news, there was growing interest. More questions were being asked now that the public's money through the licence fee would be funding the service, which was now a practical reality rather than a theoretical possibility.[1] The jolly, light-hearted articles about television and the enjoyment of such simple sights as the transmission of a doll's head began to disappear in favour of questions about programming and the practical problems, not to mention a degree of understandable regional discord relating to the London-centric transmissions. The era of accountability had begun.

Television as a Public Concern: Press Reports in 1936

By 1936 television was not only a practical reality but a broadcasting inevitability, with the publication of the previous year's report from the Television Committee. In March *The Times* published a highly critical letter that detailed the large cost of television, written by R.J. Spottiswoode, who had taken an interest in the new medium, with reservations. The letter outlined the £180,000 cost of the television service,[2] and the £40 cost of receivers. It is telling that Spottiswoode claims that 'None of these difficulties is insuperable; most of them have already been mentioned by the Television Committee. But they have since been swept away by a wave of public enthusiasm, and for the moment are disregarded.'[3] This mention of a 'wave of public enthusiasm' indicates that, by 1936, there was a perceived public appetite for a television service, something substantiated by the interest in the demonstration of sets at that year's radio festival Radiolympia, even though it has already been demonstrated that the opinions of the audience were somewhat mixed upon seeing the sets themselves.

By the time official broadcasts were close to realisation in 1936 there had been a change of attitude in the popular press. The 'public wave of enthusiasm' may have been overstating the case slightly, but there was certainly a sense of anticipation. Newspapers began to educate their readers on what to expect. On 24 March 1936 *The Times* featured an article from an unnamed correspondent that endeavoured to outline the immediate future of television, some eight months before its launch. The article did not seem to be particularly well researched, as evidenced by some vagueness or apparent assumptions such as when stating that 'the sound equipment associated with the television broadcast will *presumably* form a separate item of furniture'[4] (my emphasis). The article's main aim was to counter myths regarding television. 'The idea that modern radio instruments will be rendered obsolete can be at once dispelled,' the correspondent confirms. This appears to have been quite a concern for the general public at the time, with many listeners having made relatively recent purchases of their wireless receivers.

The article is keen to point out the many obstacles that television would have to face, both with regards to technical competence and widespread acceptance by the UK market. It is understandable that emphasis should be given to the choices made by the consumer – in this case, whether to invest in television or not – but the second half of the article also assesses the technical limitations of the system at that point. The biggest obstacle for the dominance of television in the marketplace was succinctly described thus: 'Television is likely to remain the prerogative of the wealthy for some time. Fifty pounds for a complete instrument is a conservative estimate. In view of the expense of cathode ray tubes [...] it is unlikely that this figure can be decreased.'[5] Certainly the substantial cost was always going to be the most significant reasoning behind audiences choosing not to purchase their own sets, whatever other rationale there may have been, but the article continues to downplay the technical achievement and (indirectly) artistic merit of the medium by stating:

> The television picture on a cathode ray tube, which is the most likely apparatus to be used, is about 10 [inches] by 8 [inches] on the largest tubes made up to date; so on most instruments a much smaller picture may be expected – double postcard size or slightly smaller. [...] On a picture this size great detail should be avoided, and therefore simple plays and films will be shown. A scene involving hundreds of actors cannot with advantage be packed on to a small picture.[6]

It is unclear, considering the speculative nature of the forthcoming medium at this point ('No official details of the proposed programmes at the Alexandra Palace station are available') exactly why *The Times* felt it necessary to publish such an article in the first place. It may be that interest in the forthcoming broadcasts, or pressure, from their readers precipitated such action. The article came just five days after the newspaper published the news that there would be 'Television next summer – limited range at first,' so perhaps a more detailed follow-up was considered necessary. However this second (longer) article actually adds very little detail to the earlier report. It is hardly positive in its outlook:

> Television sets were bound to be expensive when they came, and it would be some time, he [Sir Stephen Tallents, Public Relations Officer of the BBC] was afraid, before television would become a popular thing in individual homes. The B.B.C. hoped to start the first television service next summer. Its range at that stage would be limited to around 35 miles from Alexandra Palace. There were all sorts of problems to be solved.[7]

If the year started with a degree of suspicion towards the medium, over the course of the next few months the press in general began to become more interested as a result of the announcement that not only would broadcasts commence soon, but in the meantime there would be an event that would result in a great deal of press coverage for television.

Radiolympia had always received a degree of press attention each year, but the demonstrations of television were particularly widely reported. The BBC's own preliminary tests of television broadcasts from Alexandra Palace had already ignited some interest, with the *Sunday Express*'s reporter explaining that he already had his own receiver that enabled him to look in on these silent tests.[8] The *Daily Herald* reported that the broadcasts indicated that the service would be ready for the Radiolympia event.[9] There were articles in the press relating to television every day over the next month as the event drew ever closer, with it being scheduled to start on 25 August. The reports were generally positive, with most criticism reserved for the vagaries of the launch date for the official service. However, the flurry of interest as Radiolympia approached resulted in many reports on the provisional tests, as well as expectations of the limited service itself and speculation on advances in the technology including a report on the Scophony system of transmitting television pictures to a larger screen suitable for public viewings.[10] *The Times* dedicated several articles to the demonstrations at that year's Radiolympia, with the main preview article appearing on 22 August anticipating the appearance of working television broadcasts which it claimed the viewer would 'rapidly become more familiar with,'[11] and certainly it seemed that the press were starting to consider television as a system with a real future.

Such was the apparent interest that seemingly anything related to the impending service was considered newsworthy. 'Children's fight seen by television,'[12] splashed the *Daily Herald* on Radiolympia's opening day, the same date that the *Daily Express* ran with the revelation that 'mice chew through wires'[13] required for the transmission of television. A hitch of a different kind was reported in the *Daily Telegraph*, relating to the shock of an 'unrehearsed act in shirt sleeves'[14] being broadcast to the reporter's receiver. Little can be made of such news items when taken at face value, but their very existence indicates the extent of interest at this point in what was still an experimental service that would generally only be viewable by those at a single radio demonstration show in London. No real distinction was being made between the commencement of these demonstrations and of any full broadcast service. This is understandable when one considers that the reach of the service at Radiolympia was scarcely less than the number of people who would be able to receive the service in their own homes three months later – perhaps even greater, when one considers that an internal memo on 26 January 1937 claimed that there was 'confidential data from the Radio

Manufacturers' Association that 425 sets have been sold to date'.[15] Rather more than 425 people tended to pass through Radiolympia, with crowds reaching a peak of 238,000 in 1934,[16] and so the event was of as much significance to the general populace as the more standard transmissions that were to follow using the same technologies. Rather presciently, the *Manchester Guardian* pointed out that this light-hearted interest from many sections of the press was likely to change the moment television became 'official'. The article is headlined 'What Next?'[17] and opens by pointing out that 'for the general public there is inevitably a sense of disappointment – anticlimax even – in the actual arrival of a technical invention.' It goes on to say:

> The exciting, the romantic period in the invention of anything is in the early stages. […] Later, there comes the useful period, when the invention can be used or enjoyed by thousands. Only the intermediate stage is dull. Sometimes, of course, the later stage is also disappointing. […] It is possible to foresee developments which will at least add to the pleasure and possibly to the knowledge of thousands of men and women, but at present one is bound to admit that television will not profoundly affect the human race. Only a few hundred will have the privilege of seeing the pictures, and they will have nothing particular to see. The interest now lies in how television will be developed, the use to which it will be put. Will it create a new art form or merely reduplicate an old one – the cinema? Or will it, like most modern inventions, find its highest place in war?[18]

The discussion of television's potential use in warfare mirrors Baird's own experiments in 'noctovision', but perhaps more importantly demonstrates an understanding that the technology could be used as a basis for more than entertainment and information dissemination. This was more prescient than the supposition that television would not 'profoundly affect the human race,' given the international importance of the medium half a century later. It is something of a contradictory attitude, in fact, to expect the system to continue to develop but play down its overall importance. The tone of some of the news reports at this point is reminiscent of those over ten years earlier, when the details of the January 1926 experiments were being relayed to the public by the invited members of the press. While there were undoubtedly concerns and questions regarding aspects of the medium, the press was not immune to the aforementioned 'wave of public enthusiasm' and were seemingly caught up in the excitement surrounding the new test broadcasts. The context had now changed, of course, and while the interest a decade earlier had been the result of Baird's very new technology, now the implementation of the technology often took equal prominence.

The story of television viewing being made available at Radiolympia was just as newsworthy as the demonstrations themselves, with many of these preview articles being based around direct experience of the system following press privileges allowing early access. It is important to stress that many of these articles were not seriously composed analyses of television's future, such was the excitement surrounding its very existence, even some ten years after Baird's demonstrations to the press. 'How it feels to be televised,'[19] an article in the *Daily Telegraph*, was representative of such interest, focussing on the marvel of the system itself as the light-hearted report told the story of the journalist L. Marsland Gander's experience of being 'an insect under the microscope'. Gander had received a first-hand impression of the broadcast of television by sitting in front of a camera for a test transmission.

There was, then, quite a degree of anticipation for the test transmissions at Radiolympia, so it is of little surprise that the level of interest was sustained when the radio show was officially opened. Several newspapers reported on 26 August that television was to begin its demonstrations that day, with *The Times* declaring that there was to be a 'newcomer at Radiolympia,'[20] while the *Daily Star* preferred to move the emphasis back to the sound receivers as it stated that 'radio marches on'[21] at the show. The day following the transmissions themselves had more in common with the lighter reports of previous experiments than the more foreboding *Manchester Guardian* report, with its questioning of television's long-term future.

'Women watch a war in first television show,'[22] was the angle chosen by the *Daily Mirror* on the 27th, when covering the previous day's inaugural broadcasts. The headline referred to one of the films shown during the demonstration, something which it intriguingly differentiated from 'actual television' which it considered to be live broadcasts. This emphasises the previous findings of the BBC where it was discovered that television was perceived as being different from transmission of films, as seen in Section Two. As Neil Robson points out, referring to pre-war audience reactions, 'the transmissions that proved truly popular were the outside broadcasts'.[23] Such immediacy of visual images had hitherto been impossible, and were what made the medium truly distinctive. It may be that the distinction was also being drawn between material designed for television broadcast and that which was originated for another medium. Although it reported that when 'the lights went up the audience asked for more,' the *Daily Mirror* article was generally detached from any excitement that the broadcasts had generated, reporting the demonstrations in a matter-of-fact manner. The news was still placed within the general news pages some way into the newspaper; little prominence was being given, an indication of the peripheral interest of television. However, other reports generally had a more enthusiastic tone, with the *Morning Post* reporting that 'Never in the history of wireless has public interest been more clearly shown than in the first demonstrations of the new television system yesterday.'[24] The focus of the report was not the system itself, but rather the interest of the crowd. If the BBC had considered the reaction to be a little muted then this was not reflected in the *Morning Post* article, where it was claimed that nearly 7000 people had seen the demonstrations, resulting in queues that were also mentioned by several other publications, most notably by the *Daily Telegraph* who chose to emphasise it by making it their headline.[25]

Aside from cursory comments regarding brief breakdowns or technical difficulties, the extent to which the coverage was positive is interesting to see considering the potentially problematic issue of funding for the new service, which took money from the pre-existing radio licence to fund a service that would be used by significantly fewer people. This issue was raised sporadically by the regional press in particular, such as in the *Western Morning News* and *Manchester Guardian*, but had not clouded the general interest and excitement surrounding the new service to this point. Nevertheless, it is important to consider that this was often a fleeting interest; there was no evidence of a particularly wide long-term audience for the system given its high cost to the viewer. Even with the official launch television seemed to be envisaged by most as a service to be enjoyed at some point in the future, rather than imminently. *The Times* even reported on the placing of a television set in the home on 28 August as a piece of news in its own right,[26] indicating that there was still a distinction being drawn between the marvel of broadcasting moving pictures wirelessly, and a device for receiving them being placed within a private residence alongside the radio set. The potential for 'ordinary' members of the public to be able to have such unrestricted access to the service is treated almost as fantastically as the concept of the technology itself. This demonstrates the extent to which it is important to consider this period of television as unique in the way that a supposedly public service was necessarily restricted in its adoption due to limiting geographical and financial factors.

1936 continued to be a generally positive year in relation to the reporting of television. There was little criticism to report, in fact, as the public showed general interest in television, even if they had not been overenthusiastic, while the technical quality of test transmissions continued to rise. There were some grumblings of dissent as the launch date of broadcasting to homes was pushed back from October to November, but wholly negative articles were rare. Considering its long-standing antipathy to the BBC that continues to this day, it should come as little surprise to see that it was the *Daily Mail* that broke the general trend of positivity. 'The truth about television'[27] was published less than a fortnight after Radiolympia opened, and was presented as an exposé of the costs relating to the domestic future of television. 'No £50 sets for five years – BBC problem of the money,' claimed the subheading, although in actual fact sets costing as little as £30 were available in the pre-war period.[28] The article stated that 'neither the BBC nor the radio trade has had time in which to prepare adequately for its "reception",' although it speaks positively of the technical innovations in television that allowed a high quality service to be launched. Nevertheless, the report claims to quote the BBC's Chief Engineer, Noel Ashbridge, as saying that 'it may be years before television can be received by the ordinary set owner,' something that was undoubtedly true and had been little disputed. The article concludes by asking where the corporation would find the millions required to run a television service of any quality, or for more than a few hours a day, bringing attention to the thorny question of licence fee money. 'The BBC, regarding television, is faced with the biggest problem of its existence,' it claimed. 'There will have to be a separate licence issued for television,' it went on to argue, while in a bold typeface it emphasised that 'Already licence-holders are complaining that their ten shillings should not go towards a service which for many years to come will be far beyond the means of the great majority to enjoy.' In some sense the viewpoint is understandable, but the *Daily Mail* article's implication that this was causing a public uprising seems unlikely as there is little evidence of any particular grievance from the general public relating to this issue. There is certainly nothing recorded in the BBC files of the period relating to general television concerns, which hold other items of private correspondence concerning the medium. Another paragraph in bold type emphasised the claim that 'Television is now in the luxury class. For some years sets will not be bought by the general public'. This fact had not escaped the attention of any of those working on the new medium, or those who had worked to decide on the best way to fund and implement the technology. There was no perfect mechanism for getting television up and running in the United Kingdom, and these factors had already been considered. However, while the BBC and the government could give the reasoning behind their decision making processes, such facts would make little difference if the press as a whole adopted the *Daily Mail*'s attitude and became more hostile towards the medium.

The Official Launch

Although regular broadcasting of high definition images did not officially launch until 2 November, the press often heralded other occasions, such as Radiolympia, which were supposedly the 'first' television broadcast. This included 2 October, when *The Times* reported that the previous day had seen the 'first' television broadcasts disrupted by technical mishaps. The tone was remarkably forgiving, perhaps understanding the complex nature of the system. This was true, but this was actually the last in a long line of experimental broadcasts that had taken place throughout the decade. Later that month, *The Times* mentioned in a headline that there were plans by Sir Harry Greer, chairman of Baird Television at this time, to investigate the commercial potential of the medium. As this announcement took place during the company's seventh Ordinary General Meeting it seems likely that the point was made to placate the members of the board who may have been concerned about the large cost of setting up the television system. In retrospect the futility of many of their grand claims is now clear. Greer stated that with the official announcement of the impending launch date of television 'We can therefore say with conviction that so far as this company is concerned our long travail is ended, and we can now rejoice to feel we are about to face the commercialization of television from an aspect so far of necessity denied to us'.[29] By 'commercialization' it seems likely that Greer was principally referring to the widespread access to the medium itself, and the launching of television sets to the mass market. The time of an official, regular, service was drawing close.

More light stories on television continued to be published in the run-up to the November launch, indicating an ongoing interest in the service even when there was nothing substantial to report. However, the days leading up to the opening of the service saw a new surge of interest as the service moved into its final stages. There was still a general lack of critical judgment of the likely long-term prospects of the medium, with even the *Daily Mail* being generally positive in its appraisal of the service. 'The television baby to walk today,'[30] was the headline to a report claiming that the event was 'without a doubt an occasion', something that was true judging by the number of reports announcing its arrival. It still seems that the medium was not being taken entirely seriously, with such language as 'baby' and talks of 'godfathers', while the article cannot avoid the newspaper's own agenda as it points out that Selsdon 'saw to it that the baby should have a fair chance in life, and made due monetary provision for its kick-off. But to find means and ways of providing money for this infant's education is liable to turn any godfather's hair grey.'[31]

In fact, looking to the future was a key part of the reporting of television even when its arrival was imminent. It seemed that no-one was satisfied with the limitations of the medium, whether they be geographical, financial or in terms of quantity of broadcasts. The setting up of a single channel serving much of London seemed to have been less than some were hoping for in the long term of the medium. 'Television in London; Opening of regular service; More stations promised,' read the headline of *The Times* report of the 2 November launch. Calling television a 'special combination of science and the arts' the article also claimed that it 'held the promise of unique, if still largely uncharted, opportunities of benefit and delight to the community'.[32]

While this 'special combination' refers to the content (the 'art') and the sets themselves (the 'science') it may well be the case that this is an instance of the art predating the technology. Certainly the depictions of the television-like apparatus in science fiction indicate this possibility. For example, the French author Albert Robida had speculated on 'Le journal téléphonoscopique' (television newspaper) in his book *Le Vingtième Siècle (The Twentieth Century)*, set in 1952 but published in 1883. The illustration showed an audience recoiling in amazement, or horror, to the depiction on a screen of live images of a war. Such speculations suggest that some saw a system akin to television as highly likely in the future, while also demonstrating an idea that could then be refined into a technically workable system. Although many of the television entrepreneurs were rather more interested in the technology than the content, it is the possibility of watching the theatre from one's own home (as Robida also mentioned) that could be seen as the reason to desire the invention of television.

The Times' report also stated that there was no great difference between the Baird and Marconi-EMI systems but mentioned the problem of flicker. The article was still a largely positive one, while the mention of 'community' in the aforementioned quote, as well as the 'unique territories' of the medium itself establishes that television was now being taken seriously. No longer was the medium the preserve of the eccentric. Not only were there now considerations of its role within the spectrum of entertainment, information dissemination and broadcasting but questions were also being raised about its wider social implications. Television may not have become truly mainstream for another two decades, but the earnestness of these reports appears to indicate that it was considered to just be a matter of time. It seems likely that the ongoing, and increasing, popularity of radio highlighted that there was an appetite for new and innovative media. Under the subheading 'National interest' *The Times* stated that:

> [Postmaster General] Major Tryon said that they were launching a venture that had a great future. Few people would have dared, 14 or even 10 years ago, to prophesy that there would be nearly 8,000,000 holders or broadcast receiving licences in the British Isles today. The popularity and success of our sound broadcasting service were due to the wisdom, foresight, and courage of the governors and staff of the British Broadcasting Corporation, to which the Government entrusted its conduct 10 years ago.[33]

But it was another article in the same issue of *The Times* that truly laid bare the extent to which attitudes toward television had changed over the previous ten or fifteen years. Calling the launch a 'moment long seen afar by those of faith,' it almost seems to apologise for the sometimes negative attitude towards television formerly expressed in the paper.[34] The article states that 'Within ten or eleven years the public attitude to television has changed from an almost contemptuous disbelief in its possibility to impatience at what seemed a long delay.'[35] This contradictory attitude is well described, and it is worth considering whether it was the latter day involvement of the BBC that had altered the attitudes of those who came to be 'impatient' for television. Once more the report goes on to mention, in non-specific terms, the many problems that needed to be overcome before a system could be fully operational. However, it is also clear from the piece that it was fully accepted that television was still a fluid system that might still see change. *The Times* had drawn attention to the promise that all sets then on sale were guaranteed to be able to receive transmissions for at least two years (allowing for the possibility of change after this point) and here the point was made more explicitly still. 'Television is still experimental,' the writer pointed out, 'in five years' time we shall smile at the recollection of what we now admire'.[36] Nothing makes a consumer more ill at ease than the suggestion that they may have purchased an item that will soon become obsolete. In this sense it is perhaps fortunate that television was allowed to slowly establish consumer confidence by a gradual spread of transmissions. Despite the attention drawn to the possible changes in the system, the article is remarkably positive, even prescient. While the extent to which *Television* magazine spent its efforts emphasising what it considered to be the medium's natural potential should now be clear, this article is rather more unusual in its arguing of the positive influence of television in the popular press. The final section reads:

> Thus will all the news, all the doings of the great world, take on new life and interest. There seems to be no doubt now of the power of television to improve rapidly in the exhibition of scenes that it can light to its own needs. Improvement in the harder task of representing things as they happen in the ordinary world and our indifferent climate will make it, perhaps, an even greater power than the broadcasting of sounds.[37]

The *Daily Express* seemingly created its own story just prior to the opening of television as it ran with the headline 'Drama behind television opening today,'[38] in its entertainment page, where it claimed that it was impossible for the dignitaries to rehearse in advance of their televising as part of the first day's transmissions; not much of a drama in itself, but clearly the newspaper was looking for a hook onto which it could hang its story of the first official transmissions. Similarly the *Daily Mirror* the next day claimed that a momentary glitch in the picture had resulted in the transmission of two men appearing like 'bladders of lard'.[39] The *Daily Telegraph* took a more serious approach, giving the new medium some prestige in its handling from its 'television correspondent' Gander, who welcomed the new service with an extensive article detailing the history of the medium to that point and ending with some speculation towards the future. He pointed out that television 'will not bring to the home long spectacular films made regardless of costs in the Hollywood tradition' but does not view such a restriction as a problem.[40] Indeed, there is no problem in most of the reports when it comes to defining television as a medium completely distinct from other forms of entertainment. It is viewed in its own right, with cinema and radio mentioned merely as comparative factors. This demonstrates the extent to which the medium had formed its own identity not only before it achieved mass appeal some two decades later but also before it had even begun its own broadcasts. There had been a slow realisation of what television would be, and while there had never been a definitive tipping point whereby the future and use of television became clear, the drip-feeding of developments slowly revealed what television was to be. The involvement of the BBC, the findings of the Selsdon Committee and the types of programmes shown at Radiolympia had resulted in the formation of an opinion that television would continue to have a range of fifteen to thirty minute programmes of different types and genres.

In the midst of its many articles on television around this time, *The Times* ran very few which could be said to have called the medium to account and discussed the difficulties that the system presented. The day after the first transmissions had it declare that there was a 'problem of intimacy'[41] inherent in the style of presentation. 'At the present some of their staff show a fondness for broad gesture and very artificial coyness (what is, in effect, over acting) that embarrasses the "viewer" – the official BBC term – some miles away in the intimacy of his home.'[42] In respect of the entertainment itself, the reviewer kindly claims that 'It is too early yet to criticise at all sternly the programmes of the television service,' before giving the previous day's broadcasts a generally warm reception. This genial approach was in common with most of the other newspaper reports of the opening of the service. There were no harsh criticisms, and it seemed that the service would be allowed to grow away from the glare of constant analytical criticism.

Three weeks later the *Evening Standard* seemingly felt that it was time to draw attention to the deficiencies of the system at the same time that they claimed that the King was to have a set installed at Buckingham Palace. Perhaps influenced by an article in the *Wireless Trader* on 21 November which claimed 'Television programming criticised – "Retarding sales" say dealers,'[43] the article said that:

The number of orders that manufacturers are receiving for sets are gratifying. Sales could be more brisk, however, if the programme value of the broadcasts was higher. Complaints are being received from dealers that the entertainment quality of the programmes is so poor that it is difficult to interest potential customers. [...] Another trouble is that the BBC regard television as another form of education. It was hoped that television would be one hundred per cent entertainment. Instead of that, however, the bulk of programmes are educational.[44]

The report also points out that many were uninterested in newsreels that they could see at the cinema. In line with the *Evening Standard*'s views, the *Daily Telegraph* stated on the same day that a 'professional touch'[45] was needed. Television had been granted an extended honeymoon period from the press, but once the initial excitement subdued it was briskly called to account. Many of the articles referred to the opening as 'historic' or similar, but this sense of occasion could not support a service without strong programming, and as will be seen in the next section, programming was an issue that required some practical and theoretical consideration.

One of television's chief supporters had been the *Daily Express,* having maintained its privileged position with Baird ever since it had been one of the first newspapers to have the system demonstrated to them in 1926. They were still well disposed to the medium when the service itself launched in 1936, but the following year adopted a somewhat Bairdian perspective on the issue of the BBC's commitment to the service. On 6 September 1937, Jonah Barrington wrote an article where he called television a 'thriving lusty baby ... too heavy for them', the 'them' being the corporation themselves.[46]

> Consider the lesson of Radiolympia. There we saw manufacturers making magnificent gestures by dropping the price of television receivers and increasing their efficiency. But do the BBC reciprocate by increasing their programme service? There is no definite news. They may do this and they may do that. Gentlemen – we need action. And quickly. Because the present programme allowance – two hours daily and a demonstration film in the morning – is woefully, ridiculously, inadequate.[47]

Barrington not only expressed concerns, but offered a solution. Namely, he suggested what Asa Briggs claims was a 'widely canvassed' opinion at this time, which was the simultaneous transmission of radio programmes on television, with vision. A grossly impractical suggestion, it was also one which highlighted the extent to which television was perceived as 'radio with pictures', a perception that would stay with the medium until the 1960s, even (perhaps especially) from senior staff at the BBC.

Overall Impressions

There was not, then, a sea change of opinion regarding the new medium between these two periods; rather there was a shift of focus. Newspapers had little to fear from television, with live news bulletins still some two decades away, and so there was no benefit to them in suppressing it. It is difficult to sense if the 'wave of optimism' had driven the newspapers to their positivity, or whether such public interest (even excitement) had been caused by the generally upbeat media reports of its development. Perhaps the best way of analysing such reports is by humanizing them, and keeping in mind that behind each anonymous article was a person who was privileged to be one of the first people in the country to see what was an inherently new system of broadcast. Such an event must have been exciting for even the most jaded of journalists, and the result of such an interesting insight into a new form of entertainment would inevitably result in a positive write-up. The constant stream of 'firsts' for television (first broadcast of shadows, of a human face, of film, of live programming, synchronous sound and vision, etc.) allowed this same trick to be repeated over time. Newspapers covered yet more developments without having been given the opportunity to ever refer to anything more than a single test viewing of the previous advancement, and so there was little chance to do anything other than report the inherently interesting or useful aspects of the previously seen demonstration in the manner of a novelty. The attitudes of the press remained largely unmoved while television itself was changing in line with these new advancements. It would take until Radiolympia for the press to be able to view and discuss television as a complete form of ongoing transmissions (with the event lasting for two weeks) rather than as a one-off item of interest. It can be no coincidence that this was the point at which the newspapers became less in thrall of the technology and started to question its long-term usefulness. However, perhaps the biggest surprise was that, in spite of the many potentially problematic aspects of the service, the attitude rarely became wholly negative. Television had largely developed in a secure and private manner, away from issues of public funding and intrusive questioning of its eventual use. The medium had been allowed to develop without interference because of its ever-changing status, with the official confirmation from the Selsdon Committee having been made after most of the groundwork had been established; in short, by the time television moved into the public sphere, and so became more suitable for newspaper comment, it had already largely established itself. It was only now that it was firmly established as an ongoing public service that it could be analysed in more depth and questioned more vigorously. The medium would now be forced to justify its own existence after more than just individual demonstrations; instead, it could now be dissected every single day by viewers and journalists from the comfort of their own homes.

Points to Consider

1) To what extent might the press reports on television have been important to its general development?

2) Can you detect any general trends in the way that television was written about in the press during this early period?

3) Was it naive of the press not to have perceived television as a rival?

4) Do the reports give the sense that television as a concept was well known about?

5) Given all that you know from previous sections, was the press fair in its attitude towards television, in its coverage of the medium's successes and failures?

6) What impression do you think the press gives of the differing attitudes towards television from Baird and the BBC?

7) Do you think that television was taken seriously as a development with long-term potential?

8) How might the formal decision to continue television under the BBC have influenced the way that television was reported?

9) How does the coverage differ from what you might now expect?

10) Do the reports give the impression of television being experimental or an accomplished fact?

Television Goes Public

9

Programming for the Public

Television's official launch was not the first time that the content of its broadcasts had been considered, but it once more raised the question of the specific programming in relation to the medium's long-term future. Baird's test transmissions had normally run for up to five days a week, while the summer broadcasts for Radiolympia required several hours of television each day, although the programmes could be repeated and were not all live broadcasts. The programming on the 30-line service had been typical of light entertainment, featuring self-contained acts that could be found at small theatres around the country. The material shown for the Radiolympia broadcasts had arguably even less thought put into it, such were the time restraints for preparation. A selection of film material and a handful of outside broadcasts (for the Marconi-EMI system) linked by talking heads was the height of its complexity. Now that television would be an ongoing system more thought had to be put into the type of programming to be used, and how schedules would be structured. Radio provided some sort of precedent, but for television the emphasis on the visual would make technical limitations more apparent. Careful consideration was required if television was to appeal to the public, and the BBC had been offered little guidance.

The Selsdon Committee's report had made it clear that the question of programming was outside their jurisdiction, so the BBC was left to make its own decisions regarding the content of television broadcasts. In some respects, such considerations can be seen as the concluding moments of the early development of television in the United Kingdom. In order for us to properly trace attitudes and expectations around television's early history, it is also important to determine exactly what the result of these discussions was when television became a reality on 2 November 1936. The political, institutional and personal developments have already been analysed, but how had these affected the actual content of broadcasts? The assessment of early programming is not a straightforward task, but is both important and rewarding in that it gives further insight into the question of what was expected of television in this period.

That the vast majority of original material created for pre-war television no longer exists is a considerable problem for those wishing to analyse this period of television. However, Jason Jacobs has shown in *The Intimate Screen* that original documentation can be effectively used to 'reconstruct' programmes from the first decades of television. He analyses examples of British television drama up to 1955 in great detail, examining exactly what would be seen by the television viewer. This section sets out to do the same in part, but looks at pre-war productions of all types to demonstrate the full (and often unusual) range of television seen by the early adopters of television sets. Pre-war television was often very different from programming even one or two decades later.

The Range of Programming

When it comes to pre-war television, possibly the most infamous transmission was not even a television programme at all – a fact that is indicative of the range of material being shown. When the television service was interrupted on 1 September 1939 due to the impending war it is popularly believed that a Mickey Mouse cartoon was pulled off air without warning, although more recent research reveals that this is almost certainly not the case, and the cartoon was likely broadcast uninterrupted.[1] This somewhat apocryphal piece of trivia has been recounted many times but rarely (if ever) has the significance of the programme itself been considered. Given the emphasis on the BBC's public service commitments in the run up to the launch, and the retrospective importance ascribed to original programming, where does a character such as Mickey Mouse fit in to our understanding of early television? In its broadest sense, the Disney creation can be justified as a public service broadcast as he would entertain a general audience and supply some wholesome family entertainment. Nevertheless, he is not a creation original to television, nor did he have any educational purpose or even have his roots in British culture. This, perhaps, makes him less interesting to the television historian. However, while no single day's broadcasts can be considered a wholly representative schedule, more consideration must be given to what the viewers would have actually seen on their television sets, including linking continuities and non-original filmed material such as newsreels and cartoons.

There has always been more of an emphasis on drama than any other genre in television analyses (as shown by the existence of Jacobs' book, with no similar tome covering non-drama productions), but it would be misguided to give excessive weight to dramatic productions when considering the overall programming. It is more accurate and useful to consider exactly what appeared on the public's television sets day in and day out rather than cherry-picking the most interesting or groundbreaking examples. Recognising the transmission of all programmes, including Mickey's escapades, is crucial to this and demonstrates the actual culmination of the discussions about television. John Caughie has touched on this issue, as he wrote of the DIY demonstrations occasionally placed in the schedule, 'such items, though they may have been programme fillers, give a sense of the homeliness of television's early notion of the domestic and the delicacy with which the BBC intruded on the home.'[2] Television's relationship with its audience was not fully developed, and so in many respects early broadcasts were distinct from those that would follow. This book requires an examination of all aspects of the television broadcasts in order to discuss how the corporation reacted to the comments from the Selsdon enquiry and test broadcasts.

Comments by Gerald Cock, the inaugural Director of Television, indicate the perceived importance of tackling a range of programmes during the early years of television. As he put it when writing in *Ariel*, 'We go on learning. I cannot see how to avoid trial by the 'hit and miss' method, though some of the programme failures have been due entirely to practical conditions over which we had no control'.[3] This pluralism was not just an attempt to satisfy as many audiences as possible with programming specifically aimed at different tastes and backgrounds, but also because those producing television could not be entirely sure of what would work until it was attempted. Television had no fixed set of regulations or overall plan of content. At this point it was most important to simply get *anything* on air and then, as Cock indicates, an attempt could be made to see what worked and what did not over time while still testing the limits of the new technology. With all of the technical concerns the problem of content had been little addressed. Learning how to make the best of these 'practical conditions' was a crucial part of this learning process. Public service broadcasting could have been taken to mean solely semi-educational programming rather than catering to a broad range of tastes. Instead, the service drew on other media and entertainment forms to broadcast a unique collection of distinctive productions and acts. While radio was the obvious model to draw on, and television was certainly influenced by the wireless' range of programming, from the start it was clear that television needed to emphasise its visual credentials in order to appeal to its potential audience. The specifics of this were less clear, as roller skating dancers and restless chimpanzees were broadcast as readily as opera singers and extracts from Shakespeare.

Analysing Early Television Programmes

It is not possible to fully assess programming that no longer exists with absolute confidence that the nuances of the individual productions can be completely and accurately captured. No reconstruction of television programming can hope to be entirely authentic, but that is not to say that there can be no assessment at all. The analysis simply needs to be drawn from other sources rather than directly from programme recordings. Examinations of television tend to only increase in specificity and detail once the mid-1950s are reached, the point at which the first complete recordings were made, albeit infrequently with the preservation of dramas remaining sporadic for another twenty years. On the whole, programming was rarely pre-recorded until the 1960s, and even then videotape was expensive and so was normally reused.[4] An analysis can be performed, however, which draws on the peripheral material that still exists in many cases. Camera scripts for many television dramas remained stored at the BBC's own Written Archive Centre, but even more useful can be the material in the production's programme file. This will sometimes provide details such as floorplans (which detail the exact placement of sets and cameras) and breakdowns of the shots and use of insert material, such as pre-filmed material and sound effects. However, analysis of television content is about more than just individual programmes. It is just as important to understand the range of programming available, and this is best revealed by a close examination of the published schedules. While details in the *Radio Times* may generally be thin, there is sufficient detail to demonstrate the range of programming, more details of which can be found in the corporation's own Programme as Broadcast documents, which reveal details of exactly what was broadcast and when. There is also the BBC's own publicity for the service, which showcased the breadth of material available to view, a particularly useful example of which is consulted later in this section.

One person who has pointed out the relative lack of analysis of early television programming is Lez Cooke, who has written that 'Until recently, television drama in Britain before 1955 was largely unexplored territory'.[5] Certainly there is a temptation to take 1950s drama as a starting point for either television generally or drama specifically. Twenty years is a long time when it comes to refining inventions, even before one considers the inevitable stylistic changes or aesthetic developments. Technology, and the way in which technology is used, tend to improve at a considerable rate in the early years of an invention, especially when viewed retrospectively. This is as true of the arts as it is of industry. Consider, for example, the difference between the Lumière actualities of the late nineteenth century and *The Cabinet of Dr Caligari*, from 1920 (d. Robert Wiene, Germany: Decla-Bioscop), or *The Kid* (d. Charles Chaplin, US: Charles Chaplin Productions) in 1921. These are sophisticated pieces with narrative and technical nuances significantly advanced from much of 'early film' which existed to showcase the technology rather than operate as a piece of narrative or artistic expression. The medium was initially led by its technology's limitations, and then through experimentation it reached a point where it could command interest because of more than just the ingenuity of the physical processes of filming and exhibition of moving pictures. While television did not experience such a rapid stylistic advance, there were significant artistic and technical changes to the production of programming. The lack of recordings is a problem that should not be underestimated. As a point of comparison, it is worth considering how we might analyse films from the 1920s if we did not have the advantage of being able to view any of the preceding efforts. What if first-hand viewings of film could not pre-date this point as none of the earlier productions were still in existence? While it has been estimated that up to ninety per cent of silent films no longer exist, there is a wide selection that remain viewable and so can demonstrate the changes that cinema underwent. It would surely be difficult to properly appreciate the work undertaken and advances made by those in the movie industry during the early 1900s without having this context, and without being able to simply illustrate the progressions made. Television does not have this advantage.

The First Television Programmes

When television launched on 2 November 1936, it may have been perceived that it was the culmination of over a decade of anticipation and concerted work. To an extent this was true, but the relatively short notice that was given for the start of the service proper nevertheless meant that there was something of a scramble for suitable programmes. Radiolympia had been a useful testing ground, but now television had to present new programming night after night (except for Sundays). Following a weather forecast, a scheduled newsreel and a short interval television makes its first movements into variety, starring musical comedy star Adele Dixon, comedians and dancers Bucks and Bubbles, and Chinese jugglers The Lai Founs. Dixon sang a musical number composed specially for the opening night simply called *Television*.

The song described television as 'A mighty maze of mystic rays', a 'wonder' that was also referred to as 'the latest of the arts', an assertion that seemed optimistic considering how dismissive some had been of the medium's value. The showcasing of the 'television orchestra' on the first night at the end of this variety showcase may have been an attempt to highlight the potential artistic worth of the medium. After the first hour's programming was repeated for the Marconi-EMI system, there was a break in transmission until the programming resumed at 9pm, where it first showed a programme summary and then the short documentary film *Television Comes to London*, which would be re-shown several times in the coming weeks. At 9.20, the premiere episode of *Picture Page* (1936–39, 1946–52) was shown, a production that would come to be an important part of early programming.

What was not on the schedule for this first night was drama, something that highlights the importance of considering television programming as a whole. The service was surviving on a small budget of around £1,000 per week for programming, and television dramas were inherently more expensive than simple talk shows, or variety acts that required nothing more than an empty studio.[6] Those running television openly confessed that they were not sure what types of programming would be the most popular or garner the most impact, something made absolutely clear when considering the large variety of programming in these earliest years.

The existence of a *Television Demonstration Film* ('A survey of television production during the first six months of operation') is of considerable assistance here. Although a comprehensive checking of the Programmes as Broadcast documents allows a simple list to be formed of which programmes and acts were seen on television on which dates, the film serves a different purpose. It is of little use as a statistical tool, but does have something to offer as an insight into which elements of the early television broadcasts were considered to be of most interest to the audience and so most worth promoting. The film came about because retailers of television sets to the general public found it difficult to sell a service that most potential customers had not had the opportunity to see. For most of its existence television has not broadcast programming throughout the entire day, with the 1983 appearance of the BBC's *Breakfast Time* signalling the beginning of the daytime television trend.[7] And so it was that, with the exception of a single hour between three and four in the afternoon, there was nothing scheduled during the opening hours of most shops selling television sets. Clearly this was a considerable problem, and would only hinder the movement of television into the mainstream. As a result, the BBC recorded special excerpts of various acts and programmes onto film, which was then pieced together to form something of a showreel for the service. This film was then broadcast during the day so as to demonstrate the technology to potential purchasers, although the announcers featured were at pains to point out that it was not an exact reproduction of the main service. The film featured:

The Television Orchestra
John Piper, art critic
The Bavera Trio, a dance troupe wearing full evening dress while on
   rollerskates
A **golfing demonstration** from Alexandra Park
Leonard Henry, comedian
David Seth Smith, from London Zoo, who shows off animals in the studio
Sherkot, comedian/mime artist
Sidonie Goossens, harp player

The Rt. Hon. Leslie Hore-Belisha MP
Margot Fonteyn, Royal Ballet
Bruce Bairnsfather, quick-draw artist
Irene Prador, singer
Dr Charlotte Wolff, palm reader.
Johnny Nit, dancer
Dress Parade, where models show off the latest fashions
Ann De Nys, piano player and singer
Alex Moore & Pat Kilpatrick, dance lessons
The Irish Players, performers and actors
Lisa Minghetti, violinist
Pipe Major Matthews, bagpipe player
Leonie, the 'vagabond violinist'
Harry, a muffin man
Colonel Hughes, showing his collection of British army regimental head-
   wear
Oliver Oldfield, who cleans London statues
Pearly King and Queen, Mr & Mrs Tindsley
Sergeant Major Lynch
John Cairns, a London street musician
English folk dancers society
A selection of players from **'Old Time Music Hall'**
Thomas & Sally, an opera

It should come as no surprise that the chosen acts and programmes were somewhat eclectic. The film manages to showcase the sort of visual elements that would mark it out as truly offering something that radio couldn't, such as with the ballet dancer Margot Fonteyn, whose appearance on a basic sound-stage indicated the theatrical tradition of the visuals.

The film also demonstrated that television was not just for the elite, however. The appearances of the Pearly King and Queen and Harry the muffin man offered an insight into the lives of individual members of the public, while it also showed that television's vision of public service broad-casting tallied with that of radio, which the BBC made sure appealed to a broad cross-section of the public. This was achieved though both through specialist programmes and shows that tapped in to broad trends and interests. The desire to demonstrate a range of programming also meant that certain sections of the film now appear rather idiosyncratic, such as Dr Wolff's entirely serious take on palm reading.

On the film, such acts were also shown almost entirely as-is, with only rudi-mentary attempts to dress the sets, indicating that the BBC were not too concerned that prospective television viewers wanted particularly extravagant

Fig. 9.1: *Margot Fonteyn in the* Television Demonstration Film

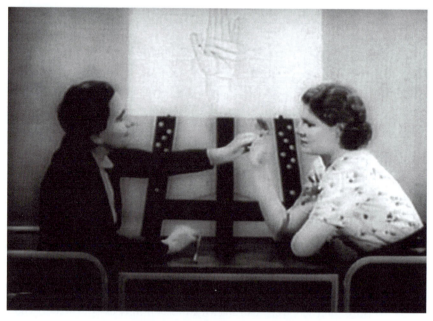

Fig. 9.2: *Dr Charlotte Wolff, the palm reader, in the*
Television Demonstration Film

visuals – had they thought so the film would have been rather counter-productive. Rather, they wished to showcase the range of programming available. Television's more limited broadcasting hours might have meant that it could not offer such variety on a daily basis, but less mainstream interests were not altogether neglected. *Picture Page* was an interview show that featured members of the public with an 'interesting' story to tell alongside the better-known, showcasing people like Harry. The programme allowed television to ensure that its programming was inclusive rather than exclusive, even if the reality was somewhat different in the early years as only the reasonably wealthy could afford a set. In time the issue of regionalisation would become important, as the BBC attempted to be less London-centric, but it would ultimately be independent commercial television in 1955 that mostly redressed this change. At this point, the limited range of television broadcasts made the emphasis on the capital a sensible practical position to take. When *Picture Page* broadcast its fiftieth programme in April 1937, the *Radio Times* featured a double page spread of photographs highlighting the diversity of guests, accompanied by an explanation of the programme and its aims:

> Ever since the televising of the first edition on [the] opening day of the regular service from Alexandra Palace [...] human interest has been the keynote; the famous have been presented with the insignificant, the one quality being they should be personalities with a story to tell. Among the hundreds of characters have been an Atlantic airwoman, Breton onion sellers, an ice-skating champion, a prima ballerina, a racing tipster, the lord mayor's coachman, a Sudanese princess, a circus ringmaster, a silkworm breeder, herring girls and a Red Indian dancer.[8]

The showcasing of special guests, and the use of existing variety acts, indicates the extent to which original productions for television were little explored in the early years, with the programming instead being used as a showcase for pre-existing entertainments. This is not just the case of jugglers, acrobats and actors but also items such as fashion shows and demonstrations of all kinds. Television was seen as a way to bring these things into the home with minimal fuss. It was little more than a way of allowing people to see things that they might otherwise have had to journey some distance for. This was not just the BBC's attitude towards the best use of television, but clearly that of the viewing public as well, with the reaction from Radiolympia indicating that television was seen as 'live'. Television was a facilitator, a way of allowing the audience to witness things from the comfort of their own home. What it was not, at this point, was a distinctive original creator of material, either education or as pieces of entertainment.

Fig. 9.3: *A 1937 photograph showcasing* **Picture Page***'s host Joan Miller at her switchboard alongside Bugler Cooper, who introduced the programme in its early days.*

(Courtesy of the Alexandra Palace Television Society)

It was the technology's ability to relay the images that was of most interest in these early years, with items such as the golfing demonstration highlighted by the film showing audiences something never seen before: outside broadcasts.

In this case, the outside broadcast only extended as far as the gardens of Alexandra Palace, but it demonstrated willingness to escape the confines of the small studios. Such a clip showed that television could, theoretically, broadcast from almost anywhere into the homes of those watching. While the 1953 coronation of Queen Elizabeth II made television a mainstream concern, the 1937 coronation of her father and predecessor George VI had seen his royal procession partially covered by live television in one of the first major outside broadcasts. Such ambition was welcomed by some of those working in television. Writing in 1936, Gerald Cock acknowledged that 'I suppose there will always be a demand for variety,' in the BBC staff

Fig. 9.4: *A golfing demonstration from the grounds of Alexandra Palace in the* Television Demonstration Film

magazine *Ariel*, 'but programmes with a news flavour, outside broadcasts, "Picture Page", and topical types of programme are, I think, the stuff of television'.[9]

Although television may have incorporated these diverse elements it also seemed periodically to aim for critical praise. This would take quite some time to arrive. Indeed, television has yet to achieve the cultural kudos of the theatre or cinema, but given the time taken for the latter to develop any academic or critical standing this should perhaps not come as a surprise. Note that the demonstration film opens and closes with its high cultural elements, an orchestra and an opera, and an orchestra's performance was indeed prominent in the first day's schedule in 1936. Certainly the recollections of some actors indicate the degree of snobbery aimed at those working in the new medium. As Miriam Karlin said in Kate Dunn's collection of reminiscences about early live television, *Do Not Adjust Your Set*:

I'll always remember sitting in the Arts Theatre Club with some friends, making one cup of coffee last for four or five hours, and I remember chums saying to me, "What are you doing at the moment?" "I'm doing a television" said I with great glee, and the pitying look I got from the person I

LIVERPOOL JOHN MOORES UNIVERSITY
LEARNING SERVICES

said it to was as if I was doing some really grotty fringe in the sticks. And I said, "I think it's the coming thing." I remember so distinctly saying, "I'm sure it is going to be the future." It was rather like when one used to think, *God, those people who do commercials!*[10]

The Placement of Drama on Pre-War Television

The almost complete absence of drama on the demonstration film does raise a question. Was there not an audience, perhaps theatregoers, who would be drawn to drama above all else? What were these people being offered? Although early television schedules were not built around drama in the way that they would come to be, there is no doubting that it has played an influential part in television's development, often being at the forefront of both technical and cultural breakthroughs. It is also noteworthy that even though drama was not as prevalent as it was to become, it still required significant resources. As Bruce Norman has said of pre-war television, '"Talks" were relatively easy and cheap to produce; much more complex and expensive was "Drama" which, after light entertainment, was the biggest area of production'.[11]

Norman also draws attention to the fact that in the pre-war period 'BBC Television produced a total of 326 plays,' but does go on to point out that 'The bulk of the drama output came from cut-down versions of the classics or abbreviations of current successes in the West End, and rarely lasted more than 30 minutes'.[12] However, even 326 plays meant that more often than not there was no drama on television on any given day. John Caughie has further suggested that individual dramas held a status akin to the 'big films' shown during public holidays in later decades, stating that 'the single play seems to have had the status of special attraction'.[13] The dramas may well have been a high point of interest for those who were watching the medium, but they did not underpin the rest of the schedules. That is not to understate the achievement of producing so many different dramas, but even then the number of complete, distinct, dramas is somewhat smaller than the 326 plays referenced by Norman. Nevertheless, television was always interested in the programme genre even if it lacked the resources to properly implement its ambitions. Indeed, the difficulty of the time was in having anything to show on television, without considering such complexities of original dramatic productions.[14]

Perhaps because dramatic productions were often perceived as special events, with particular requirements of multi-scene productions, they resulted in many of the most innovative and interesting moments in early television production history, but they also broke ground in terms of content. Some of these productions certainly dispute any presumption of cosy and safe programming. The stage thriller *Rope*, later to be an Alfred Hitchcock film,

Fig. 9.5: *The denouement of* **Rope**
(Courtesy of the Alexandra Palace Television Society)

was broadcast on 8 March 1939 and was presumably perceived to be a success because it was performed again in 1947, 1950 and 1953. Stage thrillers were an obvious candidate for early television drama, with theatre adaptations' relatively static staging being a blessing for cumbersome early cameras that even lacked the facility to zoom. However, *Rope*'s subject matter was leagues apart from other contemporary productions such as the popular pseudo-supernatural thriller *The Ghost Train* (TX 20/12/1937). *Rope* implicitly dealt with homosexuality and more explicitly depicted the immediate aftermath of a murder undertaken for visceral thrills. A cosy play for the evening it was not, and its placement in the schedules indicates that television was not interested in simply transmitting 'safe' productions.

Adaptations were prominent in television throughout the medium's first thirty years, as demonstrated by prominent staff writer of the 1950s Nigel Kneale's complaints that his job mainly consisted of 'touching up stage plays so they could put them on television,' and that 'a few simple rules could make a stage performance into a television one'.[15] Early television's link with the theatre was more explicit then than any other medium has been before or since. While cinema suffered from a similarly enforced static nature as early television for many years, this was not the case by the late 1930s and so there was not the interest in unmodified 'flat' recordings of stage productions, while radio's problems in achieving an accurate depiction are obvious.

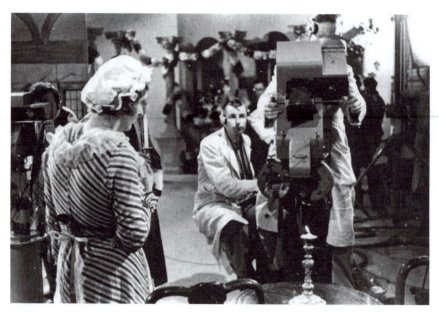

Fig. 9.6: *Adaptations included this 1938 version of* **Pride and Prejudice.**
(Courtesy of Alexandra Palace Television Society)

It is also worth considering the extent to which cinema, radio and the theatre were television's competition and the problems this would have created. For example, 1939 is one of the strongest years in cinema's history with its selection of acknowledged and enduring classics. The big screen was offering the spectacle of *Gone with the Wind* (d. Victor Fleming, US: Selznick International Pictures/MGM) and *The Wizard of Oz* (d. Victor Fleming, US: MGM) in glorious Technicolor, as well as the more understated appeal of the subtle tearjerker *Goodbye, Mr. Chips* (d. Sam Wood, UK: British MGM), a British film that spans over sixty years and many locations, a feat that would have been near-impossible in a live broadcast from a cramped studio. Similarly, television could offer a degree of intimacy, but not to the same extent as a live theatrical performance. The cramped conditions of the studio could not rival even the smallest of theatres, and certainly not the West End venues showcasing the top shows of the day. Once more, the greatest advantage of the medium was its ability to efficiently disseminate programming to the viewing masses, even if the 'masses' were not considerable in this early period, and even if the subtleties of the entertainment transmitted could often be lost. It was only when television became more confident in its creation of original productions, of all kinds, to best suit the medium that the medium could be viewed with more critical interest.

10

What the Viewer Saw

While John Reith favoured the prescriptive approach when it came to public service broadcasting, television was such an unknown territory that, as previously stated by Gerald Cock, there was a great deal of experimentation with programming needed in the early years of the service. Although the BBC had produced television programmes using Baird's 30-line system for three years, the unveiling of television as an official, high definition medium (with the increased flexibility of the new technology) meant that there needed to be more thought put in to the content of the new broadcasts, and this chapter explores what was presented to the public as 'official' television after the service was launched in 1936. As a result of the uncertainty surrounding appropriate programming the television viewers' comments were welcomed, as those producing programmes attempted to maintain the right balance between programme types while also producing them to the correct standard. Such comments indicate the subtle ways that television production changed in these early periods, and also give us our strongest indication that Cock's philosophy that the BBC could not simply get away with 'anything' on television was correct.

The *Radio Times* of 4 June 1937 contained comments from one viewer, a Mrs Jean Bartlett, who drew attention to the most exclusive element of television broadcasting.[1] 'The most important element of the television picture is, obviously, movement,' she wrote. 'We often say that if producers were reminded of this fact during every second of their preparations and rehearsals, every type of programme that has so far been televised would be successful and every failure could have been a hit.'[2] The distinctiveness of live movement was clearly not to be underestimated; it was still the technology that held the most attraction. This makes even more sense when considering the proliferation of excerpts of plays, for example, which could hold little satisfaction for many, a point that Bartlett drew attention to. The novelty of simply seeing part of a play on the television was not enough. Writing about the excerpts from Shakespearean productions, Bartlett notes that 'Non-Shakespeareans are frankly bored – they cannot get the hang of the thing before it is over; and lovers of Shakespeare are irritated by brief episodes suspended in mid-air and inevitably deprived of the play's original stagecraft, and viewed from two cameras alternately at rather uninteresting angles.'[3] Thankfully for the likes of Bartlett, drama productions would become more ambitious, with the first hour-long production showing on 11 November 1937 (R.C. Sherriff's *Journey's End*) and then 90 minute productions of *The Constant Nymph* (TX 31/5/1938) and *Cyrano de Bergerac* (TX 20/10/1938), amongst others, the following year.

Recalling the early years of television, actor James Grout has said that 'It was still very experimental, especially the drama, and nobody quite knew how to do it'.[4] While it would be unfair to take from this that those working in television were incompetent in the early years, the nature of a new medium dictates a steep learning curve, technically and artistically. There is no simple way to assess the extent of these changes but there is sufficient documentation to give an impression of the advancements made during this time. It is already clear that there was considerable advancement between the first performance of a British television drama in 1928 and the medium's official launch eight years later (and, due to its inherently complicated nature compared to light entertainment, it is sensible to discuss this type of programming despite decrying its undue prominence elsewhere). This was largely due to technical improvements and refinements, regarding both the cameras and the inherent resolution and technical specification of the system of broadcast by 1936.[5] As mentioned in the first section of this book, one of the first attempts at a drama production was a 1930 Baird production of Luigi Pirandello's one act play *The Man with the Flower in His Mouth*. The original performance no longer exists, but a 1967 reconstruction does. While it could never have been completely faithful, this more recent production used original equipment and even the same background art as the original production, giving an excellent flavour of what would have been seen.[6]

The reason for choosing to adapt Pirandello's *The Man with the Flower in His Mouth* was no doubt because of its relative brevity, as it runs to no more than twenty minutes, and the use of only three characters. It is also the case that, as with early television cameras, it is a static affair. Perhaps it may be worth also considering what the choice of Pirandello says about the perceived audience for television, being far from lowbrow. The choice implies that Baird was aspiring to artistic recognition as well as technical achievement, although as it was an experimental broadcast the number of people viewing was minimal. The style of the production itself is alien to those only familiar with modern drama, or even the live productions of television after its official launch, so different is from everything that would come later. The single camera is completely static, resolutely fixed to face a scenery flat. There is no facility to zoom in or out, with the camera instead being placed so that the only shot achievable is a medium close up of one person. The background is a simple painting that does not attempt to be realistic. One actor seats himself directly in front of the camera and says his opening line, after which there is a brief pause. A large board painted with black and white squares of sufficient size to obscure the actor and background from view is then slid between the camera and the action, an action necessary because cameras of the time found it difficult to adjust to rapidly changing shots. The board is then removed with the second actor in place ready to deliver his line. The process continues throughout the play, although the reconstruction does not cover all of it. Clearly this system was far from dynamic and would have caused considerable difficulties had it been the basis for an ongoing daily television schedule. However, by 1936 television had an inherent resolution of around a hundred times that used in the 30-line transmissions, while it also now used multiple cameras that, while not as flexible as later models, at least had some mobility which offered considerable freedom to the producers of programmes when compared to the earlier, entirely static, apparatus. The sudden leap in technical quality during the 1930s was as rapid a technical development as television has ever seen, or is likely to see again, indicating just how quickly the technology could advance.

The Practical Realities of Television Drama

Early television productions were not dissimilar to early silent movies in some aesthetic respects. There was considerably less emphasis on realism for sets, make-up and costumes in particular; rather they were painted in broader strokes, figuratively and literally. This was necessary in an age when most television screens were less than seven inches in diameter and when technical limitations meant that presenters would need to be decorated with yellow and blue make-up in order for their appearance to be visible and reasonably naturalistic at home. This is not to mention the technical considerations, with cameras incapable of broadcasting pure white, resulting in bizarre shades of makeup, and an overall lack of contrast in the received images. The lack of intricate sets and swift camera movements meant the variety performances must have owed a lot to vaudeville in style, while television's dramatic productions were little more than stage plays, an uneasy clash of style with the intimacy of television in the domestic environment. Floorplans for early television programmes demonstrate exactly where the sets, notable props and cameras would be placed. The most notable elements of these is how cramped the studios must have been, and how even items like the caption roller (for credits) needed to be accommodated, and assigned a camera; they type of elements that might get overlooked when considering the complexity of making a live drama. Making credits and changing sets would be straightforward once pre-recording and editing became

Fig. 10.1: *A photograph of the crew preparing for the broadcast of* **Western Cabaret** *in 1939, giving an idea of the somewhat confined space that early television broadcasts had to contend with.*

(Courtesy of the Alexandra Palace Television Society)

possible. Studio A, the larger of the two, was reasonably long but also narrow, creating difficulties for wider dressing of the environment.

Jason Jacobs' analysis of the drama *Clive of India* (TX 19/02/1938), for example, demonstrates the unusual complexity of live dramas, and the resulting compromises that needed to be made.[7] The top of the drama's floorplan shows the main sets, which were both small and also relatively sparse. The small screens would be forgiving of this, but the scenery was clearly basic with limited items beyond the background flats. In fact, the only other items of note appear to be the seating. The studio plan of *Clive of India* shows just two cameras operating in this half of the studio space, both of which were placed on dollies.[8] Their arrangement is unusual compared to the modern production method because of the limited scope of angles that they are set up to cover. Each 'set' is covered by only one camera, in contrast to Jean Bartlett's memories of the excerpts from Shakespearean plays being covered by 'two cameras alternately at rather uninteresting angles', and certainly it was not always the case that single cameras would be assigned to each scene on other productions. Understandably enough, this seems to have depended on the number and type of sets requiring coverage, with straight adaptations from theatre scripts often requiring just one larger set, unlike this special adaptation for television.

Jacobs' examination of the plan for *Juno and the Paycock*, also in 1938 (TX 21/10/1938), shows that both principal cameras covered the main set while they also shot other, smaller, sets individually.[9] This placing of sets around the cameras, rather than vice versa, was common at this point with the main sets often being located centrally so as to be afforded maximum coverage, with smaller setups at the periphery capable of being captured by one camera only.

In the lower half of the plan there are a further two, largely static, cameras which are configured to record smaller setups. Camera three is positioned so that it can shoot either of two live action scenes away from the main staging early in the performance, while the fourth camera is used to transmit captions.[10] The use of the last camera in this way was common practice in television production up to the 1970s, when credits and titles would be recorded alongside the main action, often live. It is difficult to properly understand how different such technical constraints would have made the production as transmitted. The entirety of the play's production was based around what the technology could achieve, rather than the converse adaptation of technology so as to achieve an artistic vision. A play consisting entirely of scenes shot using only one camera would have made for a completely different type of television production and emphasises the extent to which the cameras were sometimes present simply in order to relay pictures rather than as creative tools for expressing a visually interesting narrative.

It would be fair to describe television production as both primitive and difficult, perhaps not a conclusion that should come as a surprise to many. However, it does allow us to highlight that even once officially launched, television could not hope to satisfy all of the claims made by Baird in his publicity over the course of the previous decade. Television could not realise all of its potential due to limited facilities and the relative inflexibility of the equipment used. It had ambition, but the audience would have to content itself with live images of any sort in the medium's early years. However, the technical and practical difficulties were an influence on the type of programming seen. For example, it would have been difficult for the studios to host the 14 hours of drama that Caughie points out took place in the week before Christmas 1938; this is certainly something that would be difficult to achieve regularly.[11] The practicalities and cost of mounting these numerous productions must have put quite a strain on the television production departments. Looking at the photographs and plans of the television studios it is clear that there simply wasn't the space or equipment for multiple elaborate productions. In contrast, variety acts and talk shows could take place on simple sets that rarely required changing whatever the performing acts might be, and so it is easy to see the attraction. Nevertheless, at least *Picture Page*'s regular appearance in the schedule demonstrated that the BBC could transmit efficient, inexpensive and unproblematic productions most days.

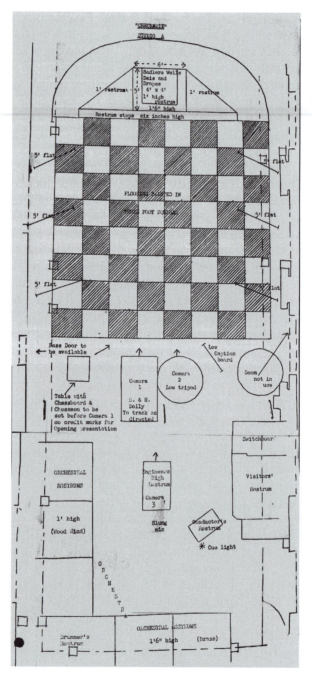

Fig. 10.2: *Floorplan for* **Checkmate** *in the larger Studio A*
(Courtesy BBC Written Archive Centre)

Case Studies

Drama's complexity understandably makes it an interesting focus for examinations of the difficulties faced in staging early television, but difficult stagings were not exclusive to the genre. An examination of a production of the ballet *Checkmate* bears this out.[12] This version was transmitted on 19 February 1939,[13] and performed again three days later. The cramped conditions at Alexandra Palace meant that there needed to be meticulous planning for such a production while, crucially, it also influenced the types of other programmes that could be shown in that evening's schedule. Such was the complexity of this programme that it not only required both the television studios, but there were even changes of set in the smaller studio B while the production was being performed live. This meant that no other even slightly complex production could take place the same evening, and indeed, Janet Bligh necessarily introduced the production from one of the studios being used for the programme itself. Short films were shown either side of the production, as there was no possibility of mounting another live programme immediately before or after, not least because there was no other available studio space – or even cameras. Studio A was used for the bulk of the programme, as this floorplan shows, with three of the four television cameras being placed in this studio.

By contrast, the second studio was principally used for cutaway shots, explaining the single camera. Cutaway shots covered a chess board and, more frequently, captions.

Even aspects of television production that may have seemed simple were made complex in their execution due to the lack of technical facilities in the early years of the medium, with the use of captions being particularly problematic. As previously noted, cameras were sometimes reserved solely for the transmission of captions, which would have to be directly shot rather than electronically overlaid. In this case it meant that for the first eighteen shots, all of which would have been relatively brief as they prefaced the ballet itself, three cameras across two studios were required simply in order to broadcast the opening credit captions and establishing shots of the chessboard and some of the principal characters. For the duration of the 85 minute production the camera script lists only a further twenty-eight separate shots to be used. Both space and facilities were limited, and this type of production stretched them to their limit. This demonstrates that other productions could be just as complex to stage as drama.

By contrast, programmes such as children's show *Puppet Parade* could be considerably more straight-forward. This was a rather more standard setup, with the main two cameras moving very little throughout.[14]

Obviously in this case the type of programme and use of puppets dictated

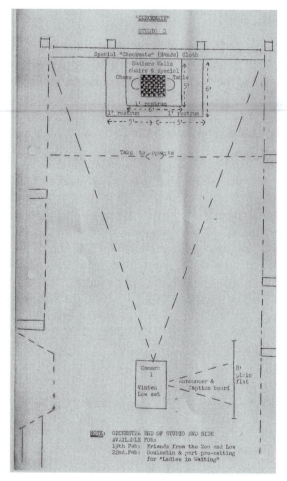

Fig. 10.3: *Floorplan for* **Checkmate** *in the smaller Studio B*

(Courtesy BBC Written Archive Centre)

that this would be possible, but it was very much a 'shoot and show' approach, whereby the cameras were not used artistically. The floorplan of the show that was transmitted on 16 June 1939 shows that the main two cameras were simply fixed on the two rostrums where the puppets 'performed' for the most part. One of these two was able to move to another scenery flat, which could also be shot by camera three, which was mainly facing the caption area for credits. The fourth camera was permanently facing a 'caption wheel', presumably used within the show rather than the end credits. With the potential (but unlikely) exception of the scenery flat each aspect of the production was covered by a single camera, with the studio laid out so

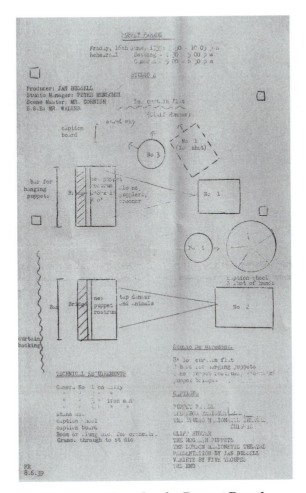

Fig. 10.4: *Floorplan for* **Puppet Parade**

(Courtesy the BBC Written Archive Centre)

that the areas being shot were very close to each other, resulting in a cramped working space. The role of the cameras was simply to show the programming as clearly as possible to the viewer at home. If this could be achieved in a single shot, then it was. They were not used to dynamically cut between different shots to create tension or humour, for example. They simply relayed the puppets to the watching children at home, in the same way that children would be watching Punch and Judy-type shows from a fixed location when seen live.

But what does learning about this type of programming actually tell us about what had resulted from the discussions about television in the years

Fig. 10.5: *Studio A in use for* **Checkmate**
(Courtesy of the Alexandra Palace Television Society)

prior to its launch? Do we simply learn that less time, money and effort was spent on aesthetics than would be the case when television became a popular medium, and that the type of content was seemingly the most important aspect? Possibly this is true, although almost certainly because of practical concerns as well as wider programming aims. In terms of this study, it demonstrates that the attitudes and expectations for television were not fully satisfied on 2 November 1936 and that there was a real drive to make the programming as impressive as possible. Productions such as *Checkmate* demonstrate how confidence increased over time, but also show that expectations were not fixed. There was an inherent ambition on both an artistic and technical level. Television cannot be neatly divided into eras, and the changes in programming are especially indicative of that. The gradual transformation of programming since 1936 shows an ongoing desire to push the limits of the medium. More recently this has meant the sacrifice of the intimacy of the studio-based drama in favour of more cinematic productions, something undreamt of when almost all of television in the United Kingdom was broadcast from two cramped studios at Alexandra Palace.

However, it is also the case that we, as modern viewers, have a different perspective on drama productions. The movement towards feature film type productions fundamentally changes the methods of production. Outside the soap opera genre, very few BBC dramas are now made as anything other than a single camera production, with each shot framed and recorded separately and later edited together, as with film. For much of television's existence, however, drama was essentially performed on a stage with multiple cameras in place of an audience, all recording simultaneously as a vision mixer cut between them to get the best shot, usually 'as live'. It may well be the ephemeral nature of the broadcasts which meant that realism was not being aimed for, instead there was an attempt at representation, in the same way that the theatre would show representations of a forest or trees and yet not expect the audience to believe that the forest or trees were real, with the sets instead acting as signifiers. Television would move towards this as it became less ephemeral, with the productions on film from ITC in the 1950s and 1960s the most prominent examples of this in the UK, as they were products to be exploited by the independent producers over time, rather than as a single evening's entertainment for one broadcaster.

It is clear from examining these plans that there is a considerable difference between the productions staged in the pre-war period and those for which recordings exist in the 1950s. Perhaps the best comparison of the differing facilities is viewing the existing material from the three *Quatermass* serials, broadcast between 1953 and 1959. Only the first serial, *The Quatermass Experiment* in 1953, was transmitted from Alexandra Palace's awkwardly shaped studios, and used many of the same facilities that had been installed at the studios prior to the 1936 launch. Film recordings of the first two episodes still exist and indicate that they were made in a transitional period for drama production. While the sets were generally cramped and simplistic, there is a single large set that is rather more impressive in both size and detail. Much of the second half of the first episode takes place around this depiction of the crash landing of a space shuttle in the middle of a London street. The devastation is well expressed, with the open-fronted houses spread cross two floors which allowed the placement of an elderly lady character on the first floor of a building.

The episodes were each transmitted live but did have a limited amount of pre-filming in order to facilitate extra space or difficult sequences. Such pre-filming would be rare, if not unheard of, in pre-war television drama, and so it is clear that *The Quatermass Experiment* cannot be seen as a fair example of 'early television', even if it was transmitted at a time that many would include in this bracket and remains one the very earliest existing examples. The sheer rate of development by 1953, much of it subtle, means that this must be one of the most diverse eras of television. When Alexandra Palace was no longer regularly used for drama productions from the mid-1950s it heralded the beginning of a new age for television. Comparing the first *Quatermass* serial with the final one made by the BBC, *Quatermass and the Pit* which ran from the end of 1958, a considerable jump in technical quality and aesthetics is evident. The sets are more intricate and noticeably larger, while the use of pre-filmed sequences is considerably more prevalent. Much of the serial took place on the 'pit' set, the site of an archaeological dig, which was pre-filmed on 35mm at Ealing Studios, giving a more epic nature to the surroundings, to an extent that would not have been achievable in a live television studio. Even the 1954 adaptation of George Orwell's *Nineteen Eighty-Four* (TX 12/12/1954) was more technically complex than the previous year's *Quatermass Experiment*, with several pre-filmed sequences (including one recorded at Alexandra Palace) while the bulk of the play was performed live from the Lime Grove studios.

There is little filmed evidence of what an Alexandra Palace television production would really look like, with the television production at the studios rarely including drama from the mid-1950s onwards, instead concentrating on news and, latterly, Open University productions. Even the material that does exist is considerably more sophisticated than the earlier productions. Because of this, there is a danger of assuming, when it comes to examining these 1950s productions, that this is what all television to this point would have been like, rather than this being a refinement of many years of developments in the industry. With the exception of some newsreader sequences, no scene in the existing two episodes from *The Quatermass Experiment* uses a single camera, unlike *Clive of India* which used a single camera for every scene.[15] Even the scenes set in the small rocket control centre cut several times between two cameras. Television had become more sophisticated by this point, and so even though the style of television in 1953 may seem rather stilted it is important to appreciate the extent to which television had already become more aware of its limitations, but also excited by the possibilities and potential in such an ambitious serial.

It is not, then, fair to use existing productions from the mid-1950s as examples of 'early' television drama. Nearly two decades of development had led to more complex and ambitious productions which took advantage of improved facilities. It is understandable that, given the research difficulties and overall lack of emphasis of this period, 'early television' should so often encompass a long period that encompassed many changes, but my comparisons support two central tenets of this book. One is that a great deal of development and thought was required before television 'arrived' in 1936. The second is that, while television in 1936 was as close to a fully formed medium as could reasonably have been expected in the circumstances, that does not mean that it remained the same for the next twenty years.

While there is no doubting the primitiveness of the *Quatermass Experiment* production in many senses it is also different from the Pirandello performance in just about every conceivable way, just as the first regular broadcasts in 1936 would have been. There are over twenty years of largely overlooked progression, as the subtleties of the medium were slowly understood. We know little about changes in the performances of the actors, for example. Instead, it is known that that by the time of *The Quatermass Experiment* the sets had started to become more refined, moving further away from a theatrical aesthetic; perhaps an indication that performances would have similarly become more suitable for the intimacy of television. In fact, the sets are properly visible, something that should not be understated when compared to the earliest dramas. The camera is able to move and so can give us more imaginative framing than simple two-shots or close-ups, and even the plot's concept is a rather ambitious one, dealing with astronauts returning from space in a crashed rocket. This is not something that would be practically achievable in the theatre. Indeed that the three BBC *Quatermass* serials were later made into feature films should come as little surprise given both their cultural impact and ambitious concepts.

Conclusions on Programming and Content

Television had come a long way since the 1920s, when content had been wholly secondary to the primitive technology, and survived the BBC attitude that the medium was lesser than radio in terms of both cultural and popular significance while also widely labelling it 'radio with pictures'. The latter problem had undoubtedly been fuelled by John Reith's complete lack of interest in (and occasional explicit dislike of) the system. 'When he did not understand something, as became painfully obvious in relation to television, he simply backed off and covered his ignorance,'[16] wrote his daughter Marista Leishman. This attitude was similar to that of many others in the BBC but, as seen in the second section's assessment of institutions, it should not be forgotten that these faceless public bodies also contain individuals who may not share the overall attitude of their colleagues and management. As the excerpt from the first edition of *Ariel* in the previous section points out, there was a real sense of segregation amongst those working in the television department, so it seems highly likely that being left alone at Alexandra Palace, a distance from Broadcasting House, helped to allow television to develop rather than be suppressed by negativity.

In the same way that television's identity as a medium was formed by an ongoing questioning of what television should be, rather than a single decisive judgement, so the programming itself was largely formed from a wide-ranging exploration of what this public service remit actually meant. This remit was embraced, but not to the detriment of providing popular entertainment and not to the extent that it particularly precluded most of the types of programming that had been popular on radio, in the cinema and at the theatre. As has already been outlined, there has been little examination of these parts of the schedule, such as cartoon films and vaudeville acts, and they were likely to have been considered to be just one of many elements of television even at the time. Nevertheless, they were part of the way that television was seen, and so considered, by the audience, however frivolous or unimportant they may have been considered at the time and since. In the same way that many television series themselves go through many changes during their early years of development, to the point that the audience forgets some of the elements that were present in earlier episodes but later dropped, so television content as a whole eventually settled into an established mix of programming. Excerpts from Shakespeare held little interest for 'Views of a Viewer' writer Jean Bartlett, clearly a widely held view as they were eventually phased out along with other theatrical extracts, with television instead showing entire productions. However, the objection to the extracts was not so strong that it merited an immediate overhaul of its placement on the schedule. We have seen evidence that viewers understood the compromises required because of television's technical restrictions at this point, but that they were generally keener to see fully fledged productions that showed off the visual aspects of the new medium to greater effect.

The piecemeal scheduling also lent an air of experimentation to the schedules as programmes were specifically designed to interest its audience even if they found the subject matter uninteresting. The same week that saw a Commander Campbell reading his *Sea Stories* (TX 05/04/1937) for ten minutes also saw a ten minute programme devoted to dress design, for example. This could be considered to be similar to the brief fashion demonstrations seen in many of daytime television's magazine shows up to the modern day; it was just enough to pique the interest but brief enough to be overlooked for those who did not care for such a topic, while still conforming to Gerald Cock's view that brevity was preferable for television programming. It would not be fair to say that television did not know what it wanted in terms of programming, but it was acknowledged by those working on it that there would inevitably be a degree of experimentation, which would inevitably include failures.

It is also worth considering the extent to which attention was paid to television programming in other media. While it is perhaps unsurprising that individual programmes were not individually deemed newsworthy, it is slightly strange that the content of the medium was so rarely considered in an assessment of television, especially when considering how the press reports seen in the previous section could explore the minutiae of television development. The publicity efforts of Baird had generally concentrated on the technology, and the 'firsts' were greeted with the most interest by the press. However, once television was a fixed prospect, there seemed to be less attention paid to its content. The prospect of broadcasts expanding to encompass more of the country ignited the most interest, but general articles on the content of broadcasts seen by just a few thousand people rarely made it into the press. More interest was shown regarding the relaying of live prearranged newsworthy events but little reference to what one could actually expect from the service otherwise. Even the preparation of the demonstration film for retailers appears to have been an afterthought as it only materialised in 1937.

With this in mind perhaps it was understandable that any reporting of news about the medium did not centre on the specifics of programmes that most readers would not have seen, or have the opportunity to see, but the almost complete absence of comments relating to even the programming schedule in general terms is a little surprising. Discussion of television at this point was based around its central principle and its potential as, eventually, a mass medium, not as an item of artistic interest. Television was so far removed from the mainstream that it was still treated as an abstract concept rather than a working practical reality. It was still being seen as a developing technology rather than a new form of entertainment or information dissemination. Arguably it would take until the 1953 coronation for this to change, this being the widely-acknowledged point where television became a mainstream product.

Points to Consider

1) How did early production methods differ from how television is now made?
2) What do you think are the reasons for the change in television style and aesthetics?
3) Why do you think the BBC decided on this particular range of programming?
4) How does the range of programming differ from what you might expect today?
5) To what extent can you clearly identify the content of early television as conforming to 'public service broadcasting'?
6) How confident can we be that we have a good understanding of exactly what was seen by viewers in the early years of television?
7) What audience do you think early television was trying to appeal to?
8) Why do you think that examinations of television so often emphasise drama?
9) How integral was the element of 'liveness' to early television?
10) In which ways could early television be described as either small-scale or ambitious?

Conclusion

The claim that the BBC's television service was the first of its kind is a statement bound up in a series of technicalities. Certainly, it was 'the first of its kind' insofar as it was the first regular, high-definition system of broadcasts.[1] However, this downplays not only the earlier experimental broadcasts in the United Kingdom, but also the international developments. We have seen that there had been the occasional test broadcasts in several countries and some had broadcast their own regular service, albeit in a low-key manner. Charles Jenkins' regular broadcasts in the United States from 14 August 1928 are especially worthy of recognition, even if they did use a low-definition system. Meanwhile, there was Germany's regular 180-line system from March 1935, and several experiments before this. France had found its own practical, and iconic, solution to broadcasting across Paris as the Eiffel Tower became a transmitter of the country's own broadcasts of a 60-line system from 13 February 1935, with a 180 line system launched in its place from November that year.

Some of these may be described as vanity products to some extent, with short-term potential at best, as the low definition of broadcasts made them more notable as examples of technical ingenuity than as a popular medium. Certainly, Germany had been keen to demonstrate its utilisation of the new technology to the world when the attention was on Berlin for the Olympics. Most of these countries had their own 'inventors' or 'fathers' of television, just as Baird had entered the British national consciousness as the lone inventor striking a blow against big business.[2] Television had no clear single inventor, such was the complexity of its development, and national pride allowed individual developments and discoveries to be emphasised as necessary. Nevertheless, none of these systems resulted in mass adoption of television by the public, and the use of public screening rooms in both Paris and Berlin indicate that widespread placement of sets in the home was seen as unlikely by many at this point. By contrast, the British model had been more thoughtfully considered, as one might expect following over a decade of discussions. The Selsdon Committee had decreed that High Definition television could only be used to describe a system broadcasting at least 240 lines with no fewer than 25 frames per second; it is probably no coincidence that this matched the Baird system exactly, although Marconi-EMI bettered it with

405 lines. More significant than these technical aspects was the confidence of television upon its launch; it was a fully-fledged service, broadcasting six days a week, juggling many forms of entertainment and information as part of its Public Service Broadcasting remit. Other countries would follow the standard set by the UK, and it was both adopted and adapted by many of those who had similarly embraced radio earlier in the century. Different locales had differing attitudes to the placement of either commercialism or 'Public Service' but the basic mixture of programming aims and content, to entertain and inform, remained key aspects of most broadcasters' schedules.

Modern Day Public Service Broadcasting

Certainly the emergence of multichannel television has meant that some of the key tenets of public service broadcasting, such as catering for niche audiences, are now covered by channels that make certain types of programming their speciality. There are channels that cater for children, for teachers, for those interested in cookery or DIY, as well as those aimed at particular cultures or users of other languages. The type of audience for these channels is dictated only by the backers of the channels themselves. Unlike traditional public service broadcasting on the main terrestrial channels, multichannel television does not have constantly try to maintain a balance. The very plurality of multiple channels, with the audience rather than the broadcaster making the choice, indicates a necessary change to the principle of public service broadcasting that was perhaps kickstarted by the arrival of Channel Four in 1982 as a markedly different alternative to the BBC and ITV. Almost unconsciously, television has been led by technology into an era of broadcasting that would have been unthinkable in 1936.

There are drawbacks to this new era of choice, however. In the early days of radio the BBC would regularly alter the schedule of programmes in an attempt to encourage the listening audience to tune in to programmes that they might not normally actively choose to hear. Such an approach seems rather nannying by today's standards, where the audience takes control (long gone are the Reithian days of the public being given what the corporation felt they needed, which was not necessarily what they wanted), but risk being ghettoised into particular types of programmes. Viewers with no natural affinity for a particular type of programme may never experience the reality of those alternatives, which they might actually enjoy, while a more thinly spread audience will inevitably influence the amount of money available for new programming. For example, it is difficult to see where brave new dramas that cannot be easily pigeonholed will sit if the BBC and Channel Four lose the ability to fund them because of a redistributed audience. Even, or perhaps especially, children's television is affected by this. While the Children's BBC (CBBC) strand on BBC1 and BBC2 was popular in the 1980s and 1990s, increasing amounts of material are now shown on the separate channels CBBC and CBeebies instead, with the children's slot on BBC1 now little over an hour a day. This compartmentalises programming for the very young and slightly older audience, providing little opportunity for children to 'graduate' from, for example, cartoons aimed at pre-schoolers, to the antics of *Shaun the Sheep* for a slightly older audience, through to dramas for secondary school students. In fact, the latter category no longer exists at the BBC, with CBBC now catering for the under-12s only. Before its demise even *Grange Hill* was notable for positioning itself towards a younger audience in its later years. Whereas previously it had been something of an introduction to adult dramas for growing children, now the leap between programming for children and those for adults is much greater. It is unclear why the BBC has felt the need to disenfranchise teenage children so completely, but it may soon find that there are long-term ramifications of this decision.

We have seen that those privately interested in television, the public institutions and the press each held different views of the medium's likely development. While the opinions and attitudes of the newspapers were largely driven by the claims of the other two groups, those working in the private sphere nevertheless had different ideas of how television could operate practically. Perhaps the most pertinent difference was that of attitude. While Baird Television emphasised the desire to have a system up and working as soon as possible, this was not a view shared by the public bodies which preferred to ensure that television was given the best chance for a long-term future. This study's analysis of these separate elements contributing to television's early development has demonstrated that there was no concerted expectation of what the medium could be and how it could operate, and as such its progress was far from pre-determined. In the Introduction we saw that the development of television in the United Kingdom as we know it, with its central tenet of Public Service Broadcasting and resultant BBC broadcasts transmitting information and entertainment to the home, was not a foregone conclusion. Baird's work actually began before the existence of Public Service Broadcasting in this country and, while it seems unlikely that the Post Office would have granted him permanent exclusive rights to broadcast television, the involvement of the BBC and adoption of the public service model was not part of their consideration at this time. It was also not the case that the BBC, still a fledgling institution, was actively looking to initiate a system of television. Although the BBC was already involved with television in various ways after its 1927 offer of limited use of its facilities, Baird himself was still acting independently. His search for assistance was almost entirely based on his precarious financial situation, and his company looked to the BBC as a silent partner rather than as the co-ordinator of efforts. The involvement of the BBC would only highlight the likelihood of television operating as a public service, and Baird's dream of an independent service was consequently less likely.

The argument that Baird could have operated his own private broadcasting company is not without its problems, however. The Post Office was reasonably open to discussions about television's future, but as a public body it would never have exclusively negotiated with Baird. There is evidence in the early internal memoranda that the BBC and the Post Office were aware that there was a good likelihood of a rival system being developed, and this raised the same problem that had been faced by the early radio broadcasters in the early part of the decade. We have seen that the limited radio wavelengths available for broadcasting would have necessitated some type of conglomerate broadcaster or broadcasters once rivals caught up with Baird. Indeed, the Selsdon Committee's report would later highlight this as one of its key reasons behind permitting a single broadcaster. The report stated that:

> We have, of course, considered the possible alternative of letting private enterprise nurture the infant service until it is seen whether it grows sufficiently lusty to deserve adoption by a public authority. This would involve the granting of licences for the transmission of sound and vision to several different firms who are pioneering in this experimental field. We should regret this course, not only because it would involve a departure from the principle of only having a single authority broadcasting a public sound service on the air [...] but also because we foresee serious practical difficulties as regards the grant of licences to the existing pioneers as well as possibly to a constant succession of fresh applicants.[3]

This does not mean that we should either underestimate Baird or presume that television needed to follow radio's path into Public Service Broadcasting through the BBC, and Baird even referred to the BBC as a 'rival' in the early years of television's development.[4] It may have been the case that commercial and public service transmissions could have operated alongside each other. Even when the BBC took control of the system in the 1930s, this was not entirely without any sense of commercialism. In fact, the Selsdon

Committee had explicitly allowed sponsorship of programmes on television and a handful of test broadcasts had followed this path. Asa Briggs points out that, for example, an October 1936 programme featured a roll call of new car models. He also writes that 'Nothing much more daring or contentious than this was attempted, and even this provoked protests'.[5] By the time of the Selsdon report the increasing strength of the BBC meant that any alternative to the corporation for television broadcasts at this stage was effectively dismissed.

Baird was instrumental in the instigation of television's more general development, not just his own technology. While the eventual pattern of television broadcasts did not conform to his personal ideology, Baird was passionate in his desire for television, and did much to rile both the Post Office and the BBC but at least the vocal manner of those associated with Baird Television meant that his voice was heard. Unfortunately for him, this also damaged the company's reputation as a serious business concern. His quest for publicity and repeated requests for assistance or licences to broadcast may have been the result of a desire for personal gain, but they nevertheless helped to instigate the development of television. Those involved with the early development were acting largely without precedent. It is perhaps understandable that Baird's work was approached with some reticence even disregarding the question of the quality of his transmissions and so it was a brave step for the BBC and the government to embrace television so readily, even if their vision differed from Baird's. The television system as we know it emerged out of these debates and often conflicting aims, and not through an innate desire for television from the corporation eventually responsible for it.

Attitudes and Expectations

If one thing is clear from this sometimes convoluted history of early television, it is that overall expectations towards television were anything but consistent. For example, while the press demonstrated some general interest in the personal story of Baird's 'struggle', with the occasional more detailed questioning of television's function and aims, this often differed between articles. Similarly, the cautious approach advocated by Peter Eckersley, Chief Engineer of the BBC, in relation to Baird's earlier work was largely embraced by the corporation while he was an employee. His departure coincided with the corporation acceding to the request of the Post Office to take Baird more seriously. This cannot simply be the result of one man's influence, but certainly the BBC had relied upon his expertise to formulate their own opinion of television's worth. With little in the way of concrete information regarding television's practical potential, or even the public's desire, it was the opinion of the very few experts that mattered so much to the BBC. The opposing view was held by Baird and his contemporaries, who instead insisted that their own stance that television could be launched imminently was beyond question, and eschewed any suggestion of further consultation. Unfortunately for them, once the Post Office had delayed the approval of a private licence to broadcast television as sought by Baird's company, television had started to slip out of the hands of the individuals who had developed it to that point. Television's emergence required the establishment of a coherent infrastructure so as to solve practical and ideological problems, something that required careful consideration. More than anything, the route to public service broadcasting for the medium was instigated by a precautionary initial consideration of the use and inherent quality of any broadcasts.

The fact that radio had already successfully followed a public service model was undoubtedly an important factor in British television's eventual progression down this path. The pre-existence of the BBC meant that there was already an institution in place that could effectively regulate and run broadcasts along similar lines. Had public radio not been a success then it is likely that the government would have looked for a different way to encourage (or even discourage) the advent of television and the formation of an audience for it. This was one factor completely external to television's own development. The decision was made largely because of experiences in other, similar, areas rather than as a result of television's own success or otherwise. There is no doubt that by the time of the BBC's involvement in the test transmissions (and especially once it had taken over the content of the broadcasts in 1932) it was almost certain that the corporation would play a central role in television. This does not mean that it remained the only possibility open; for the BBC to take control an active decision needed to be made (through the Selsdon Committee) and consideration given to the other possibilities. That they were deemed less appealing does not make them insignificant. Paradoxically, had Baird been aware that television would come under the exclusive auspices of the BBC then he might not have conducted his experiments to begin with, and the impetus for television broadcasts at all might have been lost. As it was, the radio model indicated the way in which the medium could be run administratively, plus the type and mixture of programming that could be expected. This offered a stable infrastructure for television, with no reliance on private enterprise outside the selling of sets.

There is a danger of presuming that the fitting of television into the mould of radio was achieved with ease. In fact, this placement of broadcasting as a public service was not straightforward, and it is clear from his aggressive pursuit of broadcast television that Baird, amongst others, saw strong potential for commercial and financial gain in the control of television. Baird and his enthusiastic contemporaries forced the hand of both the government and, later, the BBC, in making a decision. Unfortunately for him, it was not to be a decision that satisfied his hopes of a monopoly. The impartiality of the BBC forced equal consideration of the newer Marconi-EMI system, a method of television transmission markedly superior to the Baird company's. Given the power held by the BBC by this point, it is tempting to speculate on Baird's fortunes had he operated in another country. His company did make some attempts to explore the international market, and a sister company Baird International Television was even set up with this in mind on 25 June 1928.[6] With the exception of some test transmissions in France in 1932 little would come of this, despite several claims of negotiations. Baird needed financial backing wherever he had developed his technology, but the uniqueness of the BBC's and the government's mutual emphasis on Public Service Broadcasting is nevertheless something to be appreciated. Considering that the two institutions failed to be interested enough in television to instigate their own investigations, they nevertheless took it seriously, almost certainly because of the consideration of it as a threat (to radio and overall state control of broadcasters and, indirectly, broadcasting itself), rather than as an exciting new technology to be embraced. There were exceptions – Eckersley and his replacement Noel Ashbridge both found the basic television concept of interest, even if they were unconvinced of the workability of Baird's technology.

It is not just the underlying opinions of the large institutions that proved to be important – the significance of the attitudes of individuals runs through the whole of this book, where we see a constant battle between those advocating this new system and those who were rather more wary of it. Certainly, with all of these battling factors eventually forming television it was never going to be the case that this book could offer a definitive statement highlighting a single reason for television's development in the pre-war period. Perhaps we may get a more definitive understanding by turning the question on its head and considering which factors were eventually to play relatively minor roles in its ongoing development despite seeming to be important at earlier points. In the period from the 1930 performance of Pirandello's *The Man with the Flower in his Mouth* through to the 1936 launch and until television made the crossover to the mainstream, the success of the medium in the long term actually relied on a definite lack of viewers. While conceptually sound as a medium, the content and technology were undergoing constant refinement with relatively few people actively working on the medium, and this was best achieved away from the glare of constant widespread critical assessments of the service. As the actor Edward Jewesbury has said, 'Before the war it was just a joke because we knew that only about twelve people in the whole country had a set. You wondered if anybody was watching at all – probably not.'[7] The system had the paradoxical aim of broadcasting programming for a public who were largely unable to see it for either financial or geographical reasons, even assuming an interest in the medium itself. This did mean that the experimentation and evolution of the system could be conducted without the entire nation viewing the mistakes made or judging the system solely on its earliest endeavours. The system was not perceived as having artistic or cultural importance such was its lack of wider influence, but this would afford it a certain degree of freedom in its approach to broadcasting.

Even those appearing on the medium seemingly found it difficult to take it entirely seriously. 'Dare I say it, television was a bit of a joke,' said actor Stephen Hancock. 'In those days it was something you did when you didn't have anything better to do, the theatre was the thing. This new television business was a time filler.'[8] This statement epitomises the attitudes of many to the medium before the Second World War. There was a general sense of disdain towards the technology and its programmes, even if there was a small but vocal minority with rather more interest in the medium. Although it seems likely that she had links to the medium which made her more interested than most, it is still interesting to hear Jean Bartlett's *Radio Times* article mention that friends often enquired about television 'sympathetically, as if it were an invalid member of our family,'[9] and this is a good summation of attitudes as the general public exhibited a degree of curiosity but often failed to display any interest by actually acquiring a set of their own, even if they maintained a good natured attitude towards it.

Modern Television: A Less Ephemeral Medium

While early drama was heavily influenced by the theatrical tradition, this did not characterise a particular ideological desire of television that was later 'corrupted' by film based productions. Rather, it was simply the result of economic and technical restraints. There was a concerted drive towards making dramas and sitcoms pre-recorded rather than live when videotaping became a viable possibility in the late 1950s. Issues such as a set collapsing prematurely in a live episode of *Hancock's Half Hour* meant that live television was losing its appeal for those working on it.[10] Perhaps most importantly, the type of programming offered was increasingly trying to take advantage of television's technology, rather than predominately recycling plays and adaptations that either had been, or could be, performed in the theatre. The 1954 adaptation of *Nineteen Eighty-Four*, for example, utilised extensive pre-filmed inserts and changes of sets that would be impossible on stage. Television was outgrowing its roots, as the technology moved beyond being a simple enabler for the audience at home to watch what was happening live in a television studio in London.

These one-off plays were the backbone of early television drama, a type of programme that is now very rare in the UK, and practically unheard of on the main networks in the United States. Now series such as *24* and *State of Play* force the viewer to follow their every move, warning the audience that it faces repercussions should an episode be missed and the plot resultantly deemed unintelligible. Meanwhile series that initially seem more episodic in nature, such as *The X Files* and even *Doctor Who*, also present an underlying plot arc woven through their standalone adventures. That such underlying narratives were deemed unnecessary during the latter series' initial run from 1963 to 1989, only to become an integral part of the series by its 2005 revival, perhaps says a lot about the way that television drama changed in the 1990s. Lucy Mazdon points out in her introduction to *The Contemporary Television Serial* that many modern dramas seem formulated to specifically invite discussion and analysis (not necessarily at an academic level, but between viewers of said series).[11]

What this also means is that television is no longer solely being treated as ephemeral in the way that it was in its earliest days. Although Andrew Crisell points out that the medium is still seen as disposable in some way, and certainly not treated with the reverence of film, drama is seen (and made) differently.[12] Modern dramas are often created with the eventual DVD or Blu-Ray box set in mind to some extent; some series even shoot special scenes just for the eventual home video release.[13] Successful series are reshown and exploited for a long time after their initial run, and programmes such as *Lost* invite their audience to dissect the episodes in the sort of minute detail that would be impossible with a single viewing. At the same time, television talent shows such as *American Idol* and *The X Factor* offer the ultimate in ephemera, as they rely on live viewing and the quick discarding of winners at the close of the final show, in readiness for the next year's crop of competitors. Money and audiences are gained through short term publicity and public interest. That such programmes sit comfortably alongside dramas that require more sustained effort indicates the most notable aspect of television across the past 75 years – its diversity.

While the stances of Baird and the BBC may be relatively clear-cut, the examination of press reports indicates something more interesting. We can see from the reports that there was certainly some interest in the system from the general public. Even the BBC's own feedback from Radiolympia indicated the extent to which there was a degree of curiosity surrounding this new technology. The apparent difficulty was in television breaking away from this pigeonholing as a curiosity and becoming desirable. There was an apparent assumption that television was inevitable but, while the London broadcasts from 1936 were a modest success, there was not a clamouring for sets. In the event it was the 1953 coronation of Queen Elizabeth II which brought television into the mainstream as it offered live pictures and sound of what was a monumentally important event to much of the public. The screening of the 1937 coronation parade of her father George VI took place in television's earliest period and failed to ignite the same amount of interest, no doubt due to geographical restrictions and the lack of relatively low-cost rental sets. However, this also indicates the extent to which television's potential was increasingly appreciated over a period of time, rather than arriving as a fully formed system already fully familiar to the general public. Television would take time to establish itself as an alternative to cinema or radio. It is telling that the role that would so invigorate demand for the medium was also the one that had most interested those members of the public who witnessed test transmissions at Radiolympia in August 1936. The lack of interest in the transmission of films, as opposed to live broadcasts, already highlighted that television's biggest asset was its ability to show events in people's living rooms as they took place. The interest surrounding the broadcast of the coronation would simply confirm this earlier indication. Television allowed viewers to participate in events of national interest in a manner that they never had before; there was more intimacy than that found in a sound-only broadcast or a later screening of a film of the event. The uniqueness of the invention, so often emphasised by Baird and his contemporaries, was finally being recognised.

What was clear from the reports is that the general public were aware of the general principle of television being a means of transmitting moving images alongside sound over a distance, to be received by a television set. The concept of television had been widely recognised long before the system became a practical reality, but once it became a practical reality there arose the issues of its practical use. Had costs of sets been comparable with some of the lower priced radio sets then it might well have been the case that television could have become radio's successor at this early point in its life, rather than a parallel medium. Television had to establish itself as a permanent fixture rather than a passing fad in order for most members of the public to even consider making the investment.

Content and Technology

Television did not launch with strict criteria of programming types. Instead there was a liberating expectation that there would inevitably be some failures alongside any successes, allowing flexibility in the medium's approach to programming and content. Despite the widespread indifference towards television there was no desire within the BBC for it to fade into obscurity, and so when it launched in November 1936 it was hoped that it would be the beginning of an ongoing medium rather than simply an experiment. Television also had to prove its viability, and by slowly but surely growing more confident with more ambitious productions and broadcasts it managed to ensure the longevity of the medium. Whereas Baird appeared to assume that television as a technology could hold the interest of the audience, the BBC, which had noted the indifferent reports at Radiolympia regarding content, understood that it needed to do more than simply invest in the technology. So it was that television broadcasts boasted increased complexity with the passage of time. It needed to demonstrate itself to be an ongoing and dynamic medium with a future. Gaining the permission to broadcast the full coronation ceremony was key to giving television the kudos that it was starting to deserve, but this did not occur until nearly two decades after the service's launch. For all of this time television had slowly, and quietly, built up a stronger portfolio of programmes and started to learn what could be successfully achieved and what could not. The technology had enabled television to hold a unique position within the media, but there were also limiting factors that influenced its development. The aesthetics of television have always been directly linked to the technology of the time. Technology has operated as not only an enabler for the transmission of moving images alongside sound but also as a limiting factor for not just the quality of the reproduced image but also the artistic quality of the television productions themselves. The previous section has demonstrated how the limitations of the cameras and small, oddly proportioned, studio spaces immediately limited the types of productions that could be broadcast.

Television technology, like many innovations, relied on there being the desire for it to come into being before it could actually be devised. Significantly, there was no pressing *need* for television, but simply a growing interest from some people. Even then, this interest was not always nurtured by the available evidence relating to the technology. However exciting television had seemed to some of the interested general public and press who had witnessed specially arranged demonstrations of the apparatus at one of the radio shows or even in Selfridge's, we have also seen the broad range of opinions regarding the quality or otherwise of the demonstrations prior to the service's launch. What some felt was near-miraculous, others found to be an impractical strain on the eyes.

Interest in television and its developments was far from universal. Was there an innate desire for 'radio with pictures', or was it only the emergence of the technology that resulted in any consideration of its merits? The latter certainly seems likely when we consider the BBC's ongoing problem with deciding what should feature on television once it had been given the task of launching the system. Prior to their involvement, and the inevitable raising of the public service question, television's potential had been even broader. There are remarkably few references to original material designed for television in the pre-1936 publicity material and press reports. Rather, television was normally seen more passively, as a means of relaying events rather than an originator of artistic material.

It was only when the BBC became involved that these issues of content were given an added urgency and a proper sense of direction, despite the fact that Baird had envisaged his company as providing content for the broadcasts, initially at least. It was still the case that the technology certainly held the main interest of the press and the public for some time before this introduction of content-based issues. Early reports of television demonstrations were happy to report the physical aspects of what they could see – a face, or head and shoulders, for example. However, they were rarely interested in any further details. This is understandable as the technology was unique and exciting and so of interest in itself, but when the new glow of the technology had worn off the medium became more and more concerned with wider issues of television's use and role in society. By the time of its launch there may not have been a large viewing public, but those tuning in would be demanding something with more longevity than the simple act of transmitting a moving picture – *any* moving picture – over a distance. We can perhaps see this from Mrs Bartlett's *Radio Times* article where she is far from being a passive viewer as she meticulously listed what she felt did and did not work on the fledgling service.[14] We should not mistake the general goodwill towards television as being an indication that viewers were happy with whatever was shown. Clearly there were favourites and programmes that were less popular. Note how the talks and Shakespeare excerpts (rather than full productions) were to be seen less often as television developed, an indication that Mrs Bartlett's views tallied with at least some of those at the BBC.[15] This does demonstrate that the audience was engaging with the content rather than simply consuming it regardless of it individual merit or suitability to the medium. It may even have been that the audience were the first to realise that television was far from 'radio with pictures'.

The Multiple Factors of Television's Early History

If there is one primary answer to the question of why British television developed in the way that it did in the period prior to the Second World War then it is a bureaucratic one. The fact that there was not a single person or body in charge of the medium's development from the beginning made a considerable impact on the way that the content and technology were developed. Several factions either wanted to run television or accepted that it was part of their duty to at least contribute to its establishment. The fact that Baird felt that he would be able to launch his own system separately from the sole existing broadcaster, only to find his efforts blocked following discussions with the Post Office and the BBC, exemplifies the extent to which external influence on each of those involved with developing television had an effect. The key to television's development was the work undertaken by different groups and individuals which were then combined to make just one standard system. While Baird had worked on the early technology and, more significantly in the long term, had drawn the public's attention to television through publicity, the government and the BBC were working to establish the specifics of a system while under pressure from the (predominately amateur) enthusiasts.

One of the reasons for breaking down this book into four main sections, each examining a different aspect of early television and its development, was to allow assessment of the differing attitudes of these individuals and bodies throughout the history of the medium's development. We have seen evidence of this diversity, as each chapter has shown that there were some significantly different approaches to television's role within broadcasting. The very concept of 'television' was fluid for many years, which highlights the importance of considering the very earliest years in their own right, rather than as part of the post-war development of television when the medium was more solidified. While such examinations are more difficult, being hindered by the lack of available material, they are substantially different and so demand individual treatment.

It is the examination of the approach to television from both institutions and individual enthusiasts which most clearly shows the diversity of problems and attitudes demonstrated in the years prior to the medium's official launch, however. There was a degree of indifference and ambivalence from some as the government and the BBC slowly understood their roles in the development of this entirely new technology. This was partly due to the complications that arose from the model adopted by radio, which meant that there was already a precedent for governmental interference in broadcasting. As a result, the Post Office and latterly the BBC realised the extent of their responsibility in controlling the development and instigation of the service. However, there was no sense of urgency within these larger organisations, and no particular drive to commence television transmissions as soon as possible. This contrasts with John Logie Baird's hasty attempts to get his own Television Company up and running as soon as possible, even while the technology was in its early stages. The effect that Baird's publicity machine may have had on the perception of television was explored in the previous sections, where changing moods of the general public, the institutions and the critics were seen. By demonstrating a working system of television Baird created the sense that television was now inevitable. While most realised that sets would be expensive for some time, it seemed that 'radio with pictures' was on the horizon. To have ignored this presumption would have been difficult for the BBC in particular once it became clear that they were the expected guardians of the fledgling technology. Perhaps it was the work of Baird and his cohorts that led to the system beginning as early as it did; however, it is almost certainly the case that it was the slower and more methodical approach of the BBC that ensured the medium's longevity. While the technology has continued to be improved and refined over the seventy years of transmissions, the corporation's tests and experimentation meant that the television system that went on air in 1936 was of sufficient quality to be the predominant system in the UK for the next forty years.

These opposing forces, of sheer determination and apathy, formed the basis of much of the television system in the UK. However, it was more than this. The very fact that a public corporation had been invested with the responsibility of setting up the new medium as a public service shaped the broader decisions made about television in the UK. There was a definite aim that the system should be the best it could be, even going as far as to allow both the Baird and the Marconi-EMI systems to run on alternate weeks in the opening months. Retrospectively, it may appear that this decision is a summation of the perils of public bodies making a clear decision between two distinct options. A desire to please the greatest number of people, and so serve as much of the public as possible in the spirit of public service, resulted in a less impressive system transmitting every second week for three months despite its technical inferiority and the difficulty of the technology required to transmit it compared to Marconi-EMI.

If Baird felt that he was in the middle of a bureaucratic nightmare then this was no conspiracy; rather it was the case that no-one was automatically assigned to deal with such issues, and this assignation took time. However, the result of this careful consideration meant that the combination of the BBC's existing broadcasting infrastructure with Baird's own determination led to the United Kingdom leading the world with its 'high definition' service. It is the case that the corporation's public service remit would go on to shape the programming, but their involvement goes beyond this. The BBC offered television stability by becoming the purveyor of this fledgling system. By becoming synonymous with the new system the corporation immediately demonstrated to the wider public that this new medium was not simply a brief experiment or a low-key curiosity. The word 'experiment' was linked with many of the trials and even the early official broadcasts, and it indicated to the potential audience that the system was not ready or was just for those who were already involved. It implied an exclusivity of sorts, as did the high price tag of sets. It is also the case that the method of funding broadcasts through the licence fee furnished television with breathing space that simply would not have been possible with a commercial broadcaster, regardless of quality of programming or good intentions. The initially low uptake of television sets would have rendered such private investment unsustainable unless it was either a long-term investment, or the costs of receivers could be lowered considerably in order to encourage purchases. Television needed to settle in and establish itself as a serious contender in the entertainment and information dissemination marketplace. Once it had done so, the public could start to have more confidence in its long-term future.

Methods of Delivery

Although the basics of transmission and receiving technology have undergone only small scale modification in the last 80 years (most notably with the relatively recent proliferation of flat screen televisions, taking over from the near-century old CRT technology) this underplays the extent to which technological advances have changed the medium. Perhaps most important now is the method of delivery, not the mechanics of it. The BBC's on-demand iPlayer service was originally launched as a way to allow those in the United Kingdom to view most BBC content for a short time after broadcast (generally seven days). By mid-2010 the most requested programme on the service was an episode of *Doctor Who*, with over two million views, more than a fifth of the ten million who had watched the show the traditional way.[16]

Even ITV, a broadcaster that currently relies on traditional television viewing for its revenue, has embraced the new methods of delivery, albeit slightly inconsistently. In late 2008 the ITV website premiered the first episode of their highly publicised foray into teen television, *Britannia High,* as part of a 'cross platform launch'.[17] The all-singing all-dancing storylines failed to capture the imagination of the public, and the series was not a popular or critical success.[18] Perhaps stung by this, ITV have not gone on to use the website regularly to premiere material since. It should not be forgotten just how new this method of distribution is, and how rapidly it has become accepted as an intrinsic part of television viewing. As John Ellis has pointed out, 'By the end of the twentieth century, television had left behind the age of scarcity. [...] Television moved into an era of availability, where a choice of pre-scheduled services existed at every moment of the day and night. An era of plenty, in which choice would not depend upon the schedules of television transmission, had been envisaged during this period, but remained a commercial dream at the end of the century.'[19] This is now the reality for the future of broadcasting, as on-demand television moves from being a niche product to a commonplace mode of delivery via both computers and television sets.

Final Conclusions

The research that has explored this period has clearly shown that early television can no longer be overlooked as the lesser beginnings of a global medium, and although progress is slow there is increasing appreciation of its significance and the value of examining it. I sympathise with Charles Barr's issue with the lack of further development of early television study ever since he first appealed for more attention to be paid to it thirty years ago. This shares Jason Jacobs' and John Caughie's stance that there is value in the analysis of a period that may be more challenging to research but can offer substantial rewards, such is the diversity and interest of the material waiting to be uncovered and analysed. This is especially true when one considers the extent to which the various national systems of television across the globe differed from the established models, showcasing the influence of the British broadcasts.

The focus of this book has not only allowed us to understand the behind the scenes rationale for television's development, but also indicated the variety of programming on the fledgling service. Early television programming was simultaneously ambitious and limited. It was constrained by the practical environments of both studio space and its own apparatus. This period showcased a larger variety of programming than it is usually given credit for, although this included non-original programming (newsreels and cartoons, for example), which is often overlooked.

By analysing the key developments and looking at them in an almost parallel manner it is clear how the different factors often crossed paths only late in television's development. The fact that Baird was working on his television system even before the BBC was established as a public corporation just helps to indicate how quickly the landscape of broadcasting in the UK changed. For all of these important developments amongst the bodies involved with television's development, it may well have been that the key development in television history in this country was actually a gradual one, as the general public simply found themselves getting used to the idea of television transmissions. Was this the actual stumbling block to its development, a lack of understanding or interest in the medium? We should not underestimate the importance of familiarity to television's ongoing development, an element fuelled almost entirely by Baird and his relationship with the press. The popular press was understandably unconcerned with the intricacies of the different television systems, and so the eventual superseding of Baird's system by Marconi-EMI's was unimportant to the wider perception of the system. The important fact was that television had become a fixture of the perceived future broadcasting plans of the country, originating in Baird's publicity drives but being picked up by the BBC's involvement with the system and the resulting ongoing experimental broadcasts.

On 23 December 1938 *The Times* published an article 'Two Years of Television' which examined the developments in the medium and the public perception of it since its launch. 'The public have suddenly become interested in television'[20] stated the article, indicating that the long game played by the BBC and the government was beginning to pay off. That *The Times* even felt it necessary to honour a little more than two years of a limited service indicates that television did not just quietly operate from the period from its launch until its popular breakthrough in the 1950s; attention was still being paid to it and it had not been forgotten. By not demanding immediate results and running a limited, some say experimental, service in just one region it allowed familiarity with the very concept to grow gradually rather than having the medium launch nationally before it, or the public, were ready.

The period off air during the Second World War did not result in major changes to the television system upon its return in 1946, either artistically or technically. Programming continued its upward trajectory in terms of ambition, with an increase in drama and what seem to be more 'prestige' productions, but there was still room for more abstract filler material. The more bizarre acts were not extinct, as the fifteen minute broadcast of 'Koringa – the sensational circus performer with her crocodile' on the second day of the system's return demonstrated.[21] However, comparing the schedules with those of 1936 and 1937 shows that programming had become more consistent and original over time and was continuing to do so. Television was evolving, very slowly, as it has continued to do throughout its history. As programming today is subtly different from that of a decade ago, so it was then, even if the fundamentals of the service remained unchanged.

The adaptation of the short story *The Silence of the Sea* on that first night of the service's reappearance, 7 June 1946, may well have been a sign of television's slow emergence as an art form in its own right. While the story itself was not original to television, having been written as a piece of French Resistance underground fiction by 'Vercors' (a pseudonym for Jean Bruller), an adaptation had not previously appeared elsewhere, and of all the pieces of television lost in the ether due to the medium's ephemeral nature, this one is particularly missed. Bruller's story was published and distributed in the underground of occupied France in 1942 and, in the most basic terms, told the story of a French man and his niece forced to take in a German soldier whom they ignore throughout his six month stay, although he continues to speak to them about his respect for their country. After a trip to Paris the soldier returns disillusioned with Germany's vision for Europe. He is soon forced to leave, going 'off to hell', still unacknowledged by the family. Such a synopsis cannot convey the delicate nature of the very brief story, and it certainly left an impression on one viewer, 25 year old Peter Sallis, who would later go on to great success as a character actor. Writing in his autobiography Sallis recalls watching the play, a memory that has stayed with him for over sixty years:

> After the war [...] I remember the first play that was done on television. *The Silence of the Sea*, which starred Kenneth More, about a German who had been given shelter by a French couple [...] the three of them spent their time in hiding really, or at least hiding the German, and when it came to the end of the war they were able to let him go. It sounds pretty simple, put like that, but it was a very touching and moving play and many years later when I was working with Kenny More, I told him I had seen it and he could hardly believe it. I think I was the only person, apart from close members of his family, who had ever seen *The Silence of the Sea*.[22]

Perhaps it was a shame that, as Sallis points out, there were so few people watching the medium to appreciate the times when the programming was innovative and offered something that that had not been seen on film or heard on the radio. Television was putting on brave productions that could be artistic and touching, but few were able to see it. The medium took years to find its feet, but at least its soft launch had enabled many of the refinements to be carried out away from the public view. The extent of these subtle revisions should not be understated.

The last word should go to Kenneth Adam, who was to become Controller of Programmes for BBC television from 1957 to 1961, but had also worked as a journalist and in radio. Writing for the *Radio Times* in April 1937 he considers the television service to that point and speculates on its future.

> I suppose in time to come when [presenters] Leslie Mitchell has white hair and Miss Cowell and Miss Bligh are nice old ladies and all sorts of wonders march into our lifesize television screens, we shall laugh at the primitiveness of these early television programmes. But I for one shall be sorry when they lose their freshness and simplicity and become elaborate and water-tight, and Cabinet ministers no longer get black faces like [blackface performer] Eddie Cantor when the brilliance goes wrong.[23]

It may have been 'primitive', but television never completely moved away from its roots, and the global medium that we have today owes a great deal to this earliest period. Television has infiltrated and shaped popular culture throughout the globe at a rapid pace, with programming shared between countries. News events can be seen live worldwide, satellite link ups giving access to information in most countries. Certainly the medium's early years were simplistic by these modern day standards, but its continued ambition allowed the medium to eventually reach unparalleled heights. The programme content in this period may have been many things (not least quirky, inconsistent and inexpensive) but it was not dull. What could have been a medium interested solely in the highbrow or 'worthy' was instead liberal in its approach to public service broadcasting. If television was somewhat lacking in co-ordination and structure when it started, with abrupt changes of tone throughout the short schedules each afternoon and evening, this may have been partly due to not having been created by a single entity. Certainly it led to the distinctiveness of the UK system, based around the public service model, while the backing of the BBC also allowed time for television to develop its own voice rather than find itself launched as an explicitly commercial model with a heavy emphasis on finding ways to raise revenue. With its muddled origins perhaps it was this diversity, or this flexibility, that led to its ubiquity today.

Bibliography

[ANON.] 'Au Revoir, Television' in *BBC Handbook 1940*.

[ANON.] 'Coronation News for Televiewers', in *Radio Times (Television Supplement)* 30 April 1937.

[ANON.] 'Television' in *BBC Annual 1936*.

[ANON.] 'Television' in *BBC Annual 1937*.

[ANON.] 'Television in 1938' in *BBC Handbook 1939*.

[ANON.] 'Television To-Day' in *BBC Handbook 1938*.

ABRAMSON, ALBERT. *Electronic Motion Pictures: History of the Television Camera* (New York: Arno Press, 1974).

ABRAMSON, ALBERT. *The History of Television, 1880 to 1941* (Jefferson: McFarland and Co. Inc, 1988).

ABRAMSON, ALBERT. *The History of Television, 1942 to 2000* (Jefferson: McFarland & Co, 2003).

ABRAMSON, ALBERT. *Zworykin: Pioneer of Television* (Urbana: University of Illinois Press, 1995).

ADAM, KENNETH. 'Television Memories – Already!' in *Radio Times (Television Supplement)* 16 April 1937.

ALEXANDER, ROBERT CHARLES. *The Inventor of Stereo: The Life and Works of Alan Dower Blumlein* (Oxford: Focal Press, 1999).

ALKON, PAUL K. *Science Fiction Before 1900* (New York: Routledge, 2002).

ARMES, ROY. *On Video* (London: Routledge, 1988).

BAIRD, JOHN LOGIE. *Television and Me* (Edinburgh: Mercat Press, Ltd, 2004 (Revised Edition).

BAIRD, JOHN LOGIE. 'Television in 1932' in *BBC Yearbook 1933*.

BALIO, TINO (ed.). *Hollywood in the Age of Television* (London: Unwin Hyman, 1990).

BARNOUW, ERIK. *A History of Broadcasting in the United States* (vol. 1) (Oxford: Oxford University Press, 1966).

BARNOUW, ERIK. *A History of Broadcasting in the United States* (vol.2) (Oxford: Oxford University Press, 1968).

BARR, CHARLES. '"They Think It's All Over": The Dramatic Legacy of Live television', in J. Hill and M. McLoone (eds), *Big Picture, Small Screens: The Relations Between Film and Television* (Luton: University of Luton Press, 1997).

BARTLETT, JEAN. 'Views of a Viewer', in *Radio Times*, 4 June 1937.

BARWISE, PATRICK, AND EHRENBERG, ANDREW. *Television and its Audience* (London: Sage Publications, 1988).

BAX, PETER. 'Scenery for Television', in *Radio Times (Television Supplement)*, 28 May 1937.

BEADLE, SIR GERALD. *Television: A Critical Review* (London: Allen & Unwin; 1963).

BIGNELL, JONATHAN. *An Introduction to Television Studies* (London: Routledge, 2003).

BIGNELL, JONATHAN AND LACEY, STEPHEN (eds.) *Popular Television Drama* (Manchester: Manchester University Press, 2005).

BIGNELL, JONATHAN, AND ANDREAS FICKERS (eds.) *A European Television History* (Oxford: Blackwell, 2008).

BLAKESTON, OSWELL. 'Telecinema' in *Close Up* Vol.VI (1) July 1930.

BLUMLER, JAY, AND ELIHU KATZ. *The Uses of Mass Communications, current perspectives on gratifications research* (Beverly Hills: Sage, 1974).

BODDY, WILLIAM. *Fifties Television: The Industry & its Critics* (Urbana: University of Illinois Press, 1993).

BODDY, WILLIAM. 'The Beginnings of American Television', in Anthony Smith (ed.) *Television: An International History (Second Edition)* (Oxford: Oxford University Press, 1998).

BOOTH, DOUGLAS. *Australian Beach Cultures* (London: Routledge, 2001).

BRANDT, GEORGE W. *British Television Drama* (Cambridge: Cambridge University Press, 1981).

BRANSTON, GILL. 'Histories of British Television', in C. Geraghty and D. Lusted (eds.), *The Television Studies Book* (London: Arnold, 1998).

BRIGGS, ASA. *The BBC – The First Fifty Years* (Oxford: Oxford University Press, 1985).

BRIGGS, ASA. *The History of British Broadcasting in the United Kingdom* vol. I: The Birth of Broadcasting (Oxford: Oxford University Press, 1961).

BRIGGS, ASA. *The History of British Broadcasting in the United Kingdom* vol. II: The Golden Age of Wireless (Oxford: Oxford University Press, 1965).

BRIGGS, ASA. *The History of British Broadcasting in the United Kingdom* vol. III: The War of Words (Oxford: Oxford University Press, 1970).

BRIGGS, ASA. *The History of British Broadcasting in the United Kingdom* vol. IV: Sound and Vision (Oxford: Oxford University Press, 1979).

BRIGGS, ASA, AND PETER BURKE. *A Social History of the Media* (Cambridge: Polity Press, 2005 (Second Edition).

BRUCE, ROBERT V. *Bell: Alexander Graham Bell and the Conquest of Solitude* (London: Cornell University Press, 1973).

BRUNSDON, CHARLOTTE. 'What is the "Television" of Television Studies?', in Horace Newcomb (ed.) *Television: The Critical View (Sixth Edition)* (Oxford: Oxford University Press, 2000).

BRYAN, GEORGE S. *Edison: The Man and His Work* (London: Alfred A. Knopp, 1926).

BURNS, R.W. *British Television – The Formative Years* (London: Peter Peregrinus Ltd, 1986).

BURNS, R.W. *Communications: An International History of the Formative Years* (London: Institute of Electrical Engineers, 2004).

BURNS, R.W. *John Logie Baird – Television Pioneer* (London: Institute of Electrical Engineers, 2000).

BURNS, R.W. *Television – An International History of the Formative Years* (London: The Institution of Engineering and Technology, 1998).

BURNS, T. *The BBC: Public Institution & Private World* (London: Macmillan, 1977).

BUTLER, LAWRENCE, AND HARRIET JONES (eds). *Britain in the Twentieth Century (1900–1939)* (Oxford: Heinemann, 1994).

CAIN, JOHN. *The BBC: 70 Years of Broadcasting* (London: BBC, 1992).

CALDWELL, J.T. *Televisuality* (New Brunswick: Rutgers University Press, 1995).

CALDWELL, JOHN THORNTON (ed.). *Theories of the New Media: A Historical Perspective* (London: Athlone, 2000).

CARROLL, N. *Theorising the Moving Image* (Cambridge: Cambridge University Press, 1996).

CAUGHIE, JOHN. 'Before the Golden Age: Early Television Drama', in J. Corner (ed.), *Popular Television in Britain* (London: BFI Publishing, 1991).

CAUGHIE, JOHN. *Television Drama: Realism, Modernism and British Culture* (Oxford: Oxford University Press, 2000).

CHALABY, JEAN K. *Transnational Television Worldwide* (London: I.B. Tauris, 2005)..

CHUMBLEY, STEPHEN, AND HARRY HALL. *Timeline of the Twentieth Century* (London: Haus Publishing, 2006).

COASE, R.H. *British Broadcasting: A Study in Monopoly* (London : London School of Economics and Political Science, 1950).

COCK, GERALD. 'Long Shot, Alexandra Palace' in *Ariel* no.3 (Dec 1936).

COCK, GERALD. 'Televising the Coronation Procession' in *Radio Times*, 23 April 1937.

COLEMAN, JAMES A., AND BRIGITTE ROLLET (eds) *Television in Europe* (Exeter: Intellect Books, 1997).

COOKE, LEZ. *British Television Drama – A History* (London: BFI Publishing, 2003).

CORNER, JOHN. *Critical Ideas in Television Studies* (Oxford: Oxford University Press, 1999).

CORNER, JOHN. *Popular Television in Britain* (London: BFI, 1991).

CORNER, JOHN. 'Reappraising Reception: Aims, Concepts & Methods', in J. Curran and M. Gurevitch (eds.) *Mass Media and Society* (London: Arnold, 1996).

CORNER, JOHN, AND JEREMY HAWTHORN (eds.). *Communication Studies* (London: Arnold, 1993).

CRISELL, ANDREW. *An Introductory History of British Broadcasting* (London: Routledge, 2002).

CRISELL, ANDREW. *A Study of Modern Television* (Basingstoke: Palgrave Macmillan, 2006).

CURRAN, JAMES, AND MICHAEL GUREVITCH. *Mass Media and Society (2nd Ed)* (London: Arnold, 1996).

CURRAN, JAMES, AND JEAN SEATON. *Power Without Responsibility* (London: Routledge, 1988).

CURRIE, TONY. *The Radio Times Story* (Tiverton: Kelly Publications, 2001).

CURRIE, TONY. *A Concise History of British Television 1930–2000* (Tiverton: Kelly Publications, 2004).

DAVIES, ANDREW. 'Cinema and Broadcasting', in Paul Johnson (ed.) *20 Century Britain: Economic, Social and Cultural Change* (London: Longman, 1994).

DAVIS, ANTHONY. *Television: The First Forty Years* (London: Severn House Publishers, 1976).

DAVIS, ANTHONY. *Television: Here is the News* (London: Independent Television Books, 1977).

DAVIS, JOHN. *A History of Britain, 1885–1939* (Basingstoke: Macmillan, 1999).

DAY-LEWIS, SEAN. *TV Heaven: A Review of British Television from the 1930s to the 1990s* (London: Channel Four Television).

DESMOND, SHAW. 'Television and the Films' in *Television*, September 1928.

DINSDALE, ALFRED. *First Principles of Television* (London : Chapman & Hall, 1932).

DINSDALE, ALFRED. *Television* (London: Sir Isaac Pitman & Sons, 1926).

DINSDALE, ALFRED. *Television (Revised edn)* (London: Television Press Ltd., 1928).

DOUGLAS, SUSAN J. *Inventing American Broadcasting, 1899–1922* (Baltimore: John Hopkins University Press, 1987).

DOWN, RICHARD, AND CHRISTOPHER PERRY (eds). *The British Television Drama Research Guide* (Dudley: Kaleidoscope, 1997).

DUNN, KATE. *Do Not Adjust Your Set: The Early Days of Live Television* (London: John Murray, 2003).

ECKERSLEY, MYLES. *Prospero's Wireless* (Romsey: Myles Books, 1999).

EDGERTON, GARY R. *The Columbia History of American Television* (New York: Columbia University Press, 2007).

ELLIS, JOHN. *Seeing Things: Television in the Age of Uncertainty* (London: I.B. Tauris, 2000).

ELSNER, MONIKA, THOMAS MÜLLER AND PETER SPANGENBERG. 'The Early History of German Television: The Slow Development of a Fast Medium', in *Historical Journal of Film, Radio and Television* vol.10 (2), 1990.

EMMERSON, ANDREW. *Old Television* (Princes Risborough: Shire Publications Ltd, 1998).

ENTICKNAP, LEO, AND GRAHAM DOUGLAS. *Moving Image Technology* (London: Wallflower Press, 2005).

FANTHOME, CHRISTINE. *Channel 5: The Early Years* (Luton: University of Luton Press, 2003).

FELIX, EDGAR H., *Television – Its Methods and Uses* (London & New York: McGraw-Hill, 1931).

FIDDY, DICK. *Missing Believed Wiped* (London: BFI Publishing, 2001).

FISKE, JOHN. *Television Culture* (London: Methuen, 1987).

FISKE, JOHN, AND JOHN HARTLEY. *Reading Television* (London: Methuen & Co. Ltd, 1978).

FORNAS, JOHAN. *Cultural Theory and Late Modernity* (London: Sage, 1995).

FRIEDBERG, ANNE. *Window Shopping – Cinema and the Postmodern* (Berkeley: University of California Press, 1994).

FULTON, ROGER. *The Encyclopedia of TV Science Fiction* (London: Boxtree, 1995).

GERAGHTY, CHRISTINE, AND DAVID LUSTED. *The Television Studies Book* (London: Arnold Press, 1997).

GLINSKY, ALBERT. *Theremin: Ether Music and Espionage* (Urbana: University of Illinois Press, 2000).

GOLDIE, GRACE WYNDHAM. *Facing The Nation – Television and Politics 1936–1976* (London: The Bodley Head, 1977).

GOLDSMITH, MIKE. *John Logie Baird (Scientists Who Made History)* (London: Raintree, 2002).

GOODWIN, ANDREW, AND GARRY WHANNEL, (eds). *Understanding Television* (London: Routledge, 1990).

GORHAM, MAURICE. *Broadcasting and Television Since 1900* (London: Andrew Dakers, 1952).

GRAMSCI, ANTONIO. *Selections From Cultural Writings* [David Forgacs and Geoffrey Nowell-Smith, (eds), William Boelhower(trans.)] (London: Lawrence and Wishart, 1985).

HARBORD, JANE, AND JEFF WRIGHT. *40 Years of British Television* (London: Boxtree, 1995).

HARTLEY, JOHN. *Uses of Television* (London: Routledge, 1999).

HEIDE, MARGARET. *Television, Culture and Women's Lives* (Phil: University of Pennsylvania Press, 1995).

HENNESSEY, BRIAN. *Savoy Hill: The Early Years of British Broadcasting* (Romford: Ian Henry, 1996).

HERBERT, STEPHEN (ed.). *A History of Early TV* (3 Volumes) (London: Routledge, 2004).

HICKAN, TOM. *What Did You Do in the War, Auntie?* (London: BBC, 1995).

HILLIARD, ROBERT L., AND MICHAEL C. KEITH. *The Broadcasting Century and Beyond: A Biography of American Broadcasting* (Burlington: Focal Press, 2010).

HILMES, MICHELE. *The Television History Book* (London: BFI Publishing, 2003).

HOLMES, SU. *British TV and Film Culture in the 1950s* (Bristol: Intellect, 2005).

HOOD, STUART. *On Television* (London: Pluto Press, 1980).

HUBERT, PHILIP G. *Men of Achievement – Inventors* (London: Sampson Low, Marston & Company Limited, 1894 (originally published in the US by Charles Scribner's Sons, 1893).

HUGHES, PATRICK. 'Today's Television, Tomorrow's World', in A. Goodwin and G. Whannel (eds), *Understanding Television* (London: Routledge, 1990).

JACOBS, JASON. *The Intimate Screen* (Oxford: Oxford University Press, 2000).

JAMES, EDWARD. *Science Fiction in the 20 Century* (Oxford: Oxford University Press, 1994).

JAMES, EDWARD, AND FARAH MENDLESOHN. *The Cambridge Companion to Science Fiction* (Cambridge: Cambridge University Press, 2003).

JENKINS, C. FRANCIS. *Vision By Radio* (Washington, D.C.: Jenkins Laboratories, 1925).

JOHNSON, CATHERINE. 'Exploiting the Intimate Screen', in Janet Thumin (ed.) *Small Screens Big Ideas* (London: I.B. Tauris, 2002).

JOHNSON, PAUL (ed.). *20 Century Britain: Economic, Social and Cultural Change* (London: Longman, 1994).

JONES, FRANCIS ARTHUR. *Thomas Alva Edison – An Intimate Record* (Revised Edition) (London: Hodder & Stoughton Ltd, 1924).

KAMM, ANTHONY, AND MICHAEL BAIRD. *John Logie Baird: A Life* (Edinburgh: National Museums of Scotland, 2002).

KAPLAN, A.E. *Regarding Television* (Los Angeles: AFI/University Publications of America (1983).

KASZARSKI, RICHARD. *Hollywood on the Hudson* (New Brunswick: Rutgers University Press, 2008).

KUHN, RAYMOND. *The Media in France* (London: Routledge, 1994).

LACEY, STEPHEN. 'Some Thoughts on Television History and Historiography: A British Perspective', in *Critical Studies in Television* vol.1 (1) 2006, pp.2–12.

LANCASTER, BILL. *The Department Store – A Social History* (Leicester: Leicester University Press, 1995).

LANG, KURT AND GLADYS. 'The Unique Perspective of Television', in J. Corner and J. Hawthorn (eds) *Communication Studies* (London: Arnold, 1993).

LAYBOURN, KEITH (ed.). *Modern Britain Since 1906* (London: I.B. Tauris, 1999).

LAZELL, DAVID. *What's On The Box?* (Cheltenham: Evergreen, 1991).

LEISHMAN, MARISTA. *My Father: Reith of the BBC* (Edinburgh: St Andrew Press, 2006).

MAGOUN, ALEXANDER B. *Television: The Life Story of a Technology* (Westport, Connecticut: Greenwood Press, 2007).

MARWICK, ARTHUR. *A History of the Modern British Isles 1914–1999* (Oxford: Blackwell Publishers, 2000).

MASTERS, ANTHONY. *Pictures Through the Air: John Logie Baird (Super Scientists series)* (London: Hodder Wayland, 2001).

MAZDON, LUCY, AND MICHAEL HAMMOND (eds) *The Contemporary Television Series* (Edinburgh: Edinburgh University Press, 2005).

MCARTHUR, TOM, AND PETER WADDELL. *Vision Warrior* (Kirkwall: The Orkney Press, 1990).

MCLEAN, DONALD F. *Restoring Baird's Image* (London: Institute of Electrical Engineers, 2000).

MCLEAN, DONALD F. *The Dawn of Television Remembered (CD-ROM)* (London: TV Dawn, 2005).

MCLOONE, MARTIN. 'Boxed In?: The Aesthetics of Film and Television', in J. Hill and M. McLoone (eds.), *Big Picture, Small Screen: The Relations Between Film and Television* (Luton: John Libbey Media, 1997).

MIALL, LEONARD. *The Future of BBC Television* (London: BBC, 1962).

MORLEY, DAVID. *Television, Audiences and Cultural Studies* (London: Routledge, 1992).

MOSELEY, SYDNEY. *John Baird* (London: Odhams Press, 1952).

MOSELEY, SYDNEY. *The Private Diaries of Sydney Moseley* (London: Max Parrish, 1960).

MOUSSEAU, JACQUES, AND CHRISTIAN BROCHAND. *Histoire De La Télévision Française* (Paris: Fernand Nathan, 1982).

MURDOCK, GRAHAM. 'Culture, Services, Knowledge' in: Janet Wasko (ed.) *A Companion to Television* (Oxford: Blackwell, 2005).

NEWCOMB, HORACE (ed.). *Television – The Critical View* (Oxford: Oxford University Press, 1976 & 1994).

NEWCOMB, HORACE, AND PAUL M. HIRSCH. 'Television as a Cultural Forum', in H. Newcomb (ed.) *Television – The Critical View* (Oxford: Oxford University Press, 1994)).

NORDEN, DENIS. *Coming to you Live! Behind the Scenes Memories of Forties and Fifties Television* (London: Methuen, 1985).

NORMAN, BRUCE. *Here's Looking at You* (London: Royal Television Society, 1984).

PAULU, BURTON. *British Broadcasting* (Minneapolis: University of Minnesota Press, 1956).

PAULU, BURTON. *Television and Radio in the United Kingom* (Basingstoke: Palgrave Macmillan, 1981).

PIRANDELLO, LUIGI. [Frederick May (trans.)] 'The Man With The Flower In His Mouth' in *Short Stories* (Oxford: Oxford University Press, 1975).

REID, STRUAN. *John Logie Baird* (Groundbreakers) (Oxford: Heinemann, 2000).

REITH, JOHN. *Into the Wind* (London: Hodder & Stoughton, 1949).

REITH, JOHN. [Charles Stuart (ed.)] *The Reith Diaries* (London, Collins, 1975).

REYNOLDS, ROBIN. 'When We Knew What Was Good For Them' in *Ariel*, 3 October 2006.

RICHARDS, JEFFREY. 'Cinemagoing in Worktown' in *Historical Journal of Film, Radio and Television*, June 1994.

ROBERTS, ADAM. *Science Fiction* (London: Routledge, 2000).

ROBERTS, GRAHAM; TAYLOR, PHILIP M. *The Historian, Television and Television History* (Luton: University of Luton Press, 2001).

ROBIDA, ALBERT. *Le Vingtième Siècle (The Twentieth Century)* (Paris: Georges Decaux, 1883).

ROBSON, NEIL. 'Living Pictures out of Space: The Forlorn Hopes for Television in pre-1939 London', in *Historical Journal of Film, Radio and Television* vol.24 (2), 2004.

ROLLET, BRIGITTE. 'Television in France', in James A. Coleman and Brigitte Rollet (eds) *Television in Europe* (Exeter: Intellect, 1997).

ROWLAND, JOHN. *The Television Man – The Story of John L. Baird* (London: Lutterworth Press, 1966).

SALLIS, PETER. *Fading Into the Limelight* (London: Orion, 2006).

SAMUEL, RAPHAEL. *Island Stories* (London: Verso, 1998).

SANDFORD, JOHN. 'Television in Germany', in James A. Coleman and Brigitte Rollet (eds) *Television in Europe* (Exeter: Intellect, 1997).

SCANNELL, PADDY. 'Public Service Broadcasting: The History of a Concept', in: A. Goodwin and G. Whannel (eds), *Understanding Television* (London: Routledge, 1990).

SCANNELL, PADDY, AND DAVID CARDIFF. *A Social History of British Broadcasting 1922–1939* (Oxford: Blackwell Publishing, 1991).

SCHIVELBUSCH, WOLFGANG. *The Railway Journey* (Berkeley: University of California Press, 1977).

SCHWARTZ, EVAN I. *The Last Lone Inventor* (New York: Harper Collins, 2002).

SEITHER, ELLEN. *Television and New Media Audiences* (Oxford: Oxford University Press, 1999).

SEYMOUR-URE, COLIN. *The British Press and Broadcasting Since 1945* (Oxford: Blackwell, 1996 (Second Edition).

SHAW, TONY. *British Cinema and the Cold War* (London: I.B. Tauris, 2006).

SHELDON, H. HORTON, AND EDGAR NORMAN GRISEWOOD. *Television – Present Methods of Picture Transmission* (London : Library Press Ltd., 1929).

SHIERS, GEORGE. *Early Television: A Bibliographic Guide to 1940* (London: Garland Publishing, 1997).

SIEPMANN, CHARLES A. *Radio, Television and Society* (Oxford: Oxford University Press, 1950).

SILVEY, ROBERT. *Reflections on the Impact of Broadcasting* (London: BBC, 1963).

SILVEY, ROBERT. *Who's Listening: The Story of BBC Audience Research* (London: Allen & Unwin, 1974).

SLOTTEN, HUGH RICHARD. *Radio's Hidden Voice: The Origins of Public Broadcasting in the United States* (Urbana: University of Illinois Press, 2009).

SMITH, ANTHONY (ed.). *Television – An International History* (Oxford: Oxford University Press, 1995).

SMITH, ANTHONY (ed.) *Television: An International History* (2nd edn) (Oxford: Oxford University Press, 1998).

TAYLOR, A.J.P. *English History, 1914–1945* (Oxford: Oxford University Press, 1965).

THORNHAM, SUE, AND TONY PURVIS. *Television Drama* (London: Palgrave Macmillan, 2005).

THORPE, ANDREW. *Britain in the 1930s* (Oxford: Blackwell Publishers, 1992).

TIERNEY, C. 'The Future of Television' in *Television*, February 1929.

TILTMAN, RONALD F. *Baird of Television* (London: Seeley Service Ltd, 1933).

THUMIM, JANET (ed.). *Small Screens, Big Ideas* (London: I.B. Tauris, 2002).

TONESKI, WILLIAM J. 'How We Staged the World's First Television Plays', in *Historical Journal of Film, Radio and Television* vol.2 (2), 1982).

VAHIMAGI, TISE. *British Television* (Oxford: Oxford University Press, 1996).

VAN DYCK, J.G.R. *La Télévision Experimentale* (Paris: Dunod, 1932).

VAUGHAN, DAI. *BFI Television Monograph – Television Documentary Usage* (London: The British Film Institute Education Advisory Service, 1976).

VON SCHILLING, JIM. *The Magic Window: American Television 1939 – 1953* (London: Routledge, 2002).

WAGHORN, THOMAS. *The Bitter Bitter Cry of Outcast Inventors* (London: The Strand Publishing Company, 1885).

WASKO, JANET (ed.). *A Companion to Television* (Oxford: Blackwell Publishing, 2005).

WEDELL, GEORGE, AND BRYAN LUCKHAM. *Television at the Crossroads* (London: Palgrave, 2001).

WIETEN, JAN, Graham Murdock and Peter Dahlgren (eds). *Television Across Europe: A Comparative Introduction* (London: Sage, 2000).

WILLIAMS, RAYMOND. *Television – Technology and Cultural Form* (London: Routledge, 1990).

WINSTON, BRIAN. *Media, Technology and Society* (London: Routledge, 1998).

WOOD, JAMES. *History of International Broadcasting* (London: Peter Peregrinus, 1992).

WOODHEAD, LINDY. *Shopping, Seduction and Mr Selfridge* (London: Profile, 2007).

ZIELINSKI, SIEGFRIED. *Audiovisions – Cinema and Television as Entr'actes in History* (Amsterdam: Amsterdam University Press, 1999).

Journals and Periodicals

IN-DEPTH ARTICLES ARE REFERENCED ABOVE.

Amateur Wireless
Ariel
BBC Annual/Yearbook
Birmingham Daily Mail
Close Up
Daily Chronicle
Daily Express
Daily Graphic
Daily Herald
Daily Mail
Daily Mirror
Daily News
Daily Star
Daily Telegraph
English Mechanic and World of Science
Evening Standard
Glasgow Herald
Kinematograph Weekly
The Listener
Manchester Guardian
Media, Culture and Society
Monthly Review
Morning Post
Moving Picture News
Nature
New York Times
The Observer
The People
Popular Science Monthly
Popular Wireless
Radio Times
Scientific American
The Scotsman
The Spectator
Sunday Express
Sunday Times
Television
The Times
Westminster Gazette
Yorkshire Post

Archive Sources

BBC Written Archive Centre:

All reproduction courtesy The BBC Written Archive Centre.

S69 (Special file; Gas Light & Coke Company)
T/5/443 (*R.U.R.*)
T/12/304 (*Puppet Parade*)
T/13/11 (*Checkmate*)
T/16/42/1 to 8 (Baird Television)
T/16/65 (Marconi-EMI)
T/16/67 (Experimental systems 1928–9)
T/16/86 (John Baird policy)
T/16/214/1-2 (General Television Developments, 1928–36)
T/23/35/1 (TV Publicity – General)
T/23/77/1 & 2 (Radiolympia 1936)

Post Office Archives:

All reproduction courtesy The British Postal Museum & Archive.

POST 33/3852-3 (Baird system)
POST 33/5141 (Mihaly system)
POST 33/5142 (Scophony)
POST 33/5143 (General TV developments)
POST 33/5213 (Cinema reception of television)
POST 33/5271 (Baird demonstrations 1933–8)
POST 33/5474 (Baird Correspondence 1935–9)

Filmography and Teleography

24 (d. Various, FOX, 2001–2010).

American Idol (d. Various, Fox TV, 2002–).

Auntie: The Inside Story of the BBC (d. Marion Milne, BBC, 1997).

Ben Hur (d. Fred Niblo, US: MGM, 1925).

The Birth of Television: Here's Looking at You (d. Laurie John, BBC, TX 30 July 1984).

Box and Cox (Baird Television, TX 15 December 1928).

Breakfast Time (d. Various, BBC, 1983–89).

Britannia High (d.Various, ITV, 2008).

The Cabinet of Dr Caligari (d. Robert Wiene, Germany: Decla-Bioscop, 1920).

Checkmate (d. D.H. Munro, BBC, TX 8 & 13 March 1938; 19 & 22 February 1939).

Clive of India (d. George More O'Ferrall, BBC, TX 19 February 1938).

The Constant Nymph (d. George More O'Ferrall, BBC, TX 31 May 1938).

Cyrano de Bergerac (d. George More O'Ferrall, BBC, TX 20 October 1938).

The Discovery of Television (d. John Lloyd, BBC, TX 03 November 1966).

Doctor Who (d. Various, BBC, 1963–).

EastEnders (d. Various, BBC, 1985–Present).

Elstree Calling (d. Alfred Hitchcock et al, UK: British International Pictures, 1930).

From the Zoo (d. Various, BBC, 1939).

The Ghost Train (d. Jan Bussell, BBC, TX 20 December 1937).

Gone with the Wind (d. Victor Fleming, US: MGM/Selznick international Pictres).

Goodbye Mr Chips (d. Sam Wood, UK: British MGM, 1939).

Grange Hill (d. Various, BBC, 1978–2008).

Hancock's Half Hour (d.Various, BBC, 1956–1960).

Hats Off (d. Hal Roach, US: Hal Roach Studios, 1927).

Here's Looking at You (BBC, August–October 1936).

Here's Looking at You: The Birth of Television (d. Laurie John, BBC, TX 30 July 1984).

Hollywood Revue of 1929 (d. Charles Reisner, US: MGM, 1929).

Journey's End (d. George More O'Ferrall, BBC, TX 11 November 1937).

Juno and the Paycock (d. Fred O'Donovan, BBC, TX 21 October 1938).

The Kid (d. Charles Chaplin, US: Charles Chaplin Productions, 1921).

London After Midnight (d. Tod Browning, US: MGM, 1927).

The Lost World (d. Harry Hoyt, US: First National, 1925).

Lost (d. Various, ABC, 2004–2010).

The Man with the Flower in His Mouth (d. Val Gielgud, BBC, TX 14 July 1930).

Mickey's Gala Premier (d. Burt Gillett, US: Disney, 1933).

Nineteen Eighty-Four (d. Rudolph Cartier, BBC, TX 12 December 1954).

On the Spot (d. Royston Morley, BBC, TX 08 July 1938; 29 April & 05 May 1939).

Picture Page (d. Various, BBC, 1936–39, 1946–52).

Play School (d. Various, BBC, 1964–88).

Pride and Prejudice (d. Michael Barry, BBC, TX 22 May 1938).

Puppet Parade (d. Various, BBC, 1939 & 1946–48).

The Quatermass Experiment (d. Rudolph Cartier, BBC, 1953).

Quatermass II (d. Rudolph Cartier, BBC, 1955).

Quatermass and the Pit (d. Rudolph Cartier, BBC, 1958–9).

The Queen's Messenger (d. Mortimer Stewart, WGY Schenectady, TX 11 September 1928).

Rope (d. Dallas Bower, BBC, TX 08 March 1939).

Saturday Superstore (d. Various, BBC, 1982–87).

Sea Stories (d. Unknown, BBC, TX 05 April 1937).

Shaun the Sheep (d.Various, Aardman/BBC, 2007–).

The Silence of the Sea (d. Michael Barry, BBC, TX 7 June 1946).

State of Play (d. David Yates, BBC, 2007).

Television Comes to London (d. Gerald Cock/Dallas Bower, BBC: 1936).

Television Under the Swastika (d. Michael Kloft, Spiegel TV, 1999).

We Bring You Live Pictures (d. Martin L. Bell, BBC, 1984).

Western Cabaret (d. Harry Pringle, BBC, TX 10 & 12 January, 08 & 10 March 1939).

The Wizard of Oz (d. Victor Fleming, US: MGM, 1939).

The X Factor (d. Various, Fremantle Media, 2004–).

The X-Files (d. Various, Fox, 1993–2002).

References and Notes

Introduction

1. Namely, the first Lord Selsdon, William Lowson Mitchell-Thompson, who had been Postmaster General between 1924 and 1929.
2. Jason Jacobs, *The Intimate Screen* (Oxford: Oxford University Press, 2000).
3. Kate Dunn, *Do Not Adjust Your Set* (London: John Murray, 2003).
4. David Lazell, *What's on the Box* (Gloucestershire: Evergreen Press, 1991).
5. R.W. Burns, *British Television – The Formative Years* (London: Peregrinus, 1986).
6. Albert Abramson, *The History of Television: 1880 to 1941* (Jefferson: McFarland and Co. Inc, 1988).
7. Paddy Scannell, 'Public Service Broadcasting: The History of a Concept' in Andrew Goodwin (ed.) *Understanding Television* (London: Routledge, 1990).
8. Bruce Norman, *Here's Looking at You* (London: BBC & RTS, 1984).
9. Norman, *Here's Looking at You*, p.7.
10. *Dawn of Television Remembered* (CD-ROM) (Produced by Donald F. McLean, TV Dawn, 2005).
11. John Corner, *Critical Ideas in Television Studies* (Oxford: Oxford University Press, 1999), p.126.
12. Andrew Crisell, *An Introductory History of British Broadcasting* (London: Routledge, Second Edition, 2002).
13. Post Office Archives, POST 33/3853. Hutchinson to the Postmaster General, 4 January 1926.
14. John Caughie, 'Before the Golden Age: Early Television Drama' in John Corner (ed.) *Popular Television in Britain* (London: British Film Institute, 1991), p.24.
15. Charles Barr, '"They Think It's All Over": The Dramatic Legacy of Live Television' in John Hill and Martin McLoone (eds.) *Big Picture, Small Screen* (Luton: University of Luton Press, 1996).
16. Caughie, 'Before the Golden Age', p.25.
17. Raphael Samuel, *Island Stories* (London: Verso, 1998), p.186.
18. Samuel, *Island Stories*, p.186.

Chapter 1

1. *English Mechanic and World of Science*, 31 January 1879.
2. Andrew Crisell, *An Introductory History of British Broadcasting* (London: Routledge, 2002), p.77.

3. Anthony Masters, *Pictures Through the Air: John Logie Baird (Super Scientists series)* (London: Hodder Wayland, 2001).

4. Mike Goldsmith, *John Logie Baird (Scientists Who Made History)* (London: Raintree, 2002).

5. Struan Reid, *John Logie Baird (Groundbreakers)* (Oxford: Heinemann, 2000).

6. McLean's discussion of the change in attitudes towards Baird over time can be found in his book *Restoring Baird's Image* (London: Institute of Electrical Engineers, 2000), pp.269–274.

7. *The Discovery of Television* (BBC, TX. 03/11/1966).

8. Bruce Norman, *Here's Looking At You* (London: BBC & RTS Publishing, 1984), p.51.

9. *The Times*, 24 March 1925.

10. *The Guardian*, 14 August 2003; Reproduced at http://www.guardian.co.uk/netnotes/article/0,6729,1019043,00.html.

11. Lindy Woodhead, *Shopping, Seduction and Mr Selfridge* (London: Profile, 2007), p.105.

12. Tom McArthur and Pater Waddell, *Vision Warrior* (Kirkwall: The Orkney Press, 1990), p.14.

13. John Rowland, *The Television Man* (London: Lutterworth Press, 1966), pp.36–49.

14. J.L. Baird, *Television and Me* (Edinburgh: Mercat Press, 2004), p.30.

15. Baird, *Television and Me*, p.30; Baird claimed in his memoirs to have made £1600 when he wound up the company in 1919, a reasonable sum.

16. Sydney Moseley, *John Baird* (London: Odhams Press, 1952), pp.72–73.

17. Letter JLB/999/40/68 held by Hastings Museum as part of the National Archive.

18. Asa Briggs, *The History of Broadcasting in the United Kingdom Volume II: The Golden Age of Wireless* (Oxford: Oxford University Press, 1965), p.524.

19. A.J.P. Taylor, *English History 1914–1945* (Oxford: Oxford University Press, 1965), p.227.

20. Taylor, *English History 1914–1945*, p.195.

21. Taylor, *English History 1914–1945*, p.237.

22. Donald F. McLean, *Restoring Baird's Image* (London: Institute of Electrical Engineers, 2000), p.27.

23. *Nature*, 4 April 1925.

24. Albert Glinsky, *Theremin: Ether Music and Espionage* (Urbana: University of Illinois Press, 2000), p.46.

25. Albert Abramson, *Zworykin: Pioneer of Television* (Urbana: University of Illinois Press, 1995), p.54.

26. 'Motion Pictures by Wireless' in *Moving Picture News*, 27 September 1913.

27. Richard Kaszarski, *Hollywood on the Hudson* (New Brunswick: Rutgers University Press, 2008), p.415.

28. Albert Abramson, *Electronic Motion Pictures: History of the Television Camera* (New York: Arno press, 1974), p.29.

29. *Nature*, 'Distant Electric Vision', 18 June 1908.

30. Glinsky, *Theremin*, p.38.

31. Alexander B. Magoun, *Television: The Life Story of a Technology* (Westport, Connecticut: Greenwood Press, 2007), p.21. Magoun points out that, while

predominately electronic, the system used motorised generators as part of the apparatus.

32. Briggs, *The History of Broadcasting in the United Kingdom Volume II*, p.525.
33. J.L. Baird, *Television and Me* (Edinburgh: Mercat Press, 2004), p.53.
34. Baird, *Television and Me*, p.53.
35. R.W. Burns, *British Television – The Formative Years* (London: Peregrinus, 1986), p.42.
36. As referenced by E.G. Stewart in his report 'Television' in 1926. BBC Written Archive Centre, S69.
37. McLean, *Restoring Baird's Image*, p.38.
38. Albert Abramson, *The History of Television: 1880 to 1941* (Jefferson: McFarland and Co. Inc, 1988), p.87.
39. Abramson, *Zworykin*, p.57.
40. Abramson, *Zworykin*, p.57.
41. Abramson, *The History of Television: 1880 to 1941*, p.94.
42. R.W. Burns, *Television: An International History of the Formative Years* (London: Institute of Engineering and Technology, 1997), p.247.
43. Burns, *Television: An International History of the Formative Years*, p.247.
44. Burns, *Television: An International History of the Formative Years*, p.254.
45. Burns, *Television: An International History of the Formative Years*, p.255.
46. Post Office Archives, POST 33/3853. Hutchinson to the Postmaster General, 4 January 1926. Reproduced courtesy of The British Postal Museum & Archive.
47. Post Office Archives, POST 33/3853. Hutchinson to the Postmaster General, 4 January 1926. Reproduced courtesy of The British Postal Museum & Archive.
48. Post Office Archives, POST 33/3853. Untitled and anonymous Post Office memo, 7 January 1926. Reproduced courtesy of The British Postal Museum & Archive.
49. Post Office Archives, POST 33/3853. Hutchinson to the Secretary of the GPO, 11 January 1926. Reproduced courtesy of The British Postal Museum & Archive.
50. Post Office Archives, POST 33/3853. 'Engineer's notes', 27 January 1926. Reproduced courtesy of The British Postal Museum & Archive.
51. Post Office Archives, POST 33/3853. GPO to Hutchinson, 28 January 1926. Reproduced courtesy of The British Postal Museum & Archive.
52. Post Office Archives, POST 33/3853. Ibid. Reproduced courtesy of The British Postal Museum & Archive.
53. Paddy Scannell 'Public Service Broadcasting: The History of a Concept', in: A. Goodwin and G. Whannel (eds.), *Understanding Television*. (London: Routledge, 1990), p.11.
54. 'The photographs shown do not do the result justice. Much is lost in the photograph and much more is lost owing to the fact that photographs can only show a still picture, whereas the movements continually presented new aspects and the effect was obtained of much greater detail than the photograph will show.' J.L. Baird, *Television and Me* (Edinburgh: Mercat Press Ltd, 2004), p.64.
55. BBC Written Archive Centre, S69. Leslie Hardern to Norman Collins, 5 April 1948.

56. BBC Written Archive Centre, S69. 'Television', 1926 (specific date not noted).
57. BBC Written Archive Centre, S69. 'Television', 1926 (specific date not noted).
58. R.W. Burns, *John Logie Baird: Television Pioneer* (London: Institute of Electrical and Electronic Engineers, 2000), p.179.
59. BBC Written Archive Centre, S69. 'Television', 1926 (specific date not noted).
60. BBC Written Archive Centre, S69. 'Television', 1926 (specific date not noted).
61. BBC Written Archive Centre, S69. 'Television', 1926 (specific date not noted).

Chapter 2

1. Post Office Archives, POST 33/3853. Memo (author's name illegible), 4 February 1936. Reproduced courtesy of The British Postal Museum & Archive.
2. See, for example, the Post Office Archives, POST 33/3853. Leech to Phillips, 9 September 1927. The content of this memo is discussed later in the chapter.
3. Post Office Archives, POST 33/3853. Memo (author's name illegible), 4 February 1936. Reproduced courtesy of The British Postal Museum & Archive.
4. Post Office Archives, POST 33/3853. Ibid. Reproduced courtesy of The British Postal Museum & Archive.
5. Paddy Scannell, 'Public Service Broadcasting: The History of a Concept' in Andrew Goodwin and Gary Whannel (eds), *Understanding Television* (London: Routledge, 1990).
6. BBC Written Archive Centre, S69. 'Television', 1926 (specific date not noted).
7. Post Office Archives, POST 33/3853. Memo (author's name illegible), 4 February 1936. Reproduced courtesy of The British Postal Museum & Archive.
8. Post Office Archives, POST 33/3853. Ibid. Reproduced courtesy of The British Postal Museum & Archive.
9. J.L. Baird, *Television and Me* (Edinburgh: Mercat Press, 2004), p.74.
10. Baird, *Television and Me*, p.74.
11. Burns, *Television: An International History of the Formative Years*, p.213.
12. Gary R. Edgerton, *The Columbia History of American Television* (New York: Columbia University Press, 2007), p.30.
13. As an aside, it is worth remembering that widespread transition to synchronous sound in the cinema did not take place until the following year, 1929. Television's use of sound and vision was somewhat ahead of its time for most of the 1920s.
14. William Boddy discusses the relative lack of interest in considering who should be allowed to offer television broadcasts in its early years in *Fifties Television: The Industry and its Critics* (Urbana: University of Illinois, 1993), p.18.
15. Burns, *Television: An International History of the Formative Years*, p.480.
16. Burns, *Television: An International History of the Formative Years*, p.480.

17. Donald F. McLean, *Restoring Baird's Image* (London: Institute of Electrical Engineers, 2000), p.51

18. Baird, *Television and Me*, p.78.

19. Some of this material is available on Donald F. McLean's CD-ROM *The Dawn of Television Remembered* (London: TV Dawn, 2005).

20. McLean, *Restoring Baird's Image*, p.45.

21. R.W. Burns, *Television: An International History of the Formative Years* (London: Institute of Engineering and Technology, 1997), p.358.

22. *The Times*, 20 July 1928.

23. BBC Written Archive Centre, T/16/42/1. Hutchinson to Post Office, 17 August 1927.

24. Post Office Archives, POST 33/3853. Hutchinson to Post Office, 17 August 1927. Reproduced courtesy of The British Postal Museum & Archive.

25. Post Office Archives, POST 33/3853. Leech to Phillips, 9 September 1927. Reproduced courtesy of The British Postal Museum & Archive.

26. Post Office Archives, POST 33/3853. Ibid. Reproduced courtesy of The British Postal Museum & Archive.

27. Baird, *Television and Me*, p.95.

28. Baird, *Television and Me*, p.94.

29. This fact was uncovered by the late Denis Gifford during research for his sadly unpublished manuscript *The British Television Catalogue: 1923–1939*. The *British Vintage Wireless Society* recounts this and more information in their publication of the press release at http://www.bvws.org.uk/405alive/faq/prog_further_reading.html.

30. This difference of opinion is covered in more depth the next section of the book.

31. BBC Written Archive Centre, T/16/42/1; the exact date is not noted in the document itself, but a pencil marking suggests '27/2/29?' and this seems likely.

32. BBC Written Archive Centre, T/16/42/1. Ibid.

33. BBC Written Archive Centre, T/16/42/1. Whitehouse to Murray, 25 September 1928.

34. BBC Written Archive Centre, T/16/42/1. Ibid.

35. BBC Written Archive Centre, T/16/42/1. Whitehouse to Murray, 1 October 1928.

36. BBC Written Archive Centre, T/16/42/1. Ibid.

37. BBC Written Archive Centre, T/16/42/1. Ibid.

38. BBC Written Archive Centre, T/16/42/1. 'Yesterday's Television Test', memo from Eckersley to Murray, 10 October 1928.

39. Post Office Archives, POST 33/3853. Hutchinson writing to secretary, 22 August 1928. Reproduced courtesy of The British Postal Museum & Archive.

40. Post Office Archives, POST 33/3853. Message to secretary, 29 August 1928. Reproduced courtesy of The British Postal Museum & Archive.

41. Asa Briggs, *The History of Broadcasting in the United Kingdom Volume II: The Golden Age of Wireless* (Oxford: Oxford University Press, 1965), p.529.

42. Briggs, *The History of Broadcasting in the United Kingdom Volume II*, p.532.

43. Briggs, *The History of Broadcasting in the United Kingdom Volume II*, p.538.

44. Post Office Archives, POST 33/3853. Memo (author's name illegible), 4 February 1936. Reproduced courtesy of The British Postal Museum & Archive.
45. Post Office Archives, POST 33/3853; exact date not stated, but the previous note on the matter to which this was a reply was 9 September 1929. Reproduced courtesy of The British Postal Museum & Archive.
46. R.W. Burns, *British Television – The Formative Years* (London: Peregrinus, 1986), p.307.
47. *Television*, February 1929.
48. BBC Written Archive Centre, T/16/42/2. Copy of letter from Secretary of GPO to Baird Television Development Company, 27 March 1929.
49. Briggs, *The History of Broadcasting in the United Kingdom Volume II*, p.501.
50. BBC Written Archive Centre, T/16/42/2. Hutchinson to Eckersley, 15 May 1929.
51. Some of this material is available on Donald F. McLean's CD-ROM *The Dawn of Television Remembered* (London: TV Dawn, 2005).
52. Briggs, *The History of Broadcasting in the United Kingdom Volume II*, p.555.
53. Albert Abramson, *Zworykin: Pioneer of Television* (Urbana: University of Illinois Press, 1995), p.61.
54. Briggs points out that the use of sound did raise the question of proper 'censorship' of programming (Vol. II, p.549) but this seems to have been a theoretical consideration rather than one that was practically applied at this stage.
55. Briggs, *The History of Broadcasting in the United Kingdom Volume II*, p.556.
56. Post Office Archives, POST 33/3853. Baird to MacDonald, 24 September 1931. Reproduced courtesy of The British Postal Museum & Archive.
57. BBC Written Archive Centre, T/16/42/3. Minutes of meeting between Baird and the BBC, 17 August 1931.
58. Baird, *Television and Me*, p.125.
59. BBC Written Archive Centre, T/16/42/5. Baird to Reith, 31 January 1933.
60. Quoted by Bruce Norman in *Here's Looking at You* (London: RTS & BBC Publishing, 1984), p.78.
61. A copy of this flyer can be found in POST 33/5271.
62. Burns, *British Television – The Formative Years*, p.266.

Chapter 3

1. *Television*, December 1928.
2. Some of the details for the test transmissions of Fultographs (transmission of still images) were even listed in *The Listener* magazine.
3. Brigitte Rollet, 'Television in France' in Coleman, J.A and Rollet, B. (eds.) Television in Europe. (Exeter: Intellect, 1997), p.35.
4. Baird, *Television and Me*, pp.109–110.
5. Albert Abramson, *Zworykin: Pioneer of Television* (Urbana: University of Illinois Press, 1995), p.71.
6. John Sandford, 'Television in Germany' in: James A. Coleman and Brigitte Rollet (eds.) *Television in Europe*. (Exeter: Intellect, 1997), p.49.

7. Baird, *Television and Me*, p.111.
8. R.W. Burns, *Television – An International History of the Formative Years* (London: Institute of Engineering and Technology, 2004), p.188.
9. Burns, *British Television – The Formative Years* (London: Peter Peregrinus, 1986), p.218.
10. Alfred Dinsdale, *Television – Seeing by Wireless* (London: Sir Isaac Pitman & Sons, 1926).
11. Alfred Dinsdale, *Television – Seeing by Wireless* (Revised ed.) (London: Television Publishing Ltd., 1928).
12. Alfred Dinsdale, *First Principles of Television* (London: Chapman & Hall, 1932).
13. H. Horton Sheldon & Edgar Norman Grisewood, *Television – Present Methods of Picture Transmission* (London : Library Press Ltd., 1929).
14. Edgar H. Felix, *Television – Its Methods and Uses* (London & New York: McGraw-Hill, 1931).
15. Dinsdale, *Television – Seeing By Wireless* (1st Edn), p.61.
16. Baird's system would eventually use CRT sets by the time of the official ill-fated launch in 1936.
17. The searchable patents documents at http://v3.espacenet.com/ reveal in excess of 250 documents filed under Baird's name, the vast majority of which were television related.
18. Felix, *Television – Its Methods and Uses*, p.v.
19. *Television*, November 1928.
20. *Television*, November 1928.
21. *Television*, March 1928.
22. Malcolm Baird, 'Preface' in: J.L. Baird, *Television and Me* (Edinburgh: Mercat Press, 2004), p.ix.
23. R.W. Burns, *British Television – The Formative Years* (London: Peregrinus, 1986), p.169.
24. As recounted in the *Report of the Television Committee 1934–35*.
25. BBC Written Archive Centre, T/16/42/5. Notes of meeting between the BBC and GPO, 21 April 1933. Some claimed that the Baird system was superior for transmissions of films, although flicker was more noticeable.
26. BBC Written Archive Centre, T/16/42/5. Notes of meeting between the BBC and GPO, 21 April 1933.
27. Post Office Archives, POST 33/5474. Baird to Television Advisory Committee, October 1936. Reproduced courtesy of The British Postal Museum & Archive.
28. Post Office Archives, POST 33/5474. Ibid. Reproduced courtesy of The British Postal Museum & Archive.
29. Albert Abramson in Anthony Smith (ed.) *Television – An International History* (Oxford: Oxford University Press, 1995), p.13.
30. Donald F. McLean, *Restoring Baird's Image* (London: Institute of Electrical Engineers, 2000), p.193.
31. Asa Briggs, *The History of Broadcasting in the United Kingdom Volume II: The Golden Age of Wireless* (Oxford: Oxford University Press, 1965), p.552.

32. Post Office Archives, POST 33/5142, various documents. Reproduced courtesy of The British Postal Museum & Archive.
33. *Dawn of Television Remembered* (CD-ROM) (Produced by Donald F. McLean, TV Dawn, 2005).
34. Briggs, *The History of Broadcasting in the United Kingdom Volume II*, p.553.
35. Burns, *British Television – The Formative Years*, p.438.
36. *Here's Looking at You: The Birth of Television* (BBC, TX. 30/07/1984).
37. J. D. Percy in *Here's Looking at You: The Birth of Television* (BBC, TX. 30/07/1984).
38. Burns, *British Television – The Formative Years*, p.3.
39. J.L. Baird, *Television and Me* (Edinburgh: Mercat Press, 2004), p.124.

Chapter 4

1. Burton Paulu, *Television and Radio in the United Kingdom* (Basingstoke: Palgrave Macmillan, 1981), p.35.
2. Paulu, *Television and Radio in the United Kingdom*, p.36.
3. This is not a modern expression. See, for example, 'Marconi Tells What Radio Needs' in *Popular Science Monthly*, January 1928, where he is referred to as 'father of radio'.
4. Andrew Crisell, *An Introductory History of British Broadcasting* (London: Routledge, 2002), p.17.
5. Crisell, *An Introductory History of British Broadcasting*, p.17.
6. Crisell, *An Introductory History of British Broadcasting*, p.18.
7. Briggs, *The History of Broadcasting in the United Kingdom Volume II*, p.569.
8. Donald F. McLean, *Restoring Baird's Image* (London: Institute of Electrical Engineers, 2000), p.131.
9. Burns, *British Television – The Formative Years*, p.292.
10. As described in the memo 'Report on Television Demonstration at EMI', BBC Written Archives, T/16/65.
11. R.W. Burns, *Television – An International History of the Formative Years* (London: Institute of Engineering and Technology, 2004), p.447.
12. Albert Abramson, *Zworykin: Pioneer of Television* (Urbana: University of Illinois Press, 1995), p.132.
13. Albert Abramson in Anthony Smith (ed.) *Television – An International History* (Oxford: Oxford University Press, 1995), p.18.
14. Tony Currie, *A Concise History of British Television 1930–2000* (Tiverton: Kelly Publications, 2004), p.12.
15. Burns, *Television: An International History of the Formative Years*, p.437.
16. Graham Murdock, 'Culture, Services, Knowledge' in: Janet Wasko (ed.) *A Companion to Television* (Oxford: Blackwell, 2005), p.182.
17. Crisell, *An Introductory History of British Broadcasting*, pp.18–20.
18. Crisell, *An Introductory History of British Broadcasting*, pp.18–20.
19. James Wood, *History of International Broadcasting* (London: Peter Peregrinus, 1992), p.34.

20. *BBC in the 1920s*. http://www.bbc.co.uk/heritage/more/pdfs/1920s.pdf.

21. Asa Briggs, *BBC – The First Fifty Years* (Oxford: Oxford University Press, 1985), p.89.

22. The 1923 Sykes Committee dismissed commercial funding and advertising because it was felt that it would lower the standards of programmes, while also benefitting only the larger companies who could afford to advertise, while also having the potential to alienate the audience of the fledgling medium.

23. See, for example, the wealth of correspondence in the Post Office Archives.

24. Until Spring 1930 the transmissions were silent due to the lack of available bandwidth for simultaneous sound and vision broadcasts, explaining the lack of a 'Producer' for this basic text and image service.

25. Asa Briggs, *The History of Broadcasting in the United Kingdom Volume II: The Golden Age of Wireless* (Oxford: Oxford University Press, 1965), p.531.

26. BBC Written Archives, T/16/214/1. Minutes of Control Board meeting, 15 April 1928.

27. BBC Written Archives, T/16/214/1. Eckersley to Turner, 11 June 1928.

28. BBC Written Archives, T/16/214/1. Ibid.

29. R.W. Burns, *British Television – The Formative Years* (London: Peregrinus, 1986), p.95.

30. BBC Written Archives, T/16/214/1. Eckersley to Turner, 11 June 1928.

31. BBC Written Archives, T/16/214/1. Internal memo no.89, 'Telephotography and Television', 18 September 1928.

32. BBC Written Archives, T/16/42/1. Memo 'Suggested Attitude Towards Television', 8 October 1928.

33. BBC Written Archives, T/16/42/1. Ibid.

34. Briggs, *The History of Broadcasting in the United Kingdom Volume II*, p.19.

35. BBC Written Archives, T/16/42/1. Memo from Murray, 'Yesterday's Television Test'; 10 October 1928.

36. BBC Written Archives, T/16/42/1. Memo from Murray, 'Yesterday's Television Test'; 10 October 1928.

37. BBC Written Archives, T/16/42/1. Hutchinson to Murray, 21 November 1928.

38. BBC Written Archives, T/16/214/1. 'The Truth About Television' (anonymously authored memo), 3 November 1928.

39. This was often referenced in the press, where such fears would be allayed, such as on 25 January 1935 when the *Daily Telegraph* quoted the president of the RMA in order to reassure its readers in its article 'Television and the BBC. Radio sets not obsolete'.

40. Briggs, *The History of Broadcasting in the United Kingdom Volume II*, p.566. As Briggs goes on to say, 'It is difficult to imagine "experimental broadcasts" being financed for any less than this.'.

41. *The People*, 6 January 1929.

42. Briggs, *The History of Broadcasting in the United Kingdom Volume II*, p.541.

43. BBC Written Archives, T/16/42/2. 'Information' to Craygy, 30 January 1929.

44. BBC Written Archives, T/16/42/2. Ibid.

45. BBC Written Archives, T/16/42/1. 'Terms of Reference' (anon). Pencil mark indicates date of 27 February 1929.

46. BBC Written Archives, T/16/42/1. Ibid.
47. See, for example, the report of audience feedback at Radiolympia in 1936, as explored in the next chapter. BBC Written Archives, T/23/77/2. 'Report on Demonstrations of Television', Noel Ashbridge, 7 September 1936.
48. BBC Written Archives, T/16/42/1. Ibid.

Chapter 5

1.   'Television – The Position To-Day' in *Popular Wireless*, 14 July 1929, p.668.
2.   'Television – The Position To-Day' in *Popular Wireless*, 14 July 1929, p.668.
3.   'BBC and Television' in *Popular Wireless*, 14 July 1929, p.656.
4.   BBC Written Archives, T/16/42/2. 'Television', anonymous and undated.
5.   BBC Written Archives, T/16/42/2. Ibid.
6.   Tony Currie, *The Radio Times Story* (Tiverton: Kelly Publications, 2001), p.25.
7.   BBC Written Archives, T/16/42/3. Moseley to Murray, 5 October 1931.
8.   BBC Written Archives, T/16/42/3. Ibid.
9.   BBC Written Archives, T/16/42/3. Ibid.
10. BBC Written Archives, T/16/42/3. Ashbridge to Reith and Murray, 14 October 1931.
11. BBC Written Archives, T/16/42/3. Murray to Ashbridge, undated.
12. BBC Written Archives, T/16/42/3. Control Board Meeting minutes, 27 October 1931.
13. Communicated internally in memo from Ashbridge dated 19 October 1931. BBC Written Archives, T/16/42/3.
14. As expressed in an internal memo to the Director General, dated 14 October 1931. BBC Written Archives, T/16/42/3.
15. With some exceptions. For example, should Baird wish to use additional available hours for experimentation then they would bear the cost. The correspondence leading to the eventual agreement took place in the last quarter of 1931 (BBC Written Archive T/16/42/3), with the final agreement being drawn up early the next year (BBC Written Archive T/16/42/4).
16. R.W. Burns, *British Television – The Formative Years* (London: Peregrinus, 1986), p.224.
17. Burns, *British Television – The Formative Years*, p.231.
18. Asa Briggs, *The History of Broadcasting in the United Kingdom Volume II: The Golden Age of Wireless* (Oxford: Oxford University Press, 1965), p.563.
19. Donald F. McLean, *Restoring Baird's Image* (London: Institute of Electrical Engineers, 2000), p.182.
20. McLean, *Restoring Baird's Image*, p.51.
21. Arthur Marwick, *A Modern History of the British Isles* (Oxford: Blackwell, 2000), p.65.
22. Andrew Davies, 'Cinema and Broadcasting' in Paul Johnson (ed.) *20 Century Britain: Economic, Social and Cultural Change* (London: Longman, 1994), p.267.

23. Andrew Thorpe, *Britain in the 1930s* (Oxford: Blackwell Publishers, 1992), p.66.

24. Thorpe, *Britain in the 1930s*, p.110.

25. Thorpe, *Britain in the 1930s*, p.102.

26. McLean, *Restoring Baird's Image*, p.182.

27. Leo Enticknap and Graham Douglas, *Moving Image Technology* (London: Wallflower Press, 2005), p.166.

28. Briggs, *The History of Broadcasting in the United Kingdom Volume II*, p.540.

29. Briggs, *The History of Broadcasting in the United Kingdom Volume II*, p.537.

30. BBC Written Archives, T/16/67. 'For Information' (anon), 14 February 1928.

31. BBC Written Archives, T/16/67. Ibid.

32. BBC Written Archives, T/16/67. Ibid.

33. William Mitchell Thomson was Postmaster General between 1924 and 1929, Hastings Lee Smith from 1929 to 1931, while both Clement Attlee and William Ormsby-Gore also briefly held the post in 1931, followed by Kingsley Wood from 1931 to 1935 and Geoffrey Tryon from 1935 to 1940.

34. BBC Written Archives, T/16/42/5. Internal circulating memo from Ashbridge, 2 May 1933.

35. BBC Written Archives, T/16/42/5. Ibid.

36. R.W. Burns, *Communications: An International History of the Formative Years* (London: Institute of Electrical Engineers, 2004), p.554.

37. As detailed in *Report of the Television Committee 1934–35*.

38. Briggs, *The History of Broadcasting in the United Kingdom Volume II*, p.587.

39. *Report of the Television Committee 1934–35*, p.18.

40. *Report of the Television Committee 1934–35,* p.19.

41. *Report of the Television Committee 1934–35*, p.19.

42. The report also points out that special sponsorship of some programming was now permitted on the BBC and suggests this as an alternative revenue stream. Briggs claims that this was seriously considered for a time, although dismissed by the Board of Governors, and that it was occasionally employed in a limited form prior to the official launch. See the second volume of Briggs' *History of Broadcasting in the United Kingdom*, p.600.

Chapter 6

1. BBC Written Archives, T23/77/1. 'Television and the RMA' by Cock, 15 June 1936.

2. BBC Written Archives, T23/77/1. 'Television and the RMA' by Cock, 15 June 1936.

3. BBC Written Archives, T23/77/1. 'Television and the RMA' by Cock, 15 June 1936.

4. BBC Written Archives, T23/77/1. 'Television and the RMA' by Cock, 15 June 1936.

5. Specifically discussed and denied in the 'RMA Liaison Meeting' minutes, 15 June 1936 (BBC Written Archives, T/23/77/1).

6. BBC Written Archives, T/23/77/1. 'RMA Liaison Meeting' minutes, 15 June 1936.
7. BBC Written Archives, T/23/77/1. Ibid.
8. Tony Currie, *A Concise History of British Television 1930–2000* (Tiverton: Kelly Publications, 2004), p.14.
9. As indicated in the running order presented in the BBC document 'Television Programmes for the Week' (undated) in BBC Written Archives, T/23/77/2.
10. BBC Written Archives, T/23/77/2. 'Experimental Television Programmes for Radiolympia' BBC Announcement, 27 August 1936.
11. BBC Written Archives, T/23/77/2. 'Experimental Television Programmes for Radiolympia' BBC Announcement, 27 August 1936.
12. BBC Written Archives, T/32/77/1. Undated 'Announcements for Radiolympia'.
13. BBC Written Archives, T/32/77/2. Letter to J. Varley Roberts (unknown author), 27 August 1936.
14. BBC Written Archives, T/23/77/2. 'Radiolympia Television Demonstrations', Gerald Cock, 7 September 1936.
15. BBC Written Archives, T/23/77/2. 'Report on Demonstrations of Television', Noel Ashbridge, 7 September 1936.
16. R.W. Burns, *British Television – The Formative Years* (London: Peregrinus, 1986), p.302.
17. BBC Written Archives, T/23/77/2. 'Report on Demonstrations of Television', Noel Ashbridge, 7 September 1936.
18. BBC Written Archives, T/23/77/2. 'Report on Demonstrations of Television', Noel Ashbridge, 7 September 1936.
19. BBC Written Archives, T/23/77/2. 'Report on Demonstrations of Television', Noel Ashbridge, 7 September 1936.
20. BBC Written Archives, T/23/77/2. 'Radiolympia Television Demonstrations', Gerald Cock, 7 September 1936.
21. As publicised by the BBC in their official announcement of the opening of the service.
22. Currie, *A Concise History of British Television*, p.15.
23. Robert L. Hilliard and Michael C. Keith, *The Broadcasting Century and Beyond: A Biography of American Broadcasting* (Burlington: Focal Press, 2010), p.65.
24. Jonathan Bignell, *An Introduction to Television Studies* (London: Routledge, 2003), p.44.
25. William Boddy, 'The Beginnings of American Television' in: Anthony Smith (ed.) *Television: An International History (Second Edition)* (Oxford: Oxford University Press, 1998), p.26.
26. Boddy, 'The Beginnings of American Television', p.26.
27. This transition is well covered by Albert Abramson in *The History of Television: 1880 to 1941* (Jefferson: McFarland and Co. Inc, 1988), p.213.
28. Robert L. Hilliard and Michael C. Keith, *The Broadcasting Century and Beyond: A Biography of American Broadcasting* (Burlington: Focal Press, 2010), p.93.

29. Albert Abramson, *The History of Television, 1942 to 2000* (Jefferson: McFarland & Co, 2003), p.37.

30. Andrew Crisell, *An Introductory History of British Broadcasting* (London: Routledge, Second Edition, 2002), p.120.

31. Hugh Richard Slotten, *Radio's Hidden Voice: The Origins of Public Broadcasting in the United States* (Urbana: University of Illinois Press, 2009), p.241.

32. The documentary *Television Under the Swastika* (d. Michael Kloft) provides an insight into the programming offered by these early German broadcasts.

33. Albert Abramson, *Zworykin: Pioneer of Television* (Urbana: University of Illinois Press, 1995), p.175.

34. Brigitte Rollet, 'Television in France' in: James A. Coleman and Brigitte Rollet (eds.) *Television in Europe.* (Exeter: Intellect, 1997), p.35.

35. Raymond Kuhn, *The Media in France* (London: Routledge, 1994), p.120.

36. Kuhn, *The Media in France*, p.120.

37. Kuhn, *The Media in France* (, p.120. A handful of other countries also took up SECAM, most notably in the Soviet Union.

38. John Sandford, 'Television in Germany' in: James A. Coleman and Brigitte Rollet (eds.) *Television in Europe.* (Exeter: Intellect, 1997), p.49.

39. Sandford, 'Television in Germany', p.50.

40. There is a selection of models and prices at http://www.tvhistory.tv/tv-prices.htm.

41. Paul Johnson, 'Britain 1900 – 1990' in Paul Johnson (ed.) *20 Century Britain: Economic, Social and Cultural Change* (London: Longman, 1994), p. 6 (Figure for 1935–1936).

42. Asa Briggs, *The History of Broadcasting in the United Kingdom Volume II: The Golden Age of Wireless* (Oxford: Oxford University Press, 1965), p.591.

43. Jeffrey Richards, 'Cinemagoing in Worktown' in *Historical Journal of Film, Radio and Television*, June 1994.

44. Johnson, *20 Century Britain: Economic, Social and Cultural Change*, p.10.

45. Richards, 'Cinemagoing in Worktown'.

46. Tony Currie, *The Radio Times Story* (Tiverton: Kelly Publications, 2001), p.37.

47. Currie, *The Radio Times Story*, p.37.

48. John Caughie, *Television Drama: Realism, Modernism and British Culture* (Oxford: Oxford University Press, 2000), p.33.

49. *Radio Times*, 18 December 1936.

50. *Radio Times*, 18 December 1936.

51. *Ariel*, No.3, December 1936.

52. *Ariel*, No.3, December 1936.

53. *Ariel*, No.3, December 1936.

54. *Ariel*, No.3, December 1936.

55. *Ariel*, No.3, December 1936.

56. *Ariel*, No.3, December 1936.

57. Hugh Chignell, 'The BBC Handbooks: Some observations for broadcasting historians', p.4. Available at: http://www.microform.co.uk/guides/R97602.pdf.

58. Briggs, *The History of Broadcasting in the United Kingdom Volume II*, p.550.

59.   'The BBC Handbooks: Some observations for broadcasting historians', p.5. Available at: http://www.microform.co.uk/guides/R97602.pdf.

60.   *BBC Yearbook 1933*, p.442.

61.   *BBC Annual 1936*, p.149.

62.   *BBC Annual 1936*, p.149.

63.   The excellent four part BBC documentary *We Bring You Live Pictures* (1984) covers this in some depth.

64.   Paddy Scannell; 'Public Service Broadcasting: The History of a Concept' in Andrew Goodwin and Garry Whannel (eds.) *Understanding Television* (London: Routledge, 1990), p.13.

Chapter 7

1.   Donald F. McLean, *Restoring Baird's Image* (London: Institution of Electrical Engineers, 2000), p.37.

2.   Edgar H. Felix, *Television – Its Methods and Uses* (New York: McGraw-Hill Book Company Inc., 1931), p.3.

3.   *Evening Standard*, 8 January 1926.

4.   *Evening Standard*, 8 January 1926.

5.   *Daily Express*, 8 January 1926.

6.   *Daily Telegraph*, 11 January 1926.

7.   *Morning Post*, 26 January 1926.

8.   *Morning Post*, 26 January 1926.

9.   *Yorkshire Post*, 28 January 1926.

10.   *Yorkshire Post*, 28 January 1926.

11.   *Manchester Guardian*, 28 January 1926.

12.   *Manchester Guardian*, 28 January 1926.

13.   *The Times*, 28 January 1926.

14.   *Daily News*, 28 January 1926.

15.   *Daily News*, 28 January 1926.

16.   *Daily Graphic*, 27 January 1926.

17.   *Daily Mirror*, 21 April 1926.

18.   *Evening News*, 27 April 1926.

19.   *Nottingham Evening Post*, 27 April 1926.

20.   *Westminster Gazette*, 28 April 1926.

21.   *Daily News*, 11 August 1926.

22.   *Daily News*, 11 August 1926.

23.   *Daily Telegraph*, 3 September 1926.

24.   *Manchester Guardian*, 3 September 1926.

25.   *Daily Mail*, 16 December 1926.

26.   *Daily Telegraph*, 17 December 1926.

27.   *The People*, 2 January 1927.

28.   *The Observer*, 2 January 1927.

29.   *The Times*, 3 March 1936.

30.   *The Observer*, 9 January 1927.

31. *The Observer*, 9 January 1927.
32. *Glasgow Herald*, 27 May 1927.
33. *Daily Chronicle*, 8 April 1927.

Chapter 8

1. The licence fee was established along with the BBC in 1922 in order to support the service without recourse to advertisements or sponsorship, with no additional television licence until 1946.
2. An amount substantiated by R.W. Burns, *British Television – The Formative Years* (London: Peter Peregrinus, 1986), p.477.
3. *The Times*, 7 March 1936.
4. *The Times*, 24 March 1936.
5. *The Times*, 24 March 1936.
6. *The Times*, 24 March 1936.
7. *The Times,* 19 March 1936.
8. *Sunday Express*, 16 August 1936.
9. *Daily Herald*, 15 August 1936.
10. *Sunday Pictorial*, 16 August 1936.
11. *The Times*, 22 August 1936.
12. *Daily Herald*, 25 August 1936.
13. *Daily Express*, 25 August 1936.
14. *Daily Telegraph*, 25 August 1936.
15. BBC Written Archives, T/16/214/2, 26 January 1936.
16. 'Old Radio Broadcasting Equipment and Memories' http://www.btinternet.com/~roger.beckwith/bh/reg/olympia.htm.
17. *Manchester Guardian*, 25 August 1936.
18. *Manchester Guardian*, 25 August 1936.
19. *Daily Telegraph*, 24 August 1936.
20. *The Times*, 26 August 1936.
21. *Daily Star*, 26 August 1936.
22. *Daily Mirror*, 27 August 1936.
23. Neil Robson, 'Living pictures out of space: the forlorn hopes for television in pre-1939 London' in *Historical Journal of Film, Radio and Television*, vol.24 (2) 2004, p.225.
24. *Morning Post*, 27 August 1936.
25. 'Long queue for television at Radiolympia', *Daily Telegraph*, 27 August 1936.
26. *The Times*, 28 August 1936.
27. *Daily Mail*, 4 September 1936.
28. Andrew Emmerson, *Old Television* (Princes Risborough: Shire Publications, 1998), p.7.
29. Transcription of the meeting, as reproduced in *The Times*, 19 October 1936.
30. *Daily Mail*, 2 November 1936.
31. *Daily Mail*, 2 November 1936.
32. *The Times*, 2 November 1936.

33. *The Times*, 3 November 1936.
34. *The Times*, 3 November 1936.
35. *The Times*, 3 November 1936.
36. *The Times*, 3 November 1936.
37. *The Times*, 3 November 1936.
38. *Daily Express*, 2 November 1936.
39. *Daily Mirror*, 3 November 1936.
40. *Daily Telegraph*, 3 November 1936.
41. *The Times*, 3 November 1936.
42. *The Times*, 3 November 1936.
43. *Wireless Trader*, 21 November 1936.
44. *Evening Standard*, 24 November 1936.
45. *Daily Telegraph*, 24 November 1936.
46. *Daily Express*, 6 September 1937.
47. *Daily Express*, 6 September 1937.

Chapter 9

1. The PasB (Programme as Broadcast) document for the day shows that the *Mickey's Gala Premier* (d. Burt Gillett, US: Disney) was shown in its entirety at 12.05pm, following by a test signal, and then the close of the service at 12.35pm, with no closing announcement.
2. John Caughie, *Television Drama: Realism, Modernism and British Culture* (Oxford: Oxford University Press, 2000), p.34.
3. *Ariel*, No.3, December 1936.
4. Many existing programmes prior to the mid 1970s are telerecordings (film recordings), often made for international sales. The BBC archive is largely complete after the mid-1970s but even so several programmes after this point have been wiped or were never recorded, most notably many 1980s editions of children's shows such as *Play School* and *Saturday Superstore*.
5. Lez Cooke, *British Television Drama – A History* (London: British Film Institute, 2003), p.6.
6. R.W. Burns, *British Television – The Formative Years* (London: Peregrinus, 1986), p.444.
7. 17 January 1983.
8. *Radio Times*, 23 April 1937.
9. Gerald Cock in *Ariel*, No.3, December 1936.
10. Kate Dunn, *Do Not Adjust Your Set – The Early Days of Live Television* (London: John Murray Publishers, 2003), p.25.
11. Bruce Norman, *Here's Looking at You* (London: BBC & RTS, 1984), p.157.
12. Norman, *Here's Looking at You*, p.157.
13. Caughie, *Television Drama*, p.35.
14. Indeed, Norman claims that only fourteen of these productions were original to television.
15. Unpublished interview with Nigel Kneale, conducted by Andy Murray (2004).

Chapter 10

1. Evidence suggests that Bartlett may have been married to the aforementioned engineer on the early television service, Tony Bridgewater. As such, her comments should be read with this in mind, although given the range of her comments (positive and negative) there is no reason to suggest a particular agenda behind the article.

2. 'Views of a Viewer' in *Radio Times*, 4 June 1937, p.3.

3. 'Views of a Viewer' in *Radio Times*, 4 June 1937, p.3.

4. Kate Dunn, *Do Not Adjust Your Set – The Early Days of Live Television* (London: John Murray Publishers, 2003), p.25.

5. The 1930 test broadcasts were 30-line resolution at 25 frames per second; the Marconi-EMI system of 1936 was 405 lines and 50 fields (half-frames) per second.

6. The first televised drama production in the UK was of the play *Box and Cox* broadcast on 15 December 1928 to whichever budding enthusiasts had a televisor within range. Even this was actually beaten by the televising (on a similarly experimental system) in New York of *The Queen's Messenger* on 11 September the same year – a feat that made the front page of the *New York Times* the next day.

7. Jason Jacobs examines this and other early dramas in more detail in *The Intimate Screen*, which is an excellent in-depth demonstration of the practicalities of these earlier programmes.

8. Jason Jacobs, *The Intimate Screen* (Oxford: oxford University Press, 2000), p.54.

9. Jacobs, *The Intimate Screen*, p.62.

10. Jacobs, *The Intimate Screen*, p.62.

11. John Caughie, 'Before the Golden Age: Early Television Drama' in John Corner (ed.) *Popular Television in Britain* (London: British Film Institute, 1991), p.25.

12. The floorplans and other details related to this production are from the BBC Written Archive, T/13/11.

13. There were other productions in 1938 and 1947.

14. The floorplans and other details related to this production are from the BBC Written Archive, T/12/304.

15. Jacobs, *The Intimate Screen*, p.54.

16. Marista Leishman, *My Father, Reith of the BBC* (Edinburgh: Saint Andrew Press, 2006), p.68.

Conclusion

1. If one uses the definition of 'high definition' as at least 240 lines, used by the Television Committee. The German system used 180 lines, and the claim that this was not 'high definition' has been seen as a deliberate attempt to claim a British 'first'.

2. Such as the aforementioned Édouard Belin for France; Philo Farnsworth and Charles Jenkins for America; the former helped to pioneer electronic television and the latter worked on a mechanical system.

3. Report of the Television Committee 1935, p.12.

4. Asa Briggs, *The History of Broadcasting in the United Kingdom Volume II: The Golden Age of Wireless* (Oxford: Oxford University Press, 1965), p.534.

5. Briggs, *The History of Broadcasting in the United Kingdom Volume II*, p.600.

6. R.W. Burns, *British Television – The Formative Years* (London: Peter Peregrinus, 1986), p.83.

7. Kate Dunn, *Do Not Adjust Your Set – The Early Days of Live Television* (London: John Murray Publishers, 2003), p.27.

8. Dunn, *Do Not Adjust Your Set*, p.25.

9. Jean Bartlett, 'Views of a Viewer' in *Radio Times*, 4 June 1937, p.3.

10. *Hancock's Half Hour*, 'There's an Airfield at the Bottom of my Garden' (BBC, TX. 16/12/1957).

11. Lucy Mazdon, 'Preface' in: Lucy Mazdon and Michael Hammond (eds.) *The Contemporary Television Series* (Edinburgh: Edinburgh University Press, 2005) p.xi.

12. Andrew Crisell, *A Study of Modern Television* (Basingstoke: Palgrave Macmillan, 2006), p.9.

13. For example, the Blu-ray and DVD releases of *Doctor Who: The Complete Season Five* feature two scenes written and shot just for inclusion on the commercial releases.

14. *Radio Times*, 4 June 1937.

15. In fact, the simple talk (or lecture) by a single person delivered direct to camera was revived by Channel 4 in its early years. Such programmes contributed to the popular tabloid nickname of 'Channel Bore', and the talks were again phased out.

16. *Doctor Who News Page*, http://gallifreynewsbase.blogspot.com/2010/07/doctor-who-tops-june-iplayer-figures.html.

17. *The Guardian* 'Watch a trailer for ITV1's Britannia High' http://www.guardian.co.uk/media/video/2008/sep/24/itv.television?INTCMP=SRCH.

18. *The Guardian* 'Britannia High? See Me Afterwards.' http://www.guardian.co.uk/culture/garethmcleanblog/2008/oct/28/britannia-high-school-musical?INTCMP=SRCH.

19. John Ellis, *Seeing Things: Television in the Age of Uncertainty* (London: I.B. Tauris, 2000), p.61.

20. *The Times*, 23 December 1938.

21. 8 June 1946.

22. Peter Sallis, *Fading Into the Limelight* (London: Orion, 2006), p.14.

23. Kenneth Adam, 'Television Memories – already!', *Radio Times* 16 April 1937, pp.4–5.

Index